T0248074

MINNESOTA TWINS

A Curated History of the Twins

LA VELLE E. NEAL III

TRIUMPH
BOOKS

THE FRANCHISE

No part of this publication may be reproduced, stored in a retrieval system, or transmitted in any form by any means, electronic, mechanical, photocopying, or otherwise, without the prior written permission of the publisher, Triumph Books LLC, 814 North Franklin Street, Chicago, Illinois 60610.

Library of Congress Cataloging-in-Publication Data available upon request.

This book is available in quantity at special discounts for your group or organization. For further information, contact:

Triumph Books LLC
814 North Franklin Street
Chicago, Illinois 60610
(312) 337-0747
www.triumphbooks.com

Printed in U.S.A.
ISBN: 978-1-63727-577-1
Design by Preston Pisellini
Page production by Nord Compo

CONTENTS

PART 4 The Cradle of Greatness

PART 5 The Memorable Managers

PART 6 The Memorable Seasons

Foreword

The Minnesota Twins were very impactful to me as a young aspiring baseball player. I don't really remember much about my very, very young years, but as I started to be able to participate in organized baseball, watching and listening to Twins games was a huge part of my youth.

It was a little different back then. I didn't think about things like how Metropolitan Stadium compared to Yankee Stadium or what our attendance was compared to some of the other teams that were drawing more fans. I just knew that it was very real for me to be able to find players to look up to and be able to see the names that I was familiar with from other teams that came to play against my team. The growth over the decades has been remarkable. In some ways, it's just been a natural progression because it goes in sync with how the game has grown.

I remember watching the 1965 World Series at school. I was in third or fourth grade. They would roll this black-and-white TV into the classroom on a cart, and we watched some of those games on television. I don't remember if we were able to watch the whole game. If it started at a certain time, then we would be out of school before it was over. I didn't think it was overly special. It was just, *Hey, this means I don't have to do math today!*

To watch the Twins run through their time—including their first World Series in 1965 to eventually needing a new facility with the Dome, which seemed like the best thing for the sustainability for the organization, and finally coming into the modern age when we were able to complete the deal to bring Target Field to the Twin Cities—it all has been remarkable.

So I've seen the growth in the interest as far as the regional impact, especially with the Twins Caravan stops that I've made regularly for many years now. I was doing them since I came back in 1996 as a player and then staying on board with the organization in various capacities and, certainly, in my managerial years. And there are different legs to each caravan. We hit northern Minnesota, we hit the Dakotas, and then they would get down to Iowa a little bit too.

The ability to transmit our game both on TV and through the radio has just brought in a whole group of fans that we didn't have back in the beginning. And it was part of the reason that the club was able to stay afloat through all the years, including the contraction years. We have a very large market that far surpasses just the Twin Cities area.

Twins Territory is pretty much covered in this book. There's a tale about a young boy from Bismarck, North Dakota, who jumped into the station wagon with his father and rode into town to watch the Yankees when they played the Twins. He would one day become the president of that very franchise. There's another about a boy who rode his bike from his home in Bloomington to Metropolitan Stadium to watch his favorite hitter, Tony Oliva, play. He would one day play first base for the Twins. And there's one about a kid who would run into Twins catching great Earl Battey in St. Paul. That kid, me, would end up playing baseball for a living.

It was very rewarding to grow up with this franchise. And the stories in this book trace this franchise's history. The great players and coaches. The great moments. The stadiums.

Part of the pride of being a Minnesotan is to have the professional teams we do. And I think the Twins, in some ways, were at the top of the list for their ability to connect to the public. Particularly the last 25 years, how they have found a way to stay melded into the community in more ways than just presenting, hopefully, an entertaining product.

When you think about growing up in Minnesota, you can think a lot about parks and recreation, our state parks, the clean, healthy lifestyle, and the change of seasons. Professional sports are a big part of that. And for me, the Twins were always the number one thing.

And the stories here reflect that history.

Paul Molitor, a World Series champion and seven-time All-Star, played for 21 years in Major League Baseball, including with the Minnesota Twins from 1996 to 1998 before returning to manage the team from 2015 to 2018. He was named AL Manager of the Year in 2017. A first-ballot Hall of Famer, Molitor learned the game on the playgrounds and in the rec centers of St. Paul, Minnesota, and starred locally in high school and at the University of Minnesota before embarking on his major league career.

PART 1

THE ORIGIN STORY

1

Bringing Major League Baseball to the Twin Cities

By the time the 1950s arrived, Minnesota didn't just have an appetite for Major League Baseball. Local fans of the national pastime starved for it.

OK, technically, the area did have a professional team in 1884, the St. Paul Saints of the Union Association, which was recognized as a major league. The Saints jumped from the Northwestern League to complete the season of another team, going 2–6–1, all on the road. The league disbanded after one year.

During that short gap from the late 1800s to the middle of the 20th century, local baseball enjoyed the rivalry between the Minneapolis Millers and St. Paul Saints of the American

Association. The Millers played in that league from 1902 to 1960 and were affiliated with the Red Sox, the New York Giants, then the Red Sox again. The Saints played in the American Association during the same period as the Millers. They were affiliated with the Chicago White Sox, the Dodgers—Brooklyn and Los Angeles versions—and, beginning in 2021, the Minnesota Twins.

The Millers and the Saints were longtime rivals, and it was enhanced because the Giants and Dodgers were rivals in the major leagues. The teams frequently played home-and-home doubleheaders, playing one side of the metropolitan area in the morning before playing the second game on the other side of town. Nicollet Park in Minneapolis to Lexington Park in St. Paul. Disagreements turned into feuds and feuds into fisticuffs.

It was a level of play a step below the majors and more affordable. And fans were able to see some great players on their way to the majors. A 19-year-old Ted Williams hit .366 with 43 homers and 142 RBI for the Millers in 1938. Orlando Cepeda and Hoyt Wilhelm were also former Millers. Duke Snider and Roy Campanella played for the Saints in the 1940s before they moved on to the Dodgers. There would be an appearance by Babe Ruth during an exhibition game or a barnstorming event. Some great young ballplayers came and went through the Twin Cities.

But by the 1950s, there was a hunger for more. Minnesota was ready to prove it was a major league town. They were tired of seeing great players use the area as a stepping stone to the majors. They wanted to be a destination city.

Fans' eagerness to see players come and stay in Minnesota peaked in 1951. Some guy named Willie Mays had a phenomenal 35-game run, batting .477 with eight homers and 30 RBI. His OPS—on base plus slugging percentage—was a staggering 1.323. The Giants had every right to call Mays up. That type of talent can't be ignored. It didn't stop some Millers fans from writing angry letters to Giants owner Horace Stoneham, which compelled him to take out an ad in a local paper explaining how the Giants needed him. Mays ended up in the Hall of Fame, slugging 660 home runs and being lauded as one of the greatest all-around players the game has seen. But Millers fans wanted his stay in Minneapolis to last a little longer.

One thing was clear through all of this—Minnesota wasn't interested in being a minor league locale much longer. Minnesota sought a major league franchise. Reaching that goal meant sacrifices, because the movement required them to experience all the emotions that go with finding the right partner to settle down with—Ups and downs. Progress and setbacks. Flirtation and rejection. Joy and pain.

Frankly, it was time for Major League Baseball to grow up, anyway.

From 1901 to 1960, there were 16 teams in MLB, eight in each league. A few teams had relocated during this period, but in 1950, no team was farther west than St. Louis, where the Browns and the Cardinals played before the Browns shifted to Baltimore. This arrangement had gotten stagnant. In 1900, the population of the United States was roughly 76 million. By 1950, it had more than doubled to 151 million. The population of the Twin Cities and surrounding areas has swelled to over 1 million, making it one of the top 15 metropolitan areas in the country. We were a budding metropolis, large enough for a Major League Baseball franchise.

Yet the league had 16 teams during that entire time frame. It did little to improve the game or adjust to modern times. Owners simply opened the gates and counted cash.

Even the U.S. House of Representatives advocated for expansion, claiming that MLB's East Coast alignment was "intolerable." Slowly, baseball realized a growth period was inevitable. And Minnesota wanted to be part of that growth. The best way to prove it was to have a stadium ready for a tenant to move into, local leaders felt.

This was the era before hotel and car rental taxes or personal seat licenses were used as revenue generating tools to fund stadiums. A passionate sportswriter and a few well-connected businessmen could get the ball rolling on bringing a team to town.

In May of 1952, a report in the *Minneapolis Star* revealed that the Minneapolis Chamber of Commerce was looking into a project that would bring Major League Baseball to town. Baseball owners had to come through on their end and allow expansion/relocation to happen, but Minneapolis wanted to be ready for that moment. And leaders indicated that funding the project would not be much of a problem.

Another reason Minneapolis began to fan the flames of big-league baseball—Milwaukee was completing work on a 37,000-seat stadium and wanted to be ready to accept a franchise when one became available. Milwaukee County Stadium opened in 1953 and held just over 36,000 fans. A year later, capacity was increased to over 44,000.

The nation's capital did weigh in on the matter while investigating whether baseball had an unfair monopoly. It concluded, following a report of more than 1,600 pages, that the Pacific Coast should not be denied opportunities for Major League Baseball.

Bill Veeck was trying to move the St. Louis Browns to Baltimore. Milwaukee was closing in on getting the Boston Braves to move into its new stadium for the 1953 season. It was believed at the time that a team moving to Milwaukee was barrier-breaking in that the league was more open to expanding westward than ever. Alarms went off in the Twin Cities.

The Browns and the Philadelphia A's, who moved to Kansas City before the 1955 season, would have taken the Twin Cities more seriously as a potential destination if it had made progress on building a stadium.

In March 1953 a committee was formed to investigate all aspects of bringing a major league club to the Twin Cities. The six-person committee consisted of three members from Minneapolis and three from St. Paul.

By the way, just to demonstrate how some things haven't changed, the story about the committee appeared on the front page of the *Minneapolis Star Tribune*. Below it was a story about Russia claiming that a U.S. plane had flown over Siberia to spy on them. Seventy years later, Russia attacked a U.S. drone it claimed was spying on them.

Later in 1953, the committee met with White Sox general manager Frank Lane, who was chairman of Major League Baseball's realignment committee. By then, owners had already met during the winter and Minnesota was one of the first locations mentioned for placement of a franchise. Lane buoyed their hopes for landing a team, touting their market size and opportunities for growth. He also revealed facets of the business of baseball, the expenses required and potential revenue streams.

Emboldened by the meeting, the committee—named the Metropolitan Sports Area Commission—got down to business about planning a new stadium—and figuring out how to land a team.

But while the Twin Cities worked on bringing in a team, there was a race for baseball to expand to the West Coast. Everything came to a head during a meeting in New York in September 1953. Bill Veeck was turned down in his bid to move the Browns to Baltimore, but the Twin Cities, flexing its civic and business muscle, officially bid for a major league team. Veeck was offered a temporary stadium for 1954, then a permanent stadium in 1955 that would hold 35,000. And a guarantee of 700,000 fans the first year. The Twin Cities had made its intentions clear.

It didn't work. The league forced Veeck, viewed as something between a maverick and a pest by some owners, to sell his stake in the Browns. Then the Browns were allowed to move to Baltimore and become the Orioles. Minnesota would have to wait, but building a stadium, they believed, would keep them at the front of the line for a franchise. But where to build it?

In 1954, the committee met with the University of Minnesota about acquiring 42 acres of land near the state fairgrounds in Falcon Heights. It was a quality location, located between Minneapolis and St. Paul in a part of St. Paul known as the Midway neighborhood, named for obvious reasons. The school turned them down. But Herman Kossow, the mayor of nearby Bloomington, invited the committee to meet with him to discuss a stadium on a plot of land near 78th and Cedar, 160 acres of mostly farmland. It was farther away, but still within a 10-mile radius of both downtown Minneapolis and St. Paul.

The two cities had worked closely on the stadium project up to that point. They had been bitter rivals in many areas before that, going back to the 1800s. In fact, there was a battle during the 1890 census for each to be declared the bigger city in terms of population. It included U.S. Marshals raiding a hotel where Minneapolis enumerators padded their census numbers. Seven men were arrested and put on a train to St. Paul. St. Paul had hired a detective to follow Minneapolis enumerators and catch them in the act. Relations between the cities had thawed in the years following that, but there was always some semblance of a sibling rivalry between Minneapolis and St. Paul. In the 1950s, both pushed for the major league stadium. They were allies, until they weren't. The committee's decision to cozy up with Bloomington was not accepted by St. Paul.

St. Paul had approved $2 million for a stadium that would serve its community. Building it in Midway would have achieved that. Either the city couldn't or wouldn't have its money spent on a project in Bloomington. St. Paul would later offer up two other sites not far from the one near Falcon Heights. But the committee seemed to focus on Bloomington, which offered more than twice the acreage of the other offers—land that could be used for parking and other projects.

In June, a request was made to the Minneapolis City Council to issue tax-exempt revenue bonds to help pay for a stadium that would cost between $4 million and $5 million.

Charles Johnson, sports editor of the *Minneapolis Star* and *Tribune*—who was banging the drum for expansion—had just returned from talks with baseball officials, confident they would get a team once groundbreaking on a new stadium took place. Kansas City, Montreal and Toronto were working on stadium plans at the time, but the Twins were told they were the first option on baseball's list of expansion cities.

There were some twists and turns along the way, as the bonds needed to be sold in multiple waves. But enough funding was secured by May, and groundbreaking took place in June of 1955 on a stadium that would be ready by April of 1956. It would hold 15,000 seats at first but would be expandable once an MLB team was ready to move. As groundbreaking approached, New York Giants owner Horace Stoneham refuted a story that claimed he already had decided to move his team to the Twin Cities. There's a backstory here. In 1951, Stoneham purchased 40 acres of land just west of Highway 100 and just south of what is now Interstate 394 in St. Louis Park,

Minnesota. And Stoneham indicated that he would one day bring the Giants to Minnesota.

In March of 1956, MLB commissioner Ford Frick told a *Twin Cities* columnist, "Instead of switching franchises from one city to another, as has been done, there will be true expansion. There will be more big-league cities." In recent years, Boston, Chicago, New York, Philadelphia and St. Louis all had multiple teams in the league, and it became evident that some cities weren't big enough for that. So the Boston Braves moved to Milwaukee, the Philadelphia A's moved to Kansas City and the St. Louis Browns moved to Baltimore by 1956.

Meanwhile, the Minneapolis Millers christened the new ballpark on April 24, 1956, with a 5–3 loss to Wichita in front of 18,366. In July, the ballpark was officially named Metropolitan Stadium. Eventually, locals nicknamed it the Met.

Now all they needed was a major league team to move in. Would it be the Giants, led by Willie Mays? The Millers were a Giants affiliate and Stoneham raved about the new ballpark after getting a tour of the facility the day before the home opener. The Giants had even sent their head groundskeeper to Bloomington months before to oversee the creation of the playing field.

Stoneham took things to another level in May 1956 when he said he was considering a move to Minnesota. The comments came right before he was to meet with New York City mayor Robert F. Wagner about a new stadium. Even then, the leverage game was played. But Stoneham continued to think about moving the Giants. In October 1956, he announced that the Giants weren't moving to Minnesota for the 1957 but told the *Minneapolis Star*, "I would say that Minneapolis is a major league city." The wait for major league baseball continued.

The next year was pivotal in the history of major league baseball, as long-awaited expansion began to take shape.

Minnesota officials continued to court Stoneham, who reportedly told Brooklyn Dodgers owner Walter O'Malley that his intentions were to move the Giants to Minnesota. O'Malley asked Stoneham to consider moving to San Francisco.

The timeline gets fuzzy here, as it isn't known for sure who met with whom at what time and what was said to change Stoneham's mind. But San Francisco mayor George Christopher went to New York twice to meet with O'Malley and Stoneham. During one of those meetings, according to the *New York Times*, Christopher pitched a stadium deal as Stoneham sipped on Scotch. O'Malley and Stoneham, both unhappy with their current stadium situations, were closing in on becoming a package deal to move to the West Coast. Having two clubs out west made it easier for visiting teams to travel that far for two series instead of one.

On August 12, Stoneham informed the Metropolitan Sports Area Committee, "If I move the Giants in 1958, it will be to the West Coast." He had met off and on with the committee over the previous weeks to iron out details of a potential move to Minnesota. After the call on August 12, the committee began contacting other teams to seek their interest in moving to Minnesota, which had a state-of-the-art ballpark but no major league team playing in it.

On August 19, the Giants' board of directors voted 8–1 to move to San Francisco. The Twin Cities group was down on one knee, holding out a ring. And Stoneham wouldn't take it. Perhaps a stake in a Scotch distillery would have helped.

Spurned but undeterred, Gerald Moore, the chairman of the committee tasked with bringing major league baseball to the Twin Cities, made an August 21 phone call to Calvin Griffith, who, along with his sister, Thelma, had taken over the Washington Senators following the death of their uncle,

Clark, in 1955. Clark had taken in Calvin and Thelma from his brother-in-law, James, as children. And they eventually took on the Griffith name. Calvin was a batboy for the Washington Senators team that won the 1924 World Series.

Between 1956 and 1959, the Senators averaged 95 losses a season. Griffith would invest in prospect development and had a scout named Joe Cambria who tapped into Cuba for young talent. But it would be a few years before those efforts would come to fruition. Meanwhile, the Senators floundered on the field as perennial cellar-dwellers.

Calvin Griffith tried to change a few things upon his arrival. The Senators played in Griffith Stadium, located at the current site of the Howard University Hospital. It was a largely Black neighborhood. A young Duke Ellington, a big baseball fan, sold peanuts for a while at the park. He later became one of the great entertainers of his time.

Griffith Stadium was a cavernous ballpark in which the 1955 Senators hit just 20 of their 80 home runs. Griffith decided to move in the fences and shorten some parts of the fence, to make long balls more likely. The left field foul pole, previously 402 feet down the line, was shortened to 388. The left-center field power alley was a reasonable 360 feet away. But the inner fence that was put up shortened home run distances by 10 to 12 feet.

Welp, home runs jumped from 80 in 1955 to 112 in 1956. But the pitching staff's ERA rose from 4.62 to 5.33 from working in a smaller park.

Griffith also installed a beer garden before the 1957 season, not afraid to admit that he did it for revenue. But no matter how short the fences were or how cold the beer was, the Senators were hard to watch.

What didn't help was that, in 1954, the St. Louis Browns had moved to Baltimore in a renovated Memorial Stadium. The

Orioles drew over 1 million fans that season—more than twice the Senators. Not only did the Orioles cut into the Senators' market, but fans also no longer had to drive down to D.C. to watch a poor product.

Griffith sought a better situation. He had spoken to Los Angeles in 1956 about a move west, but the Dodgers and Giants jumped in and headed west before the 1958 season. Moore's call ignited discussions between the Senators and the Minneapolis committee, culminating in a bid by the end of September. Another courtship had begun. Negotiations continued into October, with the Minneapolis group making a final offer near the end of the month. That offer was rejected by the Senators' board of directors, making expansion for 1958 impossible.

There were a few things in Griffith's orbit during this time. The team was bad. The stadium was barely adequate. Gabe Murphy, a minority owner, didn't approve of how Griffith ran the team. Murphy tried to become majority owner and filed multiple lawsuits to force a sale. Another minority owner, Robert Rodenberg, filed suit in September, looking to oust Griffith and keep the team in Washington.

Griffith also was pilloried by local media. Even Griffith's wife, Natalie, preferred her D.C. lifestyle to moving to the land of 10,000 frozen lakes.

The biggest obstacle to moving the team might have been his inability to get enough support from other American League owners to vote in his favor. And their trepidation likely stemmed from Congress, which often eyed their antitrust exemption. There were concerns that pulling a team out of the nation's capital would trigger insurmountable political backlash.

Things came to a head in September of 1958 during an owners' meeting in Chicago. Griffith let it be known that he would not ask the league for permission to move to Minnesota for 1959. This marked the second time Griffith had declined to request a move to Minnesota. He still had two lawsuits from minority owners he was dealing with.

The Minneapolis committee, which had met with Griffith several times over the past year, listened to his concerns and continuously revised its offers to address those concerns. They had also received a commitment from the city to issue bonds to fund a $9 million project to expand Metropolitan Stadium to 41,000 seats. After the latest setback, the committee threw up its hands and pulled its offer from the table. They were assured by the league that they would be next in line for a franchise, but they had heard that before.

By April of 1959, Griffith began talking about moving to Minnesota—again. The committee kicked off discussion around August and presented an offer that Griffith loved: Annual profits of $430,000 in each of the first five seasons, based on attendance of at least 1 million. Griffith thought he had the votes this time but was denied by owners again. The threat of action from D.C., again, was a factor. During offseason meetings, owners discussed AL expansion that included the Senators moving to Minnesota, with an expansion club taking over in Washington to keep the political heat off owners. Officials, however, were unable to pull that plan together in time. Minnesota would have to go another year without a major league team.

But leverage was on the way in the form of the Continental League, which aimed at joining the American League and National League as a third major league. The concept was hatched after New York mayor Robert Wagner unsuccessfully tried to get another National League team in town to replace the departed Giants. The Twin Cities joined Houston, New York, Denver and Toronto as cities to have franchises as part of the proposal. Former Dodgers president Branch

Rickey—the man responsible for breaking the color barrier by signing Jackie Robinson and who also introduced innovations in player development—was named president. The Continental League announced in July of 1959 that it would begin play April 18, 1961.

After years of getting its hopes up for expansion only to have them crushed, Minnesota had committed to having a team in the Continental League. The commitment was confirmed during a January 1960 visit by Rickey and other league officials. The Minnesota ownership group was led by Wheelock Whitney, a 33-year-old vice president of J.M. Dain and Co., an investment banking firm. The Dayton Co., Theodore Hamm Brewing Company and George S. Pillsbury were also part of the impressive group.

Washington, D.C., was finalizing plans for RFK Stadium to be built. The football team was on board, but Griffith hadn't signed a lease yet and told some people he still hoped to move to Minnesota. One of Griffith's concerns was revenue. The Redskins, as they were called then, rented Griffith Stadium from him. That would not be the case at RFK, and Griffith didn't like losing revenue. While plans for the Continental League moved forward, behind the scenes the likes of Moore and Whitney continued to ask Griffith to move to the Twin Cities.

Then Rickey and his band of Continental hopefuls were invited to meeting in Chicago with the major leagues' expansion committee. On August 2, 1960, the interested parties gathered at a Chicago hotel. Rickey's pitch was clear—expand or the Continental League would compete with the AL and NL. The response: *We will expand, but you must disband. And Continental cities are not guaranteed to receive expansion teams.*

After all the work to secure funding for a stadium, reaching out to potential tenants only to see them use their site as leverage to get better deals at home, Minnesota was as hopeful as ever of getting a team. In late August, owners voted to expand to 10 teams by December 1, 1961. And the Continental League had disbanded without playing a game.

About this time, St. Paul let it be known that it was willing to expand Midway Stadium to 40,000 if the Bloomington project broke down.

Minnesota officials went to New York to attend owners' meetings on October 26. They didn't like their chances because Los Angeles and Dallas–Fort Worth had entered the pecking order for AL expansion teams. After seven years of trying to land a team, the local delegation believed it was about to be turned down again, despite having a stadium built and financing in place for expanding it. Moore, however, kept working over Griffith, touting the Twin Cities as the right place at the right time.

According to a report by *Minneapolis Star* sports editor Charles Johnson, who was in New York to cover the meeting, reporters were brought to a press conference with AL President Joe Cronin. Johnson braced for bad news. It was then announced that Washington's move to the Twin Cities had been approved.

Johnson wrote that the Minnesota delegation was "speechless" at the news. The Senators were moving for the 1961 season, while a new franchise would replace them in Washington and an expansion team in Los Angeles—the Angels—would begin play. This was after the National League announced that Houston and the New York Mets would begin play in 1962. The winds of expansion finally flowed through the major leagues. And the Twin Cities were happily caught in the jet stream. The NFL, earlier in the year, had awarded a franchise to Minnesota for the start of the 1961 season. Five years after breaking ground on Metropolitan Stadium, the area now had two new major sports franchises. Baseball was the first big fish the committee cast its line for. In the end, Griffith wound up with a nice deal that was hammered out over three meetings the night before the announcement, with the last one wrapping up around 3:00 AM. It included a guarantee of 2.5 million in attendance over the first three years, indemnity payments of $250,000 to Boston and the Dodgers for the removal of their minor league teams, plus full concession revenue and low rental. And Metropolitan Stadium's capacity had to be increased to 40,000.

In addition to stories about the league's decision, on October 27 the *Minneapolis Star* ran pictures of some of the Senators headed to the Twin Cities. It included Harmon Killebrew, Bob Allison, Earl Battey, Camilo Pascual and others—players Twins fans would come to know and love in the years ahead.

Griffith, in his biography, claimed he had no inkling that expansion was on the agenda at those 1960 meetings, although reports suggested otherwise. He apparently changed hotel rooms three times in one day to avoid reporters.

"I told Minneapolis [supporters] before the meeting there's no way there was going to be any expansion," Griffith said. "It wasn't on the agenda. Then I sat there [at the meeting] like a damn fool wondering what's going on."

What began as a dream in 1952 had finally become a reality. It was a long process, but the Minnesota committee shook off the bad losses like winning teams do.

"They always said to us, 'Well, if you just build a stadium, then we'll come.'" Whitney, who joined the recruitment team in the late 1950s, told the *St. Paul Pioneer Press*. "Well, we built a stadium, and all they did was use that against us.

"I mean, it was a racket. It was a way for major league owners around the country to ask for more parking revenue, lower rent, a higher percentage of everything. And when the league said no, they'd say, 'By gosh, we're probably going to move.'"

The Twin Cities might have been used by owners to get better deals for their clubs. But it proved it was a legitimate big-league locale by drawing more than 1 million fans in each of its first 10 seasons. The role of the Continental League can't be ignored. It forced Major League Baseball to expand. Branch Rickey's dream helped Minnesotans reach theirs.

Calvin Griffith was one of the more polarizing figures in Minnesota sports history. He was the man who brought major league baseball to the state. But it also brought him. He was well-known for his tight-fisted ways and contract squabbles with his best players.

Griffith also had no concept of public relations. He was incapable of telling people what they wanted to hear. He would tell them what was on his mind. And that occasionally landed him in hot water.

In no other moment was this clearer than when Griffith made his infamous appearance at the Waseca Lions Club on September 28, 1978. Waseca is a town about 65 miles south of the Twin Cities. Nick Coleman, then a reporter for the *Minneapolis Tribune*, was in the audience. Here's what he wrote when Griffith, who had downed a couple of cocktails, was asked about moving the team from Washington. Griffith first complained about the Twin Cities press. Then, according to Coleman, "at that point Griffith interrupted himself, lowered his voice and asked if there were any blacks around. After he looked around the room and assured himself that his audience was white, Griffith resumed his answer. 'I'll tell you why we came to Minnesota,' he said. 'It was when I found out you only had 15,000 blacks here. Black people don't go to ball games, but they'll fill up a rassling ring and put up such a chant it'll scare you to death. It's unbelievable. We came here because you've got good, hardworking white people here.'"

There were calls then for Griffith to sell the team. Civil rights groups called for boycotts of Twins games. Griffith claimed he was misunderstood, that he had downed a couple drinks and was trying to be funny. "Look, I'm no bigot," he said. But he misunderstood the impact of his words.

He continued to be an engaging character who was unfiltered with some of his comments. I met Griffith in 1998 when I joined the Twins beat. I found Griffith to be a jovial old fellow who frequently stopped by the press box to grab a hot dog. Learning about his comments infuriated me. Without being there that day in Waseca, it appears that Griffith said something that was enormously stupid in a public setting. At the very least, Griffith was ignorant and insensitive.

Griffith never made another racist comment again, but he continued to rankle some with his bluntness. And an All-Star team could have been assembled just from the players he upset during negotiations: Bert Blyleven, Camilo Pascual, Earl Battey, Rod Carew, Roy Smalley, Lyman Bostock, Larry Hisle. Griffith could scout, sign and develop impact players. He just couldn't retain them.

When Target Field opened in 2010, a statue of Griffith was erected outside one of its entrances. In 2020, a year in which race relations in America were strained by the murder of George Floyd by the Minneapolis Police Department, fans took umbrage with the Twins' decision to erect a statue of such a controversial figure. The Twins, whose owners, the Pohlad Family, donated $25 million to fight racial injustice, decided to take down the statue. The speech was Griffith's biggest blunder. Bigger than the trade of Carew before the 1979 season. Bigger than the firing of Billy Martin in 1969.

Carew released a statement the day the Twins announced the removal of the statue. "I have long forgiven Cal for his insensitive comments and do not believe he was a racist," it read. "That was NOT my personal experience with Calvin Griffith—prior to or following that day in 1978."

PART 2

THE ICONS

2

Harmon Killebrew

WHAT'S LOVABLE ABOUT NICKNAMES IS THEIR ORIGIN. ARE they descriptive of a person's looks or behavior? Are they the result of some strange occurrence? Baseball has been the platform for thousands of nicknames through its history.

Ernie Banks was the face of the Cubs during his playing career and after—so much so that he was nicknamed "Mr. Cub." Reggie Jackson was called "Mr. October" for his playoff excellence. Mike Hargrove earned the nickname "the Human Rain Delay" because of how much time he took between pitches before getting set in the batter's box.

The stories behind some nicknames are too good to be true. Jeff Leonard always projected a mean and dangerous expression. A teammate started calling him "Penitentiary Face," and it stuck. In 1986, Leonard asked the media to call him Jeffrey instead of Jeff. His nickname also was changed to "Correctional Institute Face." Jim Grant, who pitched four seasons for the Twins, got the nickname "Mudcat," unfairly. A teammate thought he was from Mississippi (he was born in L.A.) and started calling him Mudcat. Grant tried to set the record straight but ended up embracing the nickname, as he later became the first Black pitcher in the American League to win 20 games in a season. One reason Markus Lynn Betts is nicknamed "Mookie" is because his parents liked NBA player Mookie Blaylock. They weren't the only ones. Legendary grunge band Pearl Jam was initially named "Mookie Blaylock" because its members were also fans of the player. The name was changed to avoid potential legal entanglements.

Harmon Killebrew didn't like the nickname "Killer." He felt it didn't represent his character. It doesn't. While it was a play on his last name, it also represented what he did to baseballs. Similar to why Babe Ruth was called "the Sultan of Swat," Hank Aaron "Hammerin' Hank," Frank Thomas "the Big Hurt" or Frank Howard "the Capital Punisher," Killebrew didn't just hit baseballs. He killed them. Most of his 573 career blasts were high-towering drives that took several seconds to leave the park. He also crushed a few pitches that left ballparks in a hurry.

In 1960, when he was playing for the Washington Senators, Killebrew hit a ball off the facing of the upper deck in left field that bounced back all the way to shortstop. When Killebrew hit a ball, it stayed hit. If satellite television had been more prevalent during Killebrew's career, he might have hit the satellite. But he would be revered for his power like Aaron Judge and Pete Alonso were in the modern age. And he would have received more national recognition.

"Growing up in Southern California, for some reason my favorite players were Willie Mays, Carl Yastrzemski and Harmon," said fellow Hall of Famer George Brett, who played with Killebrew on the 1975 Kansas City Royals. "If Harmon had hit left-handed, he would have been Babe Ruth. It wasn't just the number of home runs, but how far they went and how high they went. He hit the highest home runs I had ever seen."

His ability to hit baseballs where no baseballs have gone before helped make Killebrew the first Twin to be elected to the Hall of Fame in 1984.

The technology to measure home run distances didn't exist at the time, so many estimates might have been a tad high. But one of the joys of discussing America's Pastime was being able to begin a sentence, "Did you hear how far he hit that ball?" That's what Killebrew brought to the game. He provided fodder for barbershop conversations. Parents would have stories for their children. Former Twin Kent Hrbek referred to Killebrew as "Paul Bunyan with a uniform on."

One of Killebrew's longest home runs—there were many of them—occurred in Kansas City at the old Municipal Stadium when he was still with the Senators. Killebrew sent a blast past the light towers, over a parking lot and to some railroad tracks. Estimates had the home run traveling over 500 feet.

When the Senators moved to Minnesota, the new fan base knew Killer was coming. Baseball fans throughout the Midwest traveled to Metropolitan Stadium to watch Killebrew. And if he hit a home run, they had something to discuss with the locals for the next week. As the Twins traveled through the league, fans were mesmerized over the tape-measure blasts off his bat. In his first year in Minnesota, he showed off his prodigious power with a 475-foot home run halfway up the batter's eye at Metropolitan Stadium.

On August 3, 1962, Killebrew became the first player to homer over the left-field roof at venerable Tiger Stadium. The two-run clout came in the fourth inning off Jim Bunning and brought the Twins back after they had fallen behind 3-0. They went on to win the game 7–4. That roof was quite a distance from home plate. The front of the roof in left-center was 455 feet from home plate, and a Tigers official said it would take a 500-foot blast to get it on the roof. Frank Howard, Cecil Fielder and Mark McGwire were the only other players to clear the left field roof of Tiger Stadium, which opened in 1912 and closed in 2001.

On May 24, 1964, Killebrew hit the longest home run in Baltimore Memorial Stadium history, an estimated 471 feet off Orioles right-hander Milt Pappas that cleared the hedges in center field. Boog Powell was the only other player to clear the shrubbery. Killebrew hit 68 homers against the Orioles in his career, tied for third most against any opponent. "Killebrew could hit the ball out of any park, including Yellowstone," Baltimore manager Paul Richards said.

In August 1965, Killebrew dislocated his left elbow, which sapped him of some of his power. He missed 48 games, then batted .184 with three home runs when he returned. He still had trouble straightening out his elbow as the 1966 season approached. But the moment Killebrew felt he was fully recovered can be traced to June 20 in Anaheim. Killebrew tore into a George Brunet pitch and sent it sailing over the wall until it landed near the base of the famous 230-foot "A" frame scoreboard. There was no estimate, but he considered it one of the longest—and hardest—home runs he'd hit to that point of his career. He was subdued as he spoke with a reporter following the game because the Twins had lost.

Killebrew also came through in the clutch. One of the biggest home runs of his career helped propel the Twins to the 1965 AL pennant. In the final game before the All-Star break, Killebrew hit a two-run home run with two outs and a 3–2 count in the ninth off Pete Mikkelsen for a 6–5 win over the Yankees. "It was a sweet one, all right," Killebrew said, biting into a slice of watermelon following the game.

The Twins led the AL by five games going into the break. The Yankees had been to the last five World Series, but Killebrew's homer put the Yankees behind by 14.5 games, and they were never heard from the rest of the season. The victory also made fans believe that the team was for real. Killebrew was 3-for-4 with two RBI and two runs scored. It was considered to be one of the best games of his career.

The day the Twins tied the major league record for most home runs hit in an inning, Killebrew was right in the middle of it. Rich Rollins and Zoilo Versalles homered off Kansas City's Catfish Hunter in the seventh inning, chasing Hunter. Tony Oliva and Don Mincher went deep off Paul Lindblad. Then John Wyatt was brought in to face Killebrew, who crushed a 3–2 pitch out to left.

Killebrew's signature blast took place on June 3, 1967, when he dug in against California's Lew Burdette with two runners on base in the fourth inning. "It was a knuckleball that started too high, and it got higher," Burdette said that day of the juicy pitch. Killebrew connected and sent a drive into the second deck of Metropolitan Stadium's left field bleachers, the first time a ball had been hit there. "This one felt good," Killebrew told the *Minneapolis Star Tribune* that day, "but then the one I hit in Detroit went over the roof." The initial estimate of 430 feet was met with objections from the Twins brass. Twins third base coach Billy Martin, who was with the Yankees the day Mickey Mantle hit a legendary 500-foot home run in 1953, claimed Killebrew's blast went farther.

Tom Mee, the Twins' public relations director, revised the distance a day later to 520 feet. (It would be revised one more time, to 522 feet.) Stadium announcer Bob Casey informed fans of the update as Killebrew stepped to the plate against Jack Sanford. Killebrew hammered the first pitch off the facing of the second deck. Mee announced the distance at 434 feet at the point of impact, with some asserting that the ball would have traveled 550 feet if it hadn't struck the facing. This was the effect Killebrew had on the game, creating arguments about home run distances in press boxes across the league. The Mall of America, the expansive shopping center that opened in 1992 in the same area where Metropolitan Stadium once stood, has marked the spot where Killebrew's June 3 blast landed with a seat from the stadium attached to a wall. Next to the seat is a sign thanking Killebrew for the memories. In 1973, one of the roads bordering the mall, 83rd Street in Bloomington, was renamed Killebrew Drive.

What is undeniable is Killebrew did things that very few others have done in the game's 120 years. Beginning in 2015, the Statcast era enabled fans to track speed of pitches, exit velocities off the bat, launch angles and home run distances. The longest home run of the Statcast era is 505 feet, hit in 2019 by Nomar Mazara of the Texas Rangers. Killebrew would have been the launch-angle champion of Statcast. Maybe technology would have taken a couple dozen feet off some of Killebrew's home run distances. But just think—it could have *added* distance. We'll never know.

Harmon Clayton Killebrew Jr. was born on June 29, 1936, in Payette, Idaho. He was the youngest of five children and son of an athletic father. Killebrew was stockily built, with strong hands and thick wrists. He believed that he got his strength from hustling 10-gallon cans of milk during his summers as a youth. True or not, Killebrew could snap the bat through the strike zone and send baseballs flying father than one could imagine. Harmon Sr. wanted his sons to play sports and encouraged them to get involved at a young age. During his Hall of Fame speech in 1984, Killebrew told the large crowd gathered on a field in Cooperstown, New York, what his childhood was like. "He was a man that took a great deal of pride in his children," Killebrew said of his father. "I'll never forget, we used to play a lot of ball out in the front yard, and my mother would say, 'You're tearing up the grass and digging holes in the front yard?' And my father would say, 'We're not raising grass here, we're raising boys.'" The audience applauded.

As a prep athlete, Killebrew lettered in football, basketball, baseball and track. He had signed with the University of Oregon to play football—he was a quarterback—while playing baseball in the spring. But it's amazing what you can learn on the grapevine. Clark Griffith, owner of the Washington Senators, often had politicians at his games. One was Herman Welker, a U.S. senator from Idaho. Griffith remarked one day about the lack of an offensive infielder on his team. Welker began bending Griffith's ear about a youngster in Idaho who might be the perfect signing. Griffith sent his scout, Ossie Bluege, who rented a car and drove through 60 miles of rain to see him play. The first game was rained out, and it rained the next day too. But the locals were aware a big-league scout was in town and promised there would be a game as soon as the rain let up. They even poured gasoline on the field and lit it to burn off the moisture. Once the game started, Killebrew connected on a long drive to left that landed in a field well beyond the fence. The next morning, Bluege walked off the distance. It was 435 feet. Bluege left town, but not before dropping off a contract offer. Killebrew signed a three-year, $30,000 contract that included a $4,000 bonus. That made Killebrew a "bonus baby," meaning that he had to spend two years on the major league roster. He played in 47 games those first two years, batting

.215 with four home runs, none in his first season. Killebrew spent most of the next three seasons in the minors, getting the seasoning he needed his first two years. But the bonus-baby program kept wealthy teams from hoarding young talent and stashing them in the minors. "Mainly, I had to learn patience and the strike zone and concentration," Killebrew said. "Those were the main things."

Killebrew had hoped he would make the major league club in 1958, but he failed to survive the roster cuts. Not only was he sent to the minors—he was sent to another organization. The Senators didn't have a Class AAA affiliate at the time, so they sent him to the White Sox outpost in Indianapolis, where a dejected Killebrew played poorly and considered quitting the sport. Bluege stepped in and assured him that things would turn out for the better if he stuck with the plan. Things got worse before they were better, as Killebrew was shipped back to the Senators' Class AA team in Charlotte. Maybe it lit a fire under Killebrew, who hit .308 with 17 home runs and 54 RBI in 86 games. It earned him 13 games in the majors at the end of the season.

Washington was out of options by 1959. The Senators had to keep Killebrew, trade him or risk losing him in a draft. Griffith had made up his mind. He traded third baseman Eddie Yost, a better defensive player than Killebrew with an outstanding batting eye, to Detroit. That allowed Killebrew to open the season at third base. Manager Cookie Lavagetto preferred Yost but followed orders. On Opening Day, Killebrew homered well into the left-field stands. That was the first of 42 home runs Killebrew hit during his first full season in the majors. He was named to both All-Star teams—there were two Midsummer Classics at the time.

So when the Senators moved to the Twin Cities for the 1961 season, Killebrew was establishing himself as one of the most feared sluggers in the game. But he had reservations. He loved playing in Washington and was not in favor of the move. He had played in Metropolitan Stadium when he was with Indianapolis, and it was no D.C. in the springtime. Also, the Senators were turning the corner after years of basement dwelling, and Killebrew felt that the fans who stuck with them deserved to see them when they became a contender.

While the Minnesota spring was as cold as he expected, the fans were warm and welcoming. "I loved the fans because they were down-to-earth Minnesota people," he said. "The people in the Upper Midwest were the same people I grew up around in Idaho." His housewarming gift in 1961 was 46 home runs and 122 RBI to go with a .288 batting average. He hit 48, 45 and 49 home runs in each of the next three seasons. Twins fans knew the routine by then. Come early to watch Killer take batting practice, then don't leave before his final at-bat. No one wanted to miss his next moonshot.

Despite injuring his elbow and missing seven weeks during the 1965 season, Killebrew helped the Twins reach the World Series. He batted .286 and belted a home run in Game 4 off Don Drysdale. Despite the Twins taking a 2–0 series lead, Los Angeles prevailed in seven games behind a dominant outing by Sandy Koufax. That Game 7 loss was the only loss at home in the three World Series in which the Twins have played. They won titles in 1987 and 1991 while going undefeated at home.

Killebrew was named to the 1967 All-Star team at first base, making him the first player ever to make the All-Star team at three different positions. He returned to the All-Star Game in 1968 despite batting .204 with 13 homers and 34 RBI at the break. But a bad season got worse when he stretched at first to catch a throw from Jim Fregosi and had his front foot give way in the soft indoor dirt as Curt Flood attempted to beat out a hit. Killebrew caught the throw but pretty much did a split while doing so. And Killebrew was not built for splits. He tore his left hamstring so badly that a piece of bone also tore off his pelvis. "You could hear it pop from the dugout," National League pitcher Don Drysdale said after the game. Killebrew missed 56 games before returning on September 1. By then, the Twins had tumbled out of the race and finished in seventh place. That 1968 season was a strange one for the Twins, Killebrew and baseball. The Twins were coming off the Great Pennant Race of 1967, when they lost the final three games of the regular season to yield the American League title to Boston. Killebrew ended up with a lost season. And baseball had become fed up with pitchers dominating. The mound was lowered for 1969. And each league expanded by two teams each, diluting the talent. An offensive surge soon followed.

In 1969, a healthy Killebrew couldn't be stopped while winning his first and only Most Valuable Player award. He hit .276 with 49 homers and a whopping 140 RBI. Cesar Tovar batted .288 that season. Rich Reese hit .322. Rod Carew hit .332. Tony Oliva hit .309 with 24 home runs and 101 RBI. There were men on base for Killer all season long. "I felt like I could have had about 240," said Killebrew, who led the team with 106 runs that season. All that firepower was no match for Mike Cuellar, Dave McNally, Earl Weaver and the Baltimore Orioles, who swept the Twins in the American League Championship Series. Harmon was at the height of his powers. His 393 home runs in the 1960s were the most of any player. But he couldn't fuel playoff success. The 1970 Twins were also swept by the Orioles, getting outscored 27–10.

By 1971, Killebrew had become the first Twin to earn a six-figure salary from frugal owner Calvin Griffith, making $115,000 that season. He hit "just" 28 homers in 1971 but led the league with 119 RBI and 114 walks. But there was a milestone moment that season.

On April 27, 1969, Killebrew hit career home run No. 400 off Gary Peters at Chicago's Comiskey Park. So No. 500—something that only nine players before him had done—seemed inevitable. For his career, Killebrew averaged a home run every 14 trips to the plate, second only to Bade Ruth, who did so every 12th trip. But that ratio was watered down in 1971. It took a little over a month for Killebrew to hit No. 499 when he connected off Boston's Luis Tiant. The Twins had held Harmon Killebrew mug night on July 6, thinking he would have reached the milestone by then. Killebrew had gone two weeks without a home run when he faced Baltimore left-hander Mike Cuellar in the first inning on August 10, 1971. "I didn't feel the pressure, if that's what you want to call it, until a couple weeks ago," Killebrew said that night. "There was that mug job, and people kept asking when I would do it. You try harder in those situations." The "when" was answered in the first inning that night when Killebrew jacked a Cuellar curveball 385 feet to left and into the stands for his 500th home run. Killebrew received a standing ovation from the crowd of 15,881 as he briskly jogged around the bases. He later tipped his cap to the audience when he arrived at the dugout. The weight lifted off his shoulders, Killebrew also homered off Cuellar in the sixth.

That milestone homer might have been the highlight of the season. Over the next three seasons, Killebrew produced only 44 home runs. A knee injury in 1973 limited him to 69 games. He battled knee problems and chronic pain in his big toe later in his career. His body was giving out on him. He was at that point in his career where it took more time to prepare for games and recover from them. It's something many ballplayers face late in their careers. For the fan, it's hard to watch your heroes no longer be heroes. Killebrew's baseball mind was sharp. His strike zone judgment was impeccable. It's hard enough hitting a baseball when fully healthy. Noted physicist Robert Adair once wrote that a batter has roughly two-tenths of a second to decide to swing at a pitch or not. Even if the batter decides to offer at a pitch, hand-eye coordination is vital to striking the ball at the right point. Once aging and physical ailments invade this process, hitters lose their groove.

This was where Killebrew was at in 1972. He was still useful, slugging 26 home runs with 74 RBI while posting an .817 on base-plus-slugging percentage. He hit just five homers in 1973 as he battled the knee problems. He batted .222 with 13 home runs and 54 RBI in 1974. The Twins, notably owner Calvin Griffith, had a problem on their hands. The designated hitter had arrived in the American League, which would have helped Killebrew play a few seasons. But the Twins already had a DH in Tony Oliva, who had undergone several knee surgeries. Killebrew would split time at DH with Oliva while making occasional appearances at first base. Making matters worse during Killebrew's final seasons with the Twins, those teams were mired in mediocrity, going 77–77 in 1972, 81–81 in 1973 and 82–80 in 1974.

Griffith couldn't stop himself from saving a buck, especially when attendance was down. And it didn't matter if it was at the expense of one of the most popular Twins of all time.

Following the 1974 season, Griffith offered Killebrew $52,000 to either be a player-coach or manager for the Twins' Class AAA team in Tacoma, Washington. Killebrew wanted to play at least one more season, so Griffith allowed him to find an opportunity elsewhere. It was a public relations blunder. Killebrew was unable to put on a Twins uniform one more time, doff his cap to fans and feel the love. He was unable to spend his entire career with one organization. Teammate Jim Kaat, who had annual contract squabbles with Griffith, told Killebrew that Stan Musial was kicked upstairs to a vice president role at the end of his career with the Cardinals. Griffith offered to kick Killebrew down to Tacoma. Killebrew then signed with Kansas City for a 1975 season that would be his last. In 106 games, he batted .199 with 14 homers. In the final plate appearance of his career, Killebrew reached on an error and was replaced by a pinch runner. The final home run of his career, fittingly, came just over a week earlier at Metropolitan Stadium against the Twins.

Killebrew weighed an offer from Japan for 1976 but declined. He reached out to Griffith about managing the Twins, but the owner sought someone with experience and went for Gene Mauch. By spring training in 1976, Killebrew had retired to join the Twins' broadcast crew. He finished his career with 573 home runs, the fifth-most ever at the time of retirement. He set Twins records for games (1,939), runs (1,047), total bases (3,412), home runs (475), RBI (1,325), walks (1,321) and strike-outs (1,314) and was the AL MVP in 1969.

Killebrew, however, would have to wait to get into the Hall of Fame. While getting 3,000 hits or 300 wins made it a cinch to get voted into the Hall, hitting 500 home runs was not on the same achievement scale. Killebrew also was knocked for his defense, as some voters pointed out that he played third base, first base and left field before becoming a designated hitter during his final seasons. This was unfair. Killebrew was willing to change positions for the good of the team. And Billy Martin, a Twins coach before managing them in 1969, maintained that

Killebrew was very good at third and up to par at first base. There was no interleague play to showcase his prodigious power to writers in National League cities. Consequently, many went by the numbers, and Killebrew's .256 career batting average was a turn-off. Killebrew was voted into the Hall of Fame on his fourth try, his wait not as long as several other candidates through the years. "I'm delighted. I love baseball, and I consider this baseball's greatest honor," Killebrew said during his induction speech in 1984.

As much as it was a well-deserved honor, it also was a spirit-lifter during trying times. After retirement, Killebrew suffered several setbacks with a handful of businesses, owing more than $900,000 to banks and eventually filing for bankruptcy. He had a dream home in Ontario, Oregon—across the Snake River from his boyhood home in Payette—that was foreclosed on when he couldn't make the $2,500 monthly payments. His marriage fell apart. "It's been a living hell," he said in a 1989 interview. "You have days where you feel you're at the bottom. You get to feeling that you are on that island by yourself. I don't feel anger, more sometimes frustration. Sadness is another. Loneliness is another one. Stressful? That's an understatement." Killebrew borrowed money from Griffith and Hall of Famers Reggie Jackson and Warren Spahn as he tried to climb out of the hole.

Health problems dogged Killebrew in the 1990s. He suffered from a collapsed lung in May 1990, had surgery to remove an abscess from behind a lung, then had part of a rib removed. An infection in the area affected his walking and led to him losing 40 pounds. He was sent to hospice care and recovered, despite concerns that he might not pull through. He then began representing the hospice care company that saved his life.

From the first time a scout laid eyes on him, through a magnificent career, through his wait to reach the Hall of Fame and post-career business failings, Killebrew remained the same person. Always had positive words to offer. Rarely lost his temper. Shared his time for community events. He traveled on the annual winter caravan, signing autographs throughout the Upper Midwest. In 1964, during a road trip to New York, Killebrew learned of an eight-year-old boy who had been in a Manhattan hospital for several weeks with burns over half his body. Killebrew agreed to visit the young man, Jack Guiney. He signed a baseball and a glove for the boy, who told him he would watch him on television that day. "Maybe I'll hit a couple for you," Killebrew said. True to his word, Killebrew hit a two-run homer in the first inning and a solo shot in the eighth.

"He was too nice to be a ballplayer," Tony Oliva said. "He was a gentleman."

In the late 1990s, the Twins reached out to Killebrew as part of their efforts to strengthen their connections with alumni. Killebrew began appearing at special events and representing the club at functions. He also appeared at spring training as a special instructor. The current generations of Twins enjoyed spending time with a man of such high character, who quickly became a mentor to them.

One of the important lessons Killebrew taught players more than 40 years younger than him: your signature is important. His autograph was a clinic in perfect penmanship. To sign as many autographs as they could as quickly as they could, players in the modern game produced signatures that often looked like graffiti. Killebrew would examine Twins players' autographs and scold them if he couldn't read their name. "I had a doctor's signature," Torii Hunter said. "I had a T and an I and a dot dot. He said, 'What the hell is this?'" Killebrew told Hunter that kids are more likely to throw the ball around in the backyard and destroy it if they can't read the signature.

Killebrew had a great sense of humor as well. I interviewed him the mid-2000s for a story on home run hitting, asking him how many homers he would hit in the modern era. "About 20 or 25," he said. "After all, I'm in my seventies."

Killebrew passed away on May 17, 2011, after being diagnosed with esophageal cancer about six months prior. He made enough progress to attend spring training that year looking a little frail but still grinning and chatting with players and staff. In passing, the timing must have come down from the heavens. The Twins were a few days away from playing an interleague series in Arizona when he passed away, and Killebrew lived in Scottdale. In the final game before the team traveled from Oakland to Arizona, the Twins scored in the first inning for the third consecutive game, hit three home runs in a game for the first time all season, and brought a three-game winning streak into the series against the Diamondbacks. You couldn't make it up.

So the Twins were able to attend No. 3's funeral service a few days later in Phoenix, with players Joe Nathan, Justin Morneau and Michael Cuddyer and manager Ron Gardenhire serving as pallbearers. The Twins placed a photo of Killebrew under home plate at Target Field. The players wore throwback jerseys from Killebrew's career for the remainder of the season.

Cuddyer, when he signed with the Colorado Rockies as a free agent following the 2011 season, announced he was going to wear No. 3 in honor of Killebrew. "The Twins organization had a pretty good player that wore number three," he said. "I ended up getting really close to Harmon Killebrew. I wanted to do something to show my respect toward him.... I've looked to make him proud...to make his family proud by wearing number three on my back. That way I feel like I'm playing for something on the front of my chest and on my back."

Killer was a Hall of Fame player. Killebrew was an even better person.

"A gentleman's gentleman," Twins president Dave St. Peter said. "The nicest big-league player I've ever encountered. The hardest day for me with the Twins on the contraction story was getting a phone call from Harmon. He asked me to explain what contraction was. Harmon was emotional. He was pissed. I reiterated to him that it wasn't done and that cooler heads could prevail. Harmon loved everything about the Twins. He was proud to be a Washington Senator, but he was even more proud to be part of a franchise that helped establish Minnesota as a major league state and the Twin Cities as a major league market. Harmon treated everyone with kindness and with a handshake. A true gentleman in every sense of the word."

3

Rod Carew

THE BAT WAS HIS BRUSH. EVERYTHING BETWEEN THE WHITE lines was his canvas. And Rod Carew spent 19 seasons painting between those lines.

He filled left, right and center with hits. He hit pitches up, down, outside and inside the strike zone wherever he wanted. He could adjust at-bat to at-bat, pitcher to pitcher and day to day. He was a pitcher's worst nightmare because he had no holes in his swing. An opponent could find where a power hitter is vulnerable or upset his timing. Carew would get out in front of a pitch and still hit the ball to an open space. White Sox announcer Harry Caray grew so aggravated with Carew's excellence he would announce him as "Here's Rod Car-roooo!", his voice dripping with disdain as Carew strolled to the plate.

Carew's bat could turn into a hammer, burying line drives into the gaps. It could become a wand as he waved it at pitches to spray hits around the field. It could become a pool cue when he bunted for 15–20 hits a season. His bat wasn't just a brush, it was whatever he needed it to be at that particular time. For Carew, it was placement over power. His style was envied during his heyday and still would have a place in the modern game as an alternative to today's infatuation with power. Luis Arraez, who, like Carew, debuted with the Twins and won a batting title with them, exhibits the same sprinkle-the-field-with-hits approach that Carew did.

No. 29 also had a batting stance for every occasion. While most hitters prefer sticking to form, to a fault, Carew would use different batting stances from game to game and at-bat to at-bat, depending on the situation or pitcher. "He knew what to do and how to do it," his close friend Tony Oliva said. "He was very, very confident in what he could do." Carew was so special that Calvin Griffith, with a long history of being tight-fisted with money, awarded him a $100,000 bonus after his 1977 season. And it was a season for the ages. Carew batted .388 with 14 home runs, 100 RBI, 38 doubles, 16 triples, 128 runs scored and 239 hits. He was voted the American League's Most Valuable Player by a comfortable margin over Al Cowens. He was on the 1967 Twins team that lost the pennant on the final day of the regular season and part of talented teams in 1969 and 1970 that couldn't get by the formidable Baltimore Orioles in the American League Championship Series.

Seven batting titles. Four 200-hit seasons. Named to the All-Star team 18 consecutive seasons. Rookie of the Year in 1967 and an MVP in 1977. He collected 3,053 hits in his career. And he was a first-ballot Hall of Famer in 1991, one of 22 players at the time to earn induction on their first try. The wizard of wood was so legendary that Major League Baseball, during the 2016 season, announced that the league batting champion would receive the Rod Carew American League Batting Championship

THE FRANCHISE: MINNESOTA TWINS

Award. The first 12 seasons of his brilliant career were spent with the Twins.

"You see guys today who swing so hard and try to hit it so hard and they try to hit it at a certain angle," former Twin and fellow Hall of Famer Paul Molitor, who grew up watching Carew from the stands, said. "His was just so much more poetic with what he did with the bat. It was just so fluid. A lot of players will tell you that when they grow up and they have these boyhood heroes who helped inspire their dreams, Rod was one of those guys for me. He was left-handed and he was from Panama, and I knew a lot about him. When you are playing against him and you are a young player and have a conversation with him, when a veteran superstar who you admired would give you the time of day and show you the respect in return it was very impactful. I was always grateful for that from Rod."

Many players in the modern age with just as much, if not more, speed than Carew should dig through the archives and watch replays of his bunting acumen. Carew spent 45 minutes a day honing his craft. If he was in a slump or if he noticed an infielder playing too far back, he had that bunt tool in his toolbox. And he weaponized it. "You know, you don't have to lay down a perfect bunt to get a hit," Carew said. "The fielder has to get in on the ball in a hurry, pick it up cleanly and make the perfect throw to get you. He's got more chances to make a mistake than you." It makes too much sense, but the bunt has gone the way of stirrup socks. You don't see much of them anymore. The modern generation of players are spared the mental and physical gymnastics that occur when preparing to face someone who likes to bunt for hits. "I do know I had to play third base against him for a long time," Molitor said. "You know, it didn't matter how much I crept in. He would just bunt it a little softer. And he got me to a point where it was a little uncomfortable for him. And then he had no problem shooting the ball past me because of the depth that I was forced to play at because of his ability to bunt."

The name Rodney Cline Carew was not planned for the baby boy born in Panama on October 1, 1945. It was a product of circumstance and gratitude. His parents, Eric and Olga, had boarded a train headed from their home in Gatún, Panama, in the Canal Zone to ride 40 miles to Ancón, where Gorgas Hospital was located. Olga was pregnant and she wanted to have the baby at the best facility possible. The baby, however, was on its own timetable. Olga went into labor right there on the train. A conductor ran into the white section of the segregated train—the Carews were in the colored section—to find a doctor. One hurried to the scene and helped with the delivery of a baby boy. The doctor's name: Rodney Cline. And that's how Rod Carew came into this world. The nurse who assisted with the delivery, Margaret Allen, became Carew's godmother.

Carew grew up hitting tennis balls with broomsticks, falling in love with making solid contact and proving he was by far the best among the kids he played with. He would listen to games on Armed Forces Radio and wondered what it would be like to play major league baseball. He then played Little League baseball, showing off his impressive skills. The only thing that could potentially shatter Carew's childhood and big-league dreams was his father, Eric. Eric drank heavily, never took an interest in his son's activities and was abusive to him, his mother and his brother.

"He never acknowledged that I was good," Carew said in his autobiography. "Never gave me a compliment. God, I think I would have kissed his feet if he had only said—just one time—'You're a nice player, son.' But I didn't exist as far he was concerned."

Olga Carew decided that the best thing for her and her children was to get away from Eric and work toward a better life. She took a job in New York at a purse factory and eventually sent for her children. Rod and his brother Dickie were the first wave. Rod was 15 at the time. He attended George Washington High School but never played baseball there. He focused on learning English and completing his schoolwork. In 1964, he hooked on with a sandlot team called the New York Cavaliers. It wasn't long before scouts appeared. Monroe Katz, whose son played with Carew, was alerted to a good-looking second baseman on the team. Katz was a bird-dog scout for the Twins. Bird-dog scouts worked in a supporting role for major league scouts. When a player was signed by a scout, and the bird-dog scout was involved, that bird-dog would get a small cut of the bonus from the team scout. So Katz tipped off Herb Stein, who was the Twins' scout. Stein began following Carew around. liked what he saw and had farm director Hal Keller fly in for a look. As other teams took notice of this fine hitting prospect, Stein arranged for him to work out for the Twins when they came to New York to play the Yankees. There, Carew met Oliva, who would later become his best friend and roommate. Carew clubbed batting practice pitches around Yankee Stadium, hitting several over the fence. Some Twins wondered how the skinny kid had so much pop. Carew met Harmon Killebrew, who was shorter than he expected. He also spoke with infielder Zoilo Versalles, who told him, "I be here a long time, kid. So forget about shortstop." That wouldn't be a problem. Playing second base was challenging enough. Carew's bat was his ticket, and the Twins were about to sign him to a $5,000 bonus. His batting practice ended successfully when manager Sam Mele yelled, "Get that kid out of there before the Yankees see him."

Twins owner Calvin Griffith wanted Carew on the Opening Day roster in 1967. Mele did what he was told, although the 1966 Twins had slumped to 89–73 one year after winning 102 games and reaching the World Series. Mele preferred to have a veteran there to give him a better chance to save his job. Carew was even in the Opening Day batting order, singling off Dave McNally for his first major league hit while going 2-for-4 at the plate. Carew led second basemen with a .313 batting average during the first half of that season and started there for the American League in the All-Star Game played in Anaheim, California. That was the start of an 18-year run of appearances in the Midsummer Classic.

Two years later, Carew won the first of seven batting titles with a .332 average while the Twins won the AL West before losing to the Orioles in the ALCS. Playing for aggressive manager Billy Martin, Carew stole home an American League–record seven times that season.

While his career began to flourish, Carew and Oliva became close and started rooming together on the road. The word "bromance" wasn't a thing in the 1970s, but that was the extent of their relationship. They met when Carew was a teenager in 1964 at that workout at Yankee Stadium, unaware of how his life would change in the coming weeks. Oliva was about to become AL Rookie of the Year, winning a batting title while also leading the league in runs, hits and total bases. He was the first rookie to win a batting title at the time. Carew had found a fellow Spanish speaker in Oliva, who helped a kid with no idea of where to go or what to do. They bonded during spring training in 1965 and started sharing a hotel room a few years later. Oliva said they roomed together for about 11 years. "He was easy to get along with," Oliva said. "He didn't play loud music or stay out late at night. We'd go to movies, have dinner then back to the hotel."

They ignored each other's idiosyncrasies. Carew could be unsocial at times, and Oliva would say little to him for a couple days if he was in one of those moods. Carew would try to go to sleep while Oliva stayed up to practice his English. Best friends in baseball they were then and still are today. Best hitters in baseball too, one could argue. Oliva and Carew combined to win 10 batting titles over a 14-year period from 1964 to '78.

Oliva won his last batting title in 1971. Carew won five of the next six seasons. Carew had a chance to make it six out of six. In a batting race for the ages, Carew, George Brett and Hal McRae were within a few hundredths of a point of each other as they entered the final series of the 1976 season. Coincidentally, Carew's Twins were in Kansas City for the showdown. Carew was batting .325, Brett was batting .328 and McRae .331. Carew went 5-for-8 over the first two games of the series and entered the final game of the season batting .329, while Brett and McRae were at .331. Carew went 2-for-4 in the final game to finish at .331. It wasn't enough, as Brett hit an inside-the-park homer in the ninth to cap a 3-for-4 day to finish the season with a .33333 average while McRae went 2-for-4 to end at .33207.

Carew was part of a different chase in 1977. He was batting .365 at the end of May, then hit .483 over the next 29 games and was batting .411 on July 1. Fans wondered if Carew would be the first player to hit .400 since Ted Williams in 1941, when he batted .406. *Time* and *Sports Illustrated* made him the cover photo of their publication during the same week. It takes a lot of good fortune to hit .400 in a season; avoiding a slump is part of it. Carew hit .304 in July, a stat most hitters would envy. For someone chasing .400, it represented a slump. Despite batting .457 over the final 24 games, Carew finished the season with a

.388 average, falling short of making history. He settled for being memorable with his best season at the plate. He also tied a career high with 14 home runs and set a career high with 100 RBI and was voted the AL's Most Valuable Player. Carew had signed a three-year contract before the season, so he provided instant returns on the investment. There was a drawback—Carew was tiring of the Twins' losing ways and grew frustrated with Calvin Griffth, who let talented teammates leave as free agents and failed to negotiate a contract extension with him.

The final straw came on September 28, 1978, when Griffith made his hair-raising speech at the Waseca Lions Club. He said Carew was a "damn fool" for accepting only a $170,000 contract. But the topper came when he spoke of the reasons why he moved the franchise to Minnesota. Nick Coleman, a reporter for the *Minneapolis Tribune* at the time, was at the event and provided an account that ran three days later—on the final game of the regular season, on the road in Kansas City.

Carew hit the roof and nearly left the team before the game against the Royals. "I will not ever sign another contract with this organization," he said. "I don't care how much money or how many options Calvin Griffith offers me. I definitely will not be back next year. I will not come back and play for a bigot. I'm not going to be another nigger on his plantation." It was the final game of his Twins career. He wrapped up his seventh batting title, with a .333 average, and was traded the following offseason to the Angels. Wounds healed with time, however. In seven seasons with the Angels, Carew batted .314 and made the All-Star team each year. He retired following the 1985 season with 3,053 hits. His 3,000th hit came off of Twins left-hander Frank Viola on August 4. That made his election into the Hall of Fame a formality, as he was part of the 1991 class in his first time on the ballot. By the time Carew was voted into the Hall, he had made peace with Griffith. And Griffith was one of the first people he called when he learned of his induction.

Carew was inducted into the Hall of Fame on a sweltering afternoon in July in Cooperstown, New York. *Minneapolis Star Tribune* columnist Patrick Reusse toured the audience and ran into a group of Twins fans on a knoll near the stage. "Don't step on that," Julian Loscalzo said. "We're going to wave it when Rod gets up there." It was a banner that read, SAVE THE MET. Loscalzo was part of a group of hearty Twins fans who abhorred indoor baseball at the Metrodome and missed roof-less ball at the old Metropolitan Stadium. It was the banner's second trip to Cooperstown after making its debut in 1984 when Harmon Killebrew was inducted. It made return trips to Cooperstown for the induction of Paul Molitor in 2004, Bert Blyleven in 2011 and Tony Oliva and Jim Kaat in 2022. It was not present for the ceremonies involving Kirby Puckett and Dave Winfield in 2001 and Jack Morris in 2018. But the banner's 38 years of occasional service was a testament to its durability—plus the desire of a group of Twins fans who continued to make a point years after the Old Met was pulverized to make way for the Mall of America. It was also fitting that Reusse, a legendary writer who grew up playing ball in the southwest Minnesota town of Fulda, ran across the group that particular Sunday afternoon. It was Reusse who, as a beat writer in the 1970s, began referring to Carew as "Sir Rodney," a nickname that stuck.

What the Save the Met gang didn't consider: What if Carew had played in the Metrodome, where hard-hit grounders could shoot through the infield for hits? Where outfielders had to play farther back to keep balls from bouncing over the heads, rolling past them or getting lost in the ceiling? Carew might have had another 20 to 25 hits a year.

The Carews settled in southern California following the end of Sir Rodney's career—Rod; wife, Marilynn; and daughters Charryse, Stephanie and Michelle. He kept busy by running a hitting school near his home for several years then serving as a hitting coach for the Angels (1992–99) and Brewers (2000–01). Michelle was diagnosed with acute nonlymphocytic leukemia in September of 1995. She needed a bone marrow transplant, but the search for a donor was a difficult one because her father was of West Indian and Panamanian decent and his mother of Russian and Jewish decent. Despite 70,000 citizens calling the registry to see if they could be a match, none was found. Michelle passed away in April 1996.

In 2015, Carew was on Hole No. 1 at Cresta Verde Golf Course in Corona, California, when he felt his chest burning and his hands feeling cold and wet. He went into the clubhouse and asked for paramedics. Carew had suffered a heart attack called the widowmaker. Those don't have a favorable survival rate. His heart had to be restarted—twice. He had a heart transplant in late 2016 and began an awareness campaign about heart health and organ donation. He also established a relationship with the family of Konrad Reuland, a former NFL tight end who died of an aneurysm in December 2016 at age 29.

Carew was eventually cleared to return to Twins spring training, where he was a special instructor. Carew and Oliva, also an instructor, are inseparable every spring. Of course, Carew wanted Twins players to bunt better. There were days during camp when a reporter would arrive at the clubhouse at 7:30 AM and see Carew on a nearby field, working with players to improve that skill. "I got a ton out of working with Rod," said outfielder Denard Span, who was with the Twins from 2008 through 2012. "He changed the way I looked at bunting from a physical and mental standpoint. I developed my base-hit bunting technique from him and used it my entire career."

Oliva and Kirby Puckett were the best all-around hitters in Twins history. Harmon Killebrew was the best power hitter the Twins ever had. Joe Mauer did things no catcher had ever done in winning three batting titles. But the best hitter for average the Twins had over their first 60-plus years in Minnesota was Sir Rodney Cline Carew.

4

Tony Oliva

Joseph Carl "Papa Joe" Cambria was born in Italy and moved to the United States as an infant. He served in World War I and, afterward, owned a laundry service. His baseball career lasted all of 140 games over two seasons with the Berlin Green Sox of the Canadian League. Then a broken leg ended his career before it gained any traction. He was a career .240 hitter.

But Joe's love of baseball led him to find ways to remain attached to the game. For that, Minnesota Twins fans are grateful. Because he brought them Tony Oliva, Mr. Twin.

Cambria first sponsored an amateur baseball team that he upgraded to semi-pro. Ownership was next. He was co-owner of the Baltimore Black Sox of the Negro Leagues. He didn't stop there. Cambria ended up owning minor league clubs on every level of professional baseball. In 1929, he purchased his first professional team, the Hagerstown Hubs of the Class D Blue Ridge League. He owned a field in Baltimore where the Hubs trained and played against the Black Sox. The 1931 Hagerstown team included three players who would go on to play in the major leagues. That's how Cambria succeeded. He bought players on the cheap, watched them develop and sold them for a profit.

In 1933 Cambria purchased the Albany Senators of the International League. From there, Cambria sold several players to major league teams while searching for prospects to sign for Albany and his other clubs. One person Cambria forged a profitable relationship with around this time: Washington Senators owner Clark Griffith.

Cambria made his first trip to Cuba in 1936 to sign players for his Albany club. He was onto something because Cubans loved baseball. They learned the game during the late 1890s from U.S. sailors porting in the country and students returning from U.S. colleges. Amateur baseball was vibrant, and fans routinely met in town squares to passionately discuss the game.

Many Latin players came to the United States because of Cambria's efforts and connections. He signed many American players as well. Those included Cal Ermer, who played for the Senators and would go on to replace Sam Mele as Twins manager during the 1967 season. Joe Haynes pitched for the Senators, married Clark Griffith's niece, Thelma, and later was an executive with the Twins when they moved from Washington, D.C., in 1961.

But Cambria's best work was establishing a pipeline for Cuban talent to flow into the United States, with many of his imports ending up with the Washington Senators. This continued even when Clark Griffith passed away in 1955 and his son Calvin took over the team. It's believed that Cambria signed upward of 500 players during his career. For the Senators, it was a way to reduce costs while adding talented ballplayers. When the Senators became the Twins in 1961, Cubans Julio

Becquer, Zoilo Versalles and José Valdivielso were infielders on the roster. Right-hander Pedro Ramos was in the rotation. So was future 20-game winner Camilo Pascual, with his devastating curveball, who was signed for all of $175.

"When we began to go around the league with that TC logo on our cap, these fans around the dugout would say, 'What's that TC stand for?'" Jim Kaat said. "I would say, 'Twenty Cubans.' The Cuban talent that Calvin had Joe Cambria sign, they were just happy to get out and play. There were no strict rules on minimum salary. That's really what made our team improve."

One of the most popular Cuban Twins of them all grew up in that mysterious country just south of Florida. He hailed from Pinar del Río, Cuba—a tobacco-rich area with a competitive amateur team—where his father carved out a ballfield for him and his friends to play on. He would learn how to whip a bat through the strike zone and make loud contact as line drives filled the outfield. No one did anything well with a baseball in Cuba without Papa Joe eventually finding out about it. And after watching Tony Pedro Oliva Lopez play, Cambria signed him for the expansion Minnesota Twins in 1961.

Oliva left the island for the Unites States on April 9. On April 17, the Cuban Democratic Revolutionary Front landed in the Bay of Pigs in an attempt to overthrow Fidel Castro.

Oliva's pursuit of a Major League Baseball career had been derailed by the conflict. He, along with his contingent of fellow Cubans, were held up for over a week in Mexico City while they waited for the necessary paperwork to enter the United States. By the time he arrived in Fernandina Beach, Florida, where the Senators trained, there were only four games left to play to impress the club. He collected seven hits in those games, but it wasn't enough. It didn't help that he was extremely raw in the field. His contract was terminated, and he was ordered to return to Cuba. But travel to Cuba had been halted because of the Bay of Pigs conflict, so he could not return home. Cambria arranged for Oliva to travel to Charlotte, N.C., to work out while the general manager there, Phil Howser, attempted to find a club for him to play on. History would have been rewritten if Howser hadn't accepted the mission. Oliva landed with a short-season rookie league team in Wytheville, Virgina.

During his Hall of Fame induction speech in 2022, Oliva broke up the audience as he described what happened next. "He [Howser] gave me the opportunity to play in the rookie league," Oliva said. "And everybody here knows everything after that was history. I went to the rookie league doing my thing. I hit .410. After that, I was Superman."

It was a hard .410, achieved over 64 games. Not because of challenges on the field. The dark-skinned Oliva was exposed to American racism and segregation. There were no hotels for Black players then, so he had to stay in a rooming house with two other Black players. He knew no English, but teammate Frank Quilici—who would play with Oliva in the majors and later manage the Twins in the 1970s—helped him with lessons. His hitting needed no translation. He batted .350 in Charlotte the next season, with just 32 strikeouts over 525 plate appearances. He was called up for nine games at the end of the season, going 4-for-9. Oliva began to dream of making the 1963 team out of spring training but was crushed when he was assigned to Class AAA Dallas-Fort Worth right before Opening Day. A frustrated Oliva had to be talked out of returning to Cuba, with fellow countryman Zoilo Versalles being one of the lead negotiators. Oliva spent the season in Texas, where Jack McKeon was the manager. It was just a few years earlier when McKeon had promised a young Jim Kaat that he was going pitch every fourth day and develop his craft. Kaat graduated to the major leagues and won 283 games. McKeon worked with Oliva to clean up his defense while watching that swing pummel pitches all over the Pacific Coast League. Oliva batted .304 with 23 homers and 74 RBI that season. "He used to hit 100 ground balls to me and 100 fly balls to me," Oliva said. "But I was very proud five years later when I won the Gold Glove in the American League."

Young Oliva as an outfielder? It was real. It was raw. It was really raw. He had an arm as strong as the best outfielders in the game but judging fly balls, getting to them and making plays were things he didn't have much experience with. And he was 22 during his first season in pro ball—not 17 or 18, where his skills could have been honed while he developed. He didn't bring a glove to America, but he sure found one there. "We laugh about it now," said Kaat, owner of 16 Gold Gloves himself. "When we were in the instructional league, when the manager would hit fungo flies to us, Tony would actually miss them all. He couldn't even get a glove on it. Because he never had that much experience at playing the outfield in Cuba. He just hit. So he probably is prouder of that Gold Glove he won in 1966 than those batting titles."

Oliva was 22 when he entered the country to chase his major league dream, but that wasn't what he told the Twins. To appear younger—which would make him more signable because he would have more time to develop—he took on the name and paperwork of his brother, Pedro, who was born in 1941. It's a trick that is not allowed today but was prevalent in previous decades as Latin players tried everything for a chance at the majors. So back then, Oliva was 20 years old, as far as baseball officials knew.

Oliva didn't have to worry about making the big-league club in 1964. He spent spring training in right field while Bob Allison, who had played exclusively in the outfield the two previous seasons, was being moved to first base. Jimmie Hall was in center. And Harmon Killebrew's knees were good enough for him to play in left. There was talk about Oliva perhaps platooning with Vic Power in the outfield. Owner Calvin Griffith nixed that. In fact, he believed Oliva was good enough to challenge for the batting title as a rookie. "He has those great wrists and can hit a ball right out of the catcher's hands," he said before the season opener. Oliva's defense was acceptable; his main challenge was going back on balls hit over his head.

Twins manager Sam Mele penciled Oliva in as the No. 2 hitter in the lineup when the Twins opened the season with a 7–6 win over Cleveland. Oliva had two hits in that game. He had three in the second game. Oliva opened the season with an eight-game hitting streak during which he batted .405. Line drives flying to all fields. He batted .441 over his first 23 games and .381 over his first 39. He was batting .383 at the end of May, then slumped to .333 by the end of June. When the 1964 All-Star Game took place at Shea Stadium, the rookie was the starting right fielder for the American League. Harmon Killebrew and Bob Allison also made the team. By the end of the year, Oliva finished with a league-leading .323 batting average to go with 32 homers and 94 RBI. He also led the league with 217 hits, 109 runs scored and 374 total bases. It was far from an inauspicious rookie campaign. And Oliva was a near-unanimous pick as American League Rookie of the Year. One vote went to Orioles pitcher Wally Bunker. Griffith saw the future. Oliva was the first rookie to lead the league in hitting. And more was coming.

Oliva repeated as batting champion in 1965, batting .321 with a league-leading 185 hits. That made him the first player ever to win batting titles in his first two seasons. Oliva's bat roared through the strike zone, thanks to his great hand and wrists. He didn't walk much but never struck out more than 72 times in a season. His hand-eye coordination allowed him to connect with pitches in and out of the strike zone. He didn't care if the pitch was six inches above, below or outside the strike zone. He did it because he could. Oliva was one of the most feared hitters in the league. Not because he hit for some power. It was because he was a tough out. In his first eight full seasons in the majors, he batted a cumulative .313 with 177 homers, 719 RBI and 1,455 hits. He won a third batting title in 1971 when he hit .337 with 22 homers and 81 RBI, also leading the league with a .546 slugging percentage. Hitting any pitch anywhere—neck high, shoe top low—it could travel 400 feet off his bat.

"We would laugh when the pitcher got ahead of Tony 0–2," Kaat said. "We'd say the pitcher doesn't know that he's in trouble. Everybody can hit the fastball, but when you get ahead of a hitter you throw them a curveball. Tony was a better breaking ball hitter because when they played over in Cuba, he said they would wad up a piece of paper and put tape on it, so the ball was moving all over the place. So he had great hand-eye coordination, and he became a great breaking ball hitter."

Oliva was part of three postseason teams. The 1965 Twins won 102 games but were held to a .195 batting average in the World Series by a Dodgers pitching effort led by Sandy Koufax and Don Drysdale. Oliva batted .192 in the series. His one homer came off Drysdale in a Game 4 defeat. He played on Twins teams that reached the ALCS in 1969 and 1970, with Oliva faring much better in those series. He batted .385 in the 1969 series, homering off Mike Cuellar. He was 6-for-12 in 1970, taking Dave McNally deep. But the Twins were swept in both series. The 1970 Twins team included Oliva, Kaat, Harmon

Killebrew, Bert Blyleven and Rod Carew—five future Hall of Famers.

The 1971 season was known for the worst possible thing happening during the best year of Oliva's career. Oliva's knees kept him from having a longer career and making him a no-doubt Hall of Famer. They became an issue on June 29, 1971, when he dived to catch a ball during a game against Oakland and wrecked his right knee on a sprinkler head. He was dominant at the plate at the time, batting .375. He missed 12 of the next 14 games and played hobbled the rest of the season. He won the batting title with a .337 average but missed the final week and a half after having torn cartilage removed from his knee. He had already undergone procedures on the knee as far back as 1966, and it would be an issue for the remainder of his career. The next season, he couldn't return to the lineup until June while rehabilitating the knee, then played in just 10 games before he had season-ending surgery, during which more than 100 cartilage fragments and two bone spurs were removed. Oliva batted .321 over those 10 games—with all that shrapnel in his knee.

Bone chips, loose cartilage, torn cartilage, torn ligaments. Eight knee surgeries. Oliva endured all of it during his career, but his balky knees were getting the upper hand late in his career. He brought massaging machines on road trips. Friends from Cuba sent home remedies. Carew once saw Oliva rubbing STP, a gasoline and oil additive, on the knee. Oliva tried everything he could think of to treat the knee, but the pain persisted. "As his roomie, I knew as much about what Tony went through with his knees as anyone," Carew told the *Minneapolis Star Tribune* in 2021. "The first thing I did when we got to our room at night was to go to the ice machine for Tony. I would hear him moaning, groaning, sometimes even crying, he was in so much pain. Then, he would play the next day, and hit a couple of line drives. He drove in 90-some runs on one leg as a DH in 1973."

The 1973 season ushered in the beginning of the designated hitter in the American League—and brought the end of Oliva's career as an outfielder. He batted .291 with 16 homers and 92 RBI that season and was the first DH to homer in a game. But he batted just .270 over the next three seasons. Oliva appeared in 67 games in 1976 as a player-coach, batting .211. One of the final highlights of his career was a four-hit night against Mark "the Bird" Fidrych, who tipped his cap to Oliva following a seventh-inning single. After a winter ball season in Mexico, Oliva decided to be more of a coach than player-coach in 1977. Oliva was done with the years of rehabilitation and maintenance on his knees. "I hit .291 on one leg in 1973," he said. "It wasn't the same, but I could still hit."

Oliva's playing career was over. A .304 career average, 220 home runs, 1,917 hits, eight All-Star Game appointments, one Rookie of the Year award and one Gold Glove. There were five years of aggravation at the end of his career. Those were preceded by eight years of brilliance at the plate. He inspired a young Kent Hrbek to bike to Metropolitan Stadium to watch his boyhood idol play. He made pitchers wince when he dug in at the plate.

"When Harmon Killebrew got in the Hall of Fame, he deserved it because of the home runs," Jim Kaat said. "Rodney [Carew] got in and he deserved it with seven batting titles. But if you asked Bill Freehan, Andy Etchebarren, Duane Josephson and those catchers back in those days, Tony was the guy they feared in clutch situations more than anybody because he was a great combination of power and average and being tough to strike out. So it was something to watch him."

Fortunately for the Twins and the Upper Midwest, this was just one phase of Oliva's life in baseball. He coached for the team in 1977 and 1978 then enjoyed a second stint as hitting coach from 1985 to '91. He was a roving minor league hitting instructor in the 1980s and was a spring training special instructor into the 2020s. He made appearances on behalf of the club well into his eighties. When the Minnesota Wild of the NHL hosted a Winter Classic, an outdoor hockey game played on New Year's Day in a selected city, in 2022, Oliva received the loudest cheers when introduced among the hockey dignitaries before the opening faceoff.

Oliva had embraced the area long before that. It dated back to his rookie season of 1964, when the Class of 1964 from Hitchcock, South Dakota, headed to the Twin Cities for a senior class trip—and Tony was about to meet a girl. Gordette DuBois was on that class trip, and that class was part of a matinee crowd of 4,390 that saw the Twins win 9–8 in 10 innings. Afterward, they waited by the stadium to get autographs when they discovered that some of the players were staying at the same hotel as they were. They headed back to the Maryland Hotel, where Oliva appeared and offered his autograph. It was during this chaperone-supervised moment that Oliva agreed to give Gordette his autograph in exchange for her phone number.

"We had a party line of six families," Gordette told the *Minneapolis Star Tribune* in 2021. "Our ring on the farm was two shorts, three longs and two shorts. We all loved baseball and the Twins in South Dakota. And when people found out that this rookie that everyone was talking about was calling a girl from Hitchcock...you could hear those clicks from other phones being picked up to check if it was 'him'. Of course, no one could understand what he was saying. I hardly could."

Oliva visited the farm during Christmas in 1965. He had just won his second batting title in two years and played in a World Series. Now, the Black Cuban was roaming around rural South Dakota while calling on a local lady. How did that go? "Great," he said. "I was a king in South Dakota." Tony and Gordette married in 1968. Sometime in the 1970s they moved into a Bloomington home tucked away in a cul-de-sac and have lived there ever since. They raised four children in that home. And it was in that home where, on December 5, 2021, he received a phone call from Jane Forbes Clark, chair of the board of directors of the National Baseball Hall of Fame and Museum, to inform him that he had been voted into the Hall.

Yes, it came 45 years after he made the final out of his career. In 15 years on the ballot voted on by the Baseball Writers Association of America, Oliva never received more than 47.3 percent of the vote, when 75 percent is required for induction. That occurred in 1988, when Oliva finished third in the voting. In his final year on the BBWAA ballot, 1996, he received 36.2 percent. He was in Cuba visiting relatives when the results of the vote were announced.

The undeniable truth was that, when he was healthy, Oliva had few peers at the plate. He was denied entry into the Hall of Fame because of his whole body of work. That included only 1,917 hits (when 3,000 guaranteed entry) and no Most Valuable Player awards (he finished second twice). After the writers failed to vote him in, his case was kicked up to the high court—the Veterans Committee. This committee consists of former players and executives, with a few writers and other contributors. As someone who has been on this committee, I know every participant takes his or her selection with great honor and considers every candidate carefully, confidentially and candidly. Oliva failed to get voted in by the Veterans Committee eight times. The last time was in 2014. Oliva and Dick Allen missed getting in by one vote, and the groans were audible in the media room at the winter meetings in San Diego when the results were announced.

I have come to believe that different committees arrive at different conclusions about players. The year that Harold Baines was elected to the Hall of Fame by the Today's Game Committee just happened to be the year that White Sox owner Jerry Reinsdorf and former White Sox manager Tony La Russa were on the committee and likely wielded their influence. When I was growing up in Chicago, Baines was my second-favorite player, behind Dick Allen. He is not a Hall of Famer.

Rod Carew has been on Veterans Committees through the years and has supported his former roommate. He compared Oliva's candidacy to Sandy Koufax. Koufax was voted in by the writers despite having his career limited to 12 seasons, six of them fabulous, because of injuries. Oliva, then 76, said before the 2014 vote that he didn't want to be voted in posthumously. After he learned that he had missed out by one vote, he said, "The Hall of Fame is not fair. For some people, it is beautiful. For a lot of people, it's not fair." That was the closest Oliva has been to being mad.

The next Golden Era Committee was delayed because of the pandemic until 2021. Oliva felt that if he didn't get the call this time, he was never going to get it. Family and friends were at his home in Bloomington when Forbes called with the news he'd waited 45 years to hear. Oliva was perhaps the best hitter of his era. He was the best person of his era during and after his playing days. He's a gentleman. He makes appearances on behalf of the club. He now signs autographs for the children and grandchildren of fans he signed autographs for 50 years ago. He's been a splendid ambassador for the Twins, Major League

Baseball, Minnesota, the Upper Midwest and Cubans. And, in 2022, Mr. Twin finally became Mr. Hall of Fame.

"Now, everywhere I walk, I've lost my name," Oliva said. "Now people call me 'Hall of Fame'. Not, 'Hey, No. 6,' or 'Hey, T.O.' Something happened to me that I thought would never happen."

5

Kirby Puckett

Sports heroes truly become sports heroes when their names start appearing around town. Buildings are named after them. Streets are named after them. Hamburgers are named after them. Statues of them are erected.

But not many have games named after them.

On October 26, 1991, the Minnesota Twins prepared for Game 6 of the World Series against Atlanta down 3–2 in the seven-game series. They had lost three consecutive games after taking a 2–0 lead but suddenly faced elimination.

Kirby Puckett would be damned if he and his Twins teammates were going to be knocked out the World Series by a delayed sweep. And Game 6 became known as the Puckett Game.

Already the most popular Twin in town, Puckett cemented his legacy with a signature performance after entering the clubhouse earlier in the afternoon ready for a war.

"Before the game he said, 'Get on board. I'm going to carry the load,'" Twins manager Tom Kelly said. Teammates and Puckett have similar recollections that Puckett said some version of "Jump on my back!" that night. By the end of the night, everyone was in awe of Puckett's greatest game. It set up a Game 7 where Jack Morris pitched 10 innings to nearly match the awe-inspiring feats Puckett had provided the night before.

Puckett blasted an RBI triple in his first at-bat of Game 6, connecting off Steve Avery. In the third inning, Atlanta's Ron Gant drove a Scott Erickson pitch toward left center. "When Ron Gant hit the ball, I knew it wasn't out," Puckett said. "I said, 'Just get back. Just get back.' Puckett reached the wall and jumped like a golden retriever leaping to catch a Frisbee. "That's about as high as I can jump," he said. The ball slammed into his glove before hitting that godforsaken plexiglass, and the Metrodome audience of 55,155 exploded with applause.

Puckett added a sacrifice fly in the fifth to break a 2–2 tie. He singled and stole second in the eighth, but the game remained tied at 3–3. Twins reliever Carl Willis pitched a scoreless ninth, then Rick Aguilera got through the 10th and the 11th. Puckett batted in the bottom of the inning, looking for a changeup from Charlie Leibrandt. After a few pitches, Puckett got one up in the zone and whacked it over the left-center wall as pandemonium broke out at the Dome. Puckett pumped a fist while yelling, "Yeah! Yeah!" as he rounded the bases. It was one of the greatest clutch at-bats in World Series history.

Somehow, the World Series has been the setting for several great Game Sixes. Boston's Carlton Fisk waving his drive down the left field line in 1975 that became a walk-off home run. Joe Carter's walk-off home run in 1993 for Toronto was the second to end a World Series. St. Louis' David Freese had a two-run triple to tie Game 6 in the ninth inning, then hit a game-winning home run in the 11th to force a Game 7 in 2011.

The Puckett Game occurred during what might have been the greatest World Series ever. Five games settled by one run. Three games needing extra innings. For one game, Puckett made the difference while setting up Morris' Game 7. "My gosh," Kelly said. "That's carrying the load and pulling the truck and everything."

Truthfully, Puckett frequently told his teammates to jump on his back. The 1991 World Series request simply added to the lore. Puckett was the first player to have go-ahead RBI in three different plate appearances in a World Series game. He was already the first major leaguer to earn $3 million in a season, so everyone was aware of how he impacted games. And Puckett already was the toast of the Twin Cities. Game 6 made him a legend.

No athlete has ever hit a market with as much charisma as the man from the projects of Chicago with the Cheshire cat grin. And they weren't just any projects. They were the Robert Taylor Homes, which were one of the largest housing projects in America, swelling to around 27,000 residents. There were 28 16-story buildings in a cluster near Chicago's Bronzeville neighborhood. They weren't maintained properly, were mismanaged and became targets for corruption. Crime, drug use, gang activity and single-parent families were prevalent there. And it was located on the other side of the Dan Ryan Expressway from Comiskey Park. *Newsweek* magazine wrote that it was "where hope went to die." It was there that Puckett grew up, on the 14th floor of a building at 4444 S. State St., the youngest of nine children. And he loved baseball as soon as he could walk and talk. It was there where he turned hope into a dream, then that dream into reality. He didn't play on the best fields—some of them being asphalt. You made do with what you had at the time.

When he wasn't playing on a team, Puckett played a game called strikeout. It took place in a schoolyard, but any place where there was a wall and some space for balls to land would do. A strike zone was either drawn on the wall with a rock or, in some cases, painted with a spray can. As few as two people would play as they tried to hit each other's pitching. Outs, singles and extra-base hits were determined by ground rules (clearing the street was a home run, past the tree was a triple, etc.). Two people could pitch to each other all day. As someone who grew up in Chicago and played the game, I learned the strike zone was important. It frequently was generously sized. So if a 15-year-old drew the strike zone, 10-year-olds would have to swing at pitches from their necks to their ankles. Watching Puckett—who played his share of strikeout as a kid—hit, I can see where he got his plate coverage from.

"He was like me," Twins great Tony Oliva said. "He did not have a strike zone and hit everything hard."

Puckett's family moved out of the projects in his teens, and he later starred at Calumet High School. He did not get a lot of exposure and went undrafted following his senior year in high school. He attended a tryout camp in Chicago held by legendary Kansas City Royals scout Art Stewart, where he was spotted and offered a scholarship to play at Bradley University in Peoria, Illinois. He played one year before transferring to Triton JC, partially because his grades suffered following the death of his father. But Puckett was playing in the Central Illinois Collegiate League during the summer when Twins scout Jim Rantz was in attendance. There was a strike in baseball in 1981, so Rantz had traveled to Illinois to watch his son play for the Peoria Pacers. "There was this little, short guy who was playing the outfield,"

Rantz said. "He stole three bases, had three hits and he threw out a guy at the plate. I said to my wife, Pearl, 'I'm going to put this guy in [as a recommendation]. It's for the January draft.' She says, 'What about our son?'" The Twins selected Puckett with the third overall pick of the January phase of the draft, offering him $5,000 to sign, which he turned down and prepared to play for Triton. The Twins still held rights to Puckett, so they could follow his progress at Triton and revisit negotiations following the season. "He goes to Triton, hits four-something and led all of junior college in batting average," Rantz said. Puckett, playing in the same Triton outfield as future major leaguer Lance Johnson, batted .472 that season with 16 homers, 78 RBI and 42 stolen bases. He was named NJCAA Player of the Year and just was inducted into the NJCAA Foundation Hall of Fame in June of 2023.

The Twins adjusted their offer to $25,000, which Puckett accepted and began his professional baseball career. Rantz's son, Mike, ended up getting a shot with Oakland. Jim Perry, a former Twins pitcher, was the one who signed him. So Rantz got the player he lusted after, and Pearl didn't leave him. Puckett displayed the charisma then that would endear him to Twins fans. "It was there from the beginning," Rantz said. "When we were in Illinois, after the game he tucked his helmet under his arm, walked over to the stands and talked to everybody. It was only about 20 people, but he was talking and smiling. The knock on Puck was that he was too small. Not that he was in bad shape, but he was not as big as he was when he got up here. I heard stories up there that he never pumped weights but was the strongest guy in the clubhouse."

Some wondered if Puckett could be another Jimmy Wynn, a height-challenged dynamo nicknamed "the Toy Cannon." Puckett said at the time that he would accept that comparison. It took 224 minor league games—just 159 following rookie ball—for Puckett to get the call to the majors. His debut was set for May 7, 1984, but Puckett endured four hours' worth of delays traveling from Portland, Maine, to meet the team in Anaheim, California. He rushed into the stadium in hurry, asking to borrow $83 to pay the cab fare from the airport. There was no "borrowing;" the club picked up the tab. Puckett debuted the next game, batting leadoff against Jim Slaton. Puckett grounded out in his first at-bat before going single, single, single, single for a 4-for-5 debut.

Puckett had joined a Twins team that baptized several players in 1982 and was waiting for them to blossom. The 1984 Twins, which included Kent Hrbek, Gary Gaetti, Frank Viola, Tim Laudner and others, were 81–81 but were just three games back from first. The 1985 and 1986 teams won 77 and 71 games, respectively, but there were signs of a turnaround. One was Puckett making the 1986 All-Star team for the first time. He batted .396 with eight homers in April—doubling his career power total in one month. By early May, Puckett had hit stardom. He led the major leagues in home runs, hits, runs, extra-base hits, total bases and slugging percentage at the time. Where was this power coming from? During the offseason, Puckett worked out with hitting coach Tony Oliva, adopting a leg kick that kept his weight back and allowed him to drive the ball better. And it kick-started a four-year run during which Puckett averaged .339 while socking 92 home runs. He had at least 200 hits in all four seasons, leading the league three times. He was the alpha of all alphas in the clubhouse, the spiritual force behind two World Series–winning teams.

Puckett made 10 consecutive All-Star teams beginning in 1986. Those were opportunities for the game's best players to get to know this human ball of happiness. Puckett became one of the game's most popular players. Puckett approached a young Ken Griffey Jr. early in his career and told him, "Your father took care of me. I'm going to take care of you." Puckett would take rookies out shopping for clothes on the road. Puckett was the one who called Yankees star Don Mattingly "Donnie Baseball" for the first time. Sportscasting legend Bob Costas was so enthralled with Puckett that his first child is named Keith Michael Kirby Costas. Puckett occasionally would shave his head when he wasn't hitting well (reporters learned it was dangerous to say the word "slump" around him), and teammates would rub it for good luck.

"I don't know where he got the energy to do that every day," said Paul Molitor, who faced Puckett for 12 seasons while with Milwaukee and Toronto. "I just remember the old days when the opposing team would stretch around the batting cage when the other team was hitting. Kirby would be taking his swings and we would be stretching on the other side. He'd come over and he'd address all the pitchers by 'Mister.' Trying to show them all this respect while, inside, he just can't wait until he sees them on the mound. So it was 'Mr. [Don] Sutton' or 'Mr. [Moose] Haas,' I can't hit you. Your curveballs are too good. I dread facing you.' We'd just go, 'Come on, Puck. We've seen this before.'"

On the field, there were so many memories Puckett provided before he took the field for Game 6 in 1991. Before the Puckett Game, there were the Puckett games in 1987. The Twins were in Milwaukee for a series against the Brewers. Al Newman was Puckett's roommate at the time. So Puckett brought Newman to a barbecue at the home of one of his sisters, who lived in Milwaukee. "Remember that Wendy's commercial when the lady says, 'Where's the beef?'" Newman asked. "Kirby was wearing an apron that had that phrase on it. It was hilarious."

On August 29, Puckett hit two home runs during a 12–3 rout at Milwaukee. The next game, Puckett went 6-for-6 with a home run and two doubles. He also jumped at the wall at County Stadium to rob Robin Yount of a grand slam. Dan Plesac got the first two outs of the ninth before striking out Greg Gagne. But strike three was a wild pitch, and Gagne beat the throw to first to reach base. That gave Puckett another plate appearance, and he blasted a two-run homer for his sixth hit of the day. The Twins won 10–6 while Puckett went 10-for-11 in the two games, setting an American League record. "That was one of my favorite times," Newman said. That season ended with the Twins winning their first of two World Series titles when they took down the Cardinals in seven games. Puckett had 10 hits in the series, batting .357. The next season, the Twins were the first American League team to draw 3 million fans in a season, with Puckett as a main attraction. They won more games but finished second in the AL West. Two seasons later, the Twins finished in last place. Puckett couldn't pitch, however, and the addition of Morris and Steve Bedrosian for 1991 helped put the Twins over the top.

There's still a belief that the Twins could have been more successful during the Puckett-Hrbek era. But players came and went. Catalyst Dan Gladden moved on after 1991. Pitching sputtered. Hrbek's body and desire to be a more hands-on father led him to leave following the 1994 season. After the 1995 team finished in last place, the Twins saw an opening and pounced. Future Hall of Famer Paul Molitor was willing to finish his career with the Twins, and the sides agreed on a two-year deal. Molitor would join Puckett, Chuck Knoblauch and some promising players in the daily lineup for the 1996 season.

The partnership with Puckett was tantalizing. "It was a huge draw," Molitor said. "I think that when you play and you've been around for a while, you kind of have it in the back of your mind, imagining different players around the league who would be tremendously enjoyable to play with. You know, Kirby was on that list. We had done some offseason events together. When I was at Toronto, we filmed some McDonald's commercials up there before a game one day. I don't know if I ever laughed as hard as I did during that take. The director was getting pissed because we wouldn't stop laughing during our lines. But yeah, to have it fall into place where I was looking forward to coming back to play and that and those four weeks that we had in spring training, those were just tremendous to be around him."

Four weeks was all Puckett and Molitor had together. Residents of and visitors to Florida that spring could hear the crack of balls off of Puckett's bat in all corners of the state. He was batting .344 in spring training—a very loud .344. He crushed balls during batting practice as well as exhibition games. Observers wondered how potent the Twins' offense could be. Then Puckett woke up on March 28 with a spot over his right eye. A day later, he was on the way to Baltimore to be examined by doctors at the renowned Johns Hopkins Medical School. He would not be available for Opening Day. By early April, glaucoma was considered one of the possible ailments. On April 12, Puckett was diagnosed with a rare form of glaucoma, a group of diseases that can damage the optic nerve and cause blurred vision or blindness. A week later, Puckett underwent exploratory laser surgery, with just a 25 percent chance of increasing blood flow to his retina and treating the glaucoma. He had two more surgeries, with minor improvements. Then one last procedure revealed irreversible damage. On July 12, at a press conference during which there was not a dry eye in the conference room, Puckett retired. "Kirby Puckett is going to be all right," he told the audience. "Don't you worry about me." He sounded reassuring to a crowd of teammates, club officials and media. And he might have been the only one not tearing up—in the entire state of Minnesota as well as among Twins fans in the Upper Midwest.

Even as his career abruptly ended, Puckett's optimism never wavered. A week before he announced his retirement, Puckett was at the Metrodome for a game between the Twins and Kansas City Royals. In the first inning, Paul Molitor lined a Mark Gubicza pitch that struck the 6'5" right-hander in his lower left leg. The collision was so hard that the ball deflected to first base. Gubicza took one step then fell over in excruciating pain. He later said he knew his leg was broken because he could hear the bones grinding against each other. He ended up being right, as he was diagnosed with a broken left tibia.

Gubicza was in the visitors' training room at the Dome following the incident when Puckett walked in with beers.

"Hey, what's up, Goobie? How you feeling?" Puckett said.

"Don't worry about me," Gubicza replied. "You're going to Johns Hopkins to have your glaucoma checked out."

"I'll be fine," Puckett said, handing him a beer. "Don't worry about me. I'll be fine."

A Royals trainer then appeared and slapped the beer out of Gubicza's hand. As Puckett looked on, the trainer told Gubicza that combining alcohol and the pain medication he was getting would be dangerous. "'He's telling me, 'You're not going to remember who you are,'" Gubicza recalled. "I said, 'That might not be a bad thing.' And Puck is laughing his head off at all of this. That was Puck."

Seven days later, Puckett announced that his playing career was over at age 36. He moved into an executive role with the club, the only African American to reach that level in club history.

Puckett collected 2,304 career hits but, since the turn of the century, no player had more hits than him—1,996—in the first 10 years of their career. While he finished in the top 10 in American League Most Valuable Player award voting seven times, he never won, finishing second once and third twice. He hit 207 home runs during his 12-year career. That's a lot, but not that eye-catching.

All of this is to point out that Puckett's numbers were a little light for someone attempting to enter the Hall of Fame. But his case, at the time, could be compared to those of Sandy Koufax and Tony Oliva, players who were among the best at what they did but had injuries curtail their careers. Koufax played 12 years before his elbow would not allow him to play anymore. Oliva played 15 years, the final five with a knee that was in flames. Like Koufax and Oliva, Puckett was considered one of the best players of his time. What was in Puckett's favor, as well, was that everyone liked him. His smile was disarming, his personality was magnetic and he could inspire a room of teammates to be great. That's how Puckett became a first-ballot Hall of Famer in 2001, part of the same class as good friend Dave Winfield. Puckett received 82.1 percent of the vote, a clear mandate as far as Hall of Fame voting goes. "And I faced odds when glaucoma took the bat out of my hands," Puckett said at his induction ceremony.

"You're not supposed to have favorites but, clearly, he made players around him better," said Andy MacPhail, the general manager during the Twins' World Series runs in 1987 and 1991. "I find it hard for me to reconcile the offseason issues that would manifest themselves later with the player I knew and how much he brought that franchise in terms of energy and enthusiasm. I swear to God he made Shane Mack a better player just by Kirby being next to him. I think if you ask Chili Davis, one of the reasons he signed with us as a free agent was the opportunity to play with Puck. He just brought so much value to the franchise even beyond what he put on the field, which was considerable."

MacPhail wasn't the only one conflicted. Puckett does have a street named after him along one of the routes that borders Target Field in Minneapolis. And there was a time McDonald's promoted a "Puck Pack," with a Quarter Pounder with Cheese as the anchor. What separated him from the pack was the Puckett Game. And there's a statue at Target Field of him pumping his first after hitting the homer in Game 6. Puckett wasn't just an icon. He was a colossus. So his post-career controversies were hard to compute.

Puckett did not ride off into the sunset. Instead, he suffered a fall from grace. During divorce proceedings with his wife, Tonya, in 2002, a woman asked for protection from Puckett after he shoved her in his Bloomington condo. She also claimed she had an 18-year relationship with him. Another woman sought protection from Tonya Puckett after receiving a death threat from the Hall of Famer's wife over an alleged affair. In September of that year, Puckett was accused by a woman of pulling her into a restroom at an Eden Prairie restaurant and grabbing her breast. Puckett was found not guilty of false imprisonment, fifth-degree criminal sexual conduct and fifth-degree assault.

Despite the not-guilty ruling, the legal entanglements shattered the image many fans had of Puckett just because of the possibility he had committed unacceptable acts. Perhaps he sensed that, as he dropped from the public eye and was increasingly withdrawn from the organization after it failed to figure out a different role for him. He sought a new direction in life. He attempted to take better care of himself, met another woman, moved to Scottsdale and planned to remarry. That chapter of his life never began. Puckett suffered a stroke on March 5, 2006, rocking the Twins, former teammates and his fans everywhere. He passed away a day later, one week before he would have turned 46 years old. A crowd of nearly 15,000 mourned him at a memorial service at the Metrodome, then were left to struggle with the final analysis.

What's undeniable is that Puckett was one of the greatest Twins in Franchise history. While his post-career life was troubling, many prefer to remember what he was in the uniform—especially when they drive down the street named after him and walk by the iconic statue of him, with that right fist punching the air.

6

Bert Blyleven

IF THERE WERE A HALL OF FAME FOR BASEBALL PRANKSTERS, voters would have waived the five-year waiting period for induction to get Bert Blyleven in as soon as he retired following the 1992 season.

Blyleven was the Lord of Levity. The Superintendent of Sabotage. A dirty bastard to some. Ripping holes in teammates' clothes. Ties cut in half. Oh, and the hotfoot. So many hotfoots. Blyleven would crawl under the dugout bench with a lighter and light teammates' shoelaces on fire during the games. No one was safe. In one game, Blyleven even got his manager, Tom Kelly.

"You've got to make sure you are winning and winning comfortably," Blyleven said of lighting up his manager. "And remember that I'm one year older than T.K., so he had to respect his elders when I lit his ass up."

Kelly is officially one year older than Blyleven. But, hey, Bert has a reputation to uphold. The story fits the narrative.

Opponents weren't safe either. Blyleven, then with the Angels, noticed Mariners manager Jim Lefebvre doing an interview near their dugout. Blyleven snuck up behind Lefebvre and lit both shoes on fire.

"He probably gave 98 percent of the guys on the team hotfoots," said Twins great Kent Hrbek, who played with Blyleven from 1985 to '88. "I know that much."

When Bert was with the Angels, the fire extinguisher in the clubhouse read, IN CASE OF BLYLEVEN. PULL.

Before Game 6 of the 1979 World Series between Pittsburgh and Baltimore, Blyleven, then with the Pirates, was walking around downtown and saw a pig's head in a meat market. Blyleven called teammate Jim Rooker "Pighead," so he purchased the head, brought it to the clubhouse, placed it on top of Rooker's uniform and stuck a cigarette in its mouth.

And these were the G-rated pranks, folks. The Motion Picture Association would have had issues with a few others.

Cutting holes in the toes of teammates' socks, hitting folks with shaving cream pies. Freezing shoes. Blyleven was in an incessant pursuit of slapstick throughout his 22-year career—and beyond.

As I write this, I'm looking at a button over my desk that reads, DON'T SAY FUCK AT THE HALL OF FAME! Blyleven is responsible for that one. Just read on.

This was also the man who wore a T-shirt that read, "I love to fart."

Former teammate Mickey Hatcher once said, "Bert was the sickest player of all time."

Rik Aalbert Blyleven was born in Zeist, Netherlands, and went to high school in California. His parents fled Holland in 1953 during the mass emigration from the country during the post–World War II era. The family first settled in Saskatchewan,

Canada, before moving to California in 1957. Bert picked up the game when he was around nine years old and was a phenom by the end of high school. He won 287 games over a 22-year career. His 3,701 strikeouts were third-most ever at the time he retired. He tossed 60 shutouts. He won World Series with the 1979 Pirates and 1987 Twins. Once his playing days were over, Blyleven became a beloved analyst while working alongside Dick Bremer during Twins television broadcasts. But Bert was the guy you slapped on the back after he pitched a great game—then watched your back to make sure he didn't slap a "kick me" sign on it.

It took 14 years of being on the ballot before Blyleven gained election to the Hall of Fame, subjecting him to experience a roller coaster of emotions as he waited for the day his plaque would be hung in Cooperstown, New York. The hang-up was that he was 13 wins short of 300 for his career. And 300 wins, for a long time, was viewed as that master key that unlocked the doors to the Hall of Fame. Blyleven won at least 15 games in 10 different seasons, but he might have been the ultimate hard-luck loser. He went 17–17 in 1974—despite a sparkling 2.66 ERA that season. As comical as Blyleven was, he was tormented by his inability to get enough votes for enshrinement.

After receiving only 23.5 percent of the vote in 2001— 266 votes shy of induction—Bert popped off. "This is a message to all the writers: Don't vote for me at all. I thought my percentage would go up to 30 to 40 percent, to tell you the truth." Fortunately for him, the writers kept him on the ballot, eventually enshrining him in 2011 as voters stopped relying on wins as a main component of a pitcher's Hall of Fame candidacy.

Blyleven wasn't afraid to speak his mind as a player and, a few times, managed to enrage hecklers while landing himself in hot water. Blyleven was real. Like many of us, he had to apologize for a few things along the way. Who doesn't have regrets?

But he was a Hall of Fame pitcher. And one of the more popular Twins ever if his television hijinks were included. He made it fun to come to the ballpark or to turn on a Twins game.

"The ultimate character," Twins president Dave St. Peter said. "For some generations of fans who knew him only as a broadcaster, they probably don't appreciate how good of a pitcher he was. Because he would make fun of how many home runs he would give up, and he would give up a bunch. But, overall, he was obviously a dominant pitcher, a Hall of Fame pitcher. And another one who never took the game too seriously and was wildly successful, I think, because of that."

The Twins selected Blyleven in the third round in 1969 out of Santiago High School in Garden Grove, California. He grew up listening to Dodgers games and the legendary radio voice of Vin Scully. Blyleven dreamed of throwing a Sandy Koufax–caliber curveball. When Blyleven made his major league debut as a 19-year-old in 1970, he had one. Blyleven threw one of the great curveballs of all time, a big breaker that would snap downward and sometimes down and away from right-handed hitters. Opposing hitters knew the pitch was coming and would still corkscrew themselves into the ground while trying to connect with it. Bob Boone, who batted .149 in 47 at-bats against Blyleven, said he could hear his curveball buzz as it approached home plate. That's how hard Blyleven spun the pitch. But if you ask Bert what his best pitch was, he often said, "My best pitch was a well-placed fastball."

Blyleven made his first start on June 5, 1970, against the Senators. And the first batter, Lee Maye, homered off him. Blyleven thought he was in trouble as manager Bill Rigney walked to the mound. Instead, Rigney reassured him, "Son, that's not the last home run you'll give up." Blyleven recovered to win that game 2–1. But he gave up a total of 430 home runs in his career, including league highs in 1986 and 1987.

Blyleven went 10–9 with a 3.18 ERA and was named the *Sporting News'* AL rookie pitcher of the year. He won between 15 and 20 games in each of the next five seasons, establishing himself as a bulldog and one of baseball's best pitchers. But just like many Twins players at the time, he had a hard time getting a nice raise from owner Calvin Griffith. Free agency had reached baseball, with players like Andy Messersmith and Dave McNally challenging the reserve clause and becoming free agents. A fed-up Blyleven was willing to let his 1976 contract run down and then sign with another team the next year. This led to the Twins trading Blyleven to Texas in June 1976. With his contract squabbles now in the papers, fans jeered him throughout his last start with the Twins on May 31. Blyleven knew he was headed to Texas by then but let jeering fans get to him as he walked off the field at Metropolitan Stadium. Blyleven left the field with an arm in the air with a middle finger extended. American League president Lee MacPhail demanded that Blyleven apologize for his gesture or be fined. Blyleven said he wanted to apologize anyway. MacPhail's son, Andy, would become general manager of the Twins and build a World Series–winning team.

Blyleven and Danny Thompson were dealt to the Rangers for Mike Cubbage, Jim Gideon, Bill Singer, Roy Smalley and $250,000. Blyleven signed a three-year deal for $150,000 annually, in addition to a bonus. A year later, on September 22, Blyleven no-hit the Angels in Anaheim. He had been out for 16 days because of a groin strain, which he tweaked in the first inning and then injured further in the eighth. There was too much pain when he threw his fastball, so he threw his curveball exclusively the rest of the game. "I was going to stay in, even if I had to throw underhanded." That was Blyleven's final game as a Ranger. Apparently, Ol' Bert had been caught on camera giving the one-finger salute again during a nationally televised game, which rankled the front office. Blyleven landed in Pittsburgh as part of a four-team, 11-player deal. The move worked out, as Blyleven was part of the "We Are Family" Pirates that won the 1979 World Series. He made two starts and one relief appearance in the postseason, allowing just three earned runs over 19 innings.

But Blyleven wasn't long for Pittsburgh. The next season, he tired of being pulled out of games early, left the team and headed home to California, where he threatened to retire if he wasn't traded. He returned in two weeks but was not a popular teammate. At the end of the year, he was dealt to Cleveland. He struggled with injuries, tearing a muscle in his right elbow that required surgery, then injuring his left elbow in a fall. He didn't pitch more than 159⅓ innings in each of his first three seasons. He recovered to go 19–7 with a 2.87 ERA in 1984 but was gone a year later when he demanded a trade and ended up back in Minnesota, where it all began.

Now in his mid-thirties, Blyleven had added a slider and changeup to his repertoire through the years. His experience and talent were just intersecting at a time when pitchers in their mid-thirties were considered ancient. Blyleven was just hitting his stride. In 1986, he went 17–14 while leading the league in innings. He also gave up a record 50 home runs. After the final game of the regular season, Blyleven grabbed a microphone and told fans the Twins could win the World Series the following year if everyone worked to have the best seasons of their careers. Blyleven had watched Tom Kelly be named interim manager for 23 games following the dismissal of Ray Miller. He was encouraged by how Kelly ran the team. Blyleven saw the future correctly. The 1987 Twins were just 85–77 during the regular season and had a negative run differential. Blyleven and Frank Viola formed a dominant partnership, the bullpen was led by Juan Berenguer and Jeff Reardon, and a great offense was led by Kirby Puckett, Gary Gaetti, Kent Hrbek and Tom Brunansky. This, plus having home field advantage throughout the playoffs, brought Minnesota its first World Series title. Blyleven beat Detroit, who was favored, twice in the ALCS. It proved he could be a big-game pitcher when needed.

Blyleven went 10–17 with a 5.43 ERA the next season, the worst year of his career, while dealing with a sore thumb. He had turned down a two-year contract extension at $1.8 million at midseason, based on some language in the contract that was unacceptable. But his future in Minnesota was up in the air—for a while. Blyleven, second all-time among Twins with 149 wins, was dealt to California following the season. He lived near Anaheim Stadium and had dreamed of playing for the Angels. Blyleven had 33 more wins in that right arm, as he pitched three seasons for California. He went 17–5 in 1989 and finished fourth in Cy Young voting.

And the pranks kept coming. One day, he noticed that every player had a stack of cards in front of their stalls to be signed. There was large stack in front of popular slugger Chili Davis'. Blyleven took the cards and displayed them all over the clubhouse. In the trainer's room, the bathroom, the visitor's clubhouse. Everywhere. Toward the end of the season, the Angels were in the dugout before a game when it was announced that the club was going to give a lucky fan a new car after the game and rolled a Chevrolet Suburban onto the field. Grounds crew members got out of the vehicle and started working on the infield. Someone then drove the Suburban around the stadium.

When it got close enough, Blyleven looked and recognized the license plate. It was his SUV. Payback.

Blyleven's career ended in 1993 during spring training when he couldn't make the Twins' Opening Day roster. He finished 287–250 with a 3.31 ERA. When he retired, his 3,701 strikeouts were the fourth-most ever, and he was one of eight pitchers with at least 3,500 strikeouts. He was not done with the Twins, however. In 1996, Blyleven agreed to join Dick Bremer to televise Twins games. Blyleven had made a couple of cameo appearances the year before. At the end of their first telecast together, Bremer complimented Blyleven on his work. Blyleven could not resist. "I thought you did a great job too, Big Dick," he replied. While it's standard practice to have a former player in the booth, Blyleven was now unleashed to perform in front of tens of thousands of Twins fans daily instead of once every five days. Blyleven offered insightful analysis but mixed in hilarious one-liners. It was the beginning of a 25-year run in his second career.

Before the 2002 season, Blyleven was given a Telestrator. It was a device that allowed broadcasters to diagram or break down plays with a pen that drew lines on the screen that viewers could see. It was great for John Madden doing football games or Mike Fratello, the "Czar of the Telestrator," during NBA games. It's hard to apply to baseball games because there is no movement until the ball is put in play. Blyleven really had no use for a Telestrator. So, as the 2002 season began in Kansas City, Blyleven spotted a Twins fan in the upper deck and circled him. He circled a few more that game, then more during the road trip. There are times when the Minnesota sports fan doesn't need much to be entertained, and this was one of them. Fans began bringing signs to Twins games and asking to be circled between innings. The 2002 Twins won the AL Central division and fans traveled well that year. On road games, hundreds of fans would rise between innings, look up to the visitors' television booth, hold up signs and scream for Blyleven to circle them. The traveling media had to explain in the press box what in the hell was going on to the local beat writers. Blyleven had created a phenomenon. He would punctuate his ritual with the phrase, "You are hereby circled!" Twins fans ate it up.

Blyleven gave Twins broadcasts credibility—except for in one game. During a pregame show on September 3, 2006, Blyleven was discussing the upcoming matchup between the Twins and Yankees when he fumbled a few lines. Frustrated, Blyleven then blurted, "We've gotta do this fucking thing again, because I just fucked it up." Blyleven didn't realize the show was live. He apologized later in the segment and even more passionately during the first inning. The Twins agreed that Blyleven had simply made a mistake but still suspended him for five games.

"I want to make sure that everyone knows that I fully understand and accept this suspension and am very much looking forward to getting back in the booth to concentrate on the team's late-season success," Blyleven said in a statement. This is the reason why buttons were printed that read DON'T SAY FUCK AT THE HALL OF FAME before Blyleven was inducted in 2011.

Anything was possible with Blyleven, especially if it was wacky. Being a broadcaster gave Blyleven access to the ballpark, where he would confer with managers, coaches and players to assist in his broadcasts. Occasionally, he would advise struggling pitchers on how to get back on track, careful not to show up the coaching staff. But he also had a clubhouse full of players to prank.

It became tradition for Blyleven to moon the entire team during the annual photo day. The Twins tried, at times, to keep the date of the photo shoot from him, but Blyleven would get tipped off by someone, appear on the field and perform the mooning while the photo was being snapped.

"I remember that hairy ass," Torii Hunter said. "And they would show the picture with our expressions when he did it. We would all have throw-up faces."

While he was beloved as a TV voice, there was a rage building inside of Blyleven. He became eligible to be elected to the Hall of Fame in 1998, drawing 17.5 percent of the vote that year. Then he drew 14.1, 17.4 and 23.5 percent the next three seasons. Blyleven, who never had a problem speaking his mind, expressed his frustration following the 2001 vote.

There was a slight diversion in 2002, when Blyleven was inducted into the Twins Hall of Fame. "This should be the first of *two* Hall of Fames he should enjoy," Dick Bremer, his television straight-man, said during a ceremony. Others saw the event at an opportunity to pay Blyleven back for his years of shenanigans. Tom Kelly was Blyleven's manager in 1986 when he gave up a league-record 50 home runs and in 1987, when he gave up 46. "Bert, I have a bill from my chiropractor for 1987," he said during his speech. "Could you please help me settle this up?"

Hall of Fame radio voice Herb Carneal introduced Blyleven this way: "Bert is one of only two pitchers to win a game before he was 20 and after he turned 40. It was those 20 years in between that were a problem."

As the years went by and Blyleven lingered on the ballot, followers of the game began to evaluate pitchers differently. The win-loss record was no longer considered a major determining factor of a pitcher's effectiveness because it didn't consider offensive support, the defensive support, ballparks, etc. The statistical revolution was coming. Sabermetrics had been around for years but was being embraced even more. No longer would a pitcher with a 23–11 record automatically be ranked above a pitcher with an 18–9 mark just because he reached the 20-win mark. There were statistics like FIP—fielding-independent pitching—which evaluates pitchers based on things they control—strikeouts, walks, hit batters and home runs. If a pitcher's FIP is lower than his ERA, it suggests that pitcher will improve. If it's higher, it suggests regression. ERA+ includes factors like ballpark effects and the level of the opponent. The figure is then adjusted to make 100 the league average. If a pitcher has an ERA+ of 130, he is 30 percent better than the league average.

Front offices were using stats like those as part of their decision-making, and they eventually became part of the hardcore baseball fan's lexicon.

Baseball writers, including this one, blundered in 2005 when Bartolo Colón was voted the winner of the Cy Young Award. It was largely because he led the American League with 21 wins against 8 losses and a 3.48 ERA. Other pitchers were better. Twins left-hander Johan Santana was 16–7. The wins weren't there, but Santana led the AL with a 2.80 FIP and an ERA+ of 155. He also led in WAR—wins above replacement—at 7.2. Santana, however, finished third in voting behind Colon and closer Mariano Rivera. Either Rivera or Santana would have been a better choice than Colon that season. For Santana, it kept him from winning three consecutive Cy Young Awards. Writers weren't quite ready to embrace these statistics.

Zack Greinke's Cy Young Award in 2009 is when evaluation turned a statistical corner. Greinke was just 16–8 for the season and tied for seventh in wins. But his ERA+ was 205, which was phenomenal, and his 2.33 FIP led the league. His 2.16 ERA didn't hurt either. Félix Hernández won the Cy Young the next season despite only 13 wins. The stat geeks had won! Sorry.

That's an unfair stereotype of curious and passionate baseball fans. But a different way to compare players had arrived.

Blyleven's case was swept up in the evolution. The knock on Blyleven was his 287 wins. He hadn't reached that mythical threshold of 300 wins that made a pitcher a lock for the Hall. But his case was looked at differently as more writers cleared that mental hurdle of relying on wins to compare pitchers. Blyleven's career ERA+ was 118 and he had an ERA+ of at least 125 an impressive 13 times. He twice led the league in FIP. And 3,701 career strikeouts—the third-most ever at the time—certainly helped his candidacy. He also was ninth in shutouts. Heck, Blyleven lost *nine* games by the score of 1–0. He had 20 no decisions in 1979 alone. Should that be held against him in the final reckoning?

Blyleven had an ally in Rich Lederer, an investment manager and huge baseball fan who ran a website called baseballanalysts .com. Lederer banged the drum for Blyleven, pointing out facts like Blyleven's career FIP of 3.19 was lower than his career ERA of 3.31.

Lederer contacted some Hall of Fame voters to make his case. But instead of beating them over the head with the next generation of statistical weaponry, he focused on some basic numbers: Blyleven was third all-time in strikeouts upon his retirement. Everyone who had pitched 50 shutouts was in the Hall; Blyleven had 60.

Lederer had taken on a noble cause, one that likely influenced many voters. Baseball followers were already starting to dig into the new numbers, so the combination likely boosted Blyleven over the 75 percent threshold. And Hall of Fame voters are a strange lot. A candidate's numbers don't improve after his playing career ends. But, to some, they look better and better as time goes by.

Blyleven was at his home in Fort Myers, Florida, when he received the call shortly after noon on January 5, 2011. He received 79.7 percent of the vote.

"It's been 14 years of praying and waiting," he said then. "I thank the baseball writers of America for—I'm going to say it—finally getting it right."

Bert deserved to take a shot at the voters. For years, he didn't get what he richly deserved. He was inducted in 2011, delivering an entertaining speech that was revealing, hilarious, thought-provoking and reflective upon his career as a player and a broadcaster. He began and ended his speech with, "You are all hereby circled."

7

Jim Kaat

My love affair with baseball began in the early 1970s. Growing up in Chicago, I had two teams and one choice.

I watched a Cubs game on WGN, channel 9. I was seven years old, so I wanted to know why there were plants on the outfield walls at Wrigley Field and why the Cubs wore strange uniforms. Although the Cubs finished over .500 those seasons, most of the times I watched them they lost. And I'm not wrong; the Cubs were 303–337 from 1972 to 1975, the time I was deciding which club to support.

I flipped over to WFLD, channel 32, to watch the White Sox. And they had this slugging first baseman who had the forearms of life and seemingly hit home runs with a flick of his wrists. He also wore the same glasses as my father. I chose Dick Allen and the White Sox.

When the 1973 season came along, the White Sox were trying to stop being a sub-.500 team but were on their way to a

77–85 season. In August, it was announced that the White Sox had picked up a pitcher on waivers from the Minnesota Twins.

I looked at the name and wondered, *Who is this Cat guy?* It was Jim Kaat. He spelled his name with a *K*, but I pronounced it like it was a *C*. Thanks to legendary announcer Harry Caray, we learned how to pronounce *Kaat* with respect to its Dutch origins and learned that he used to be pretty good when he was with the Twins. Kaat went 4–1 with 4.22 ERA in seven starts that season. In 1974, Kaat went 21–13 with a 2.92 ERA. What were the Twins thinking?

Kaat won at least 20 games in each of his two full seasons in Chicago. Here was this tall man with blazing red hair who strutted to the mound as if he were a New York stockbroker. He had impeccable command, threw nasty breaking balls and pitched deep into games. He played for a manager in Chuck Tanner who let players be themselves as long as they showed up to the ballpark ready to give their best. Kaat also became good friends with Allen, who was the AL MVP in 1972. And Kaat went 93–78 after Griffith let him go, his miserly ways keeping him from waiting and getting something in return for the left-hander. Who knows—If Griffith had been patient and let Kaat regain his form, he might have never left the Twins. Maybe.

After two-plus seasons in Chicago, the White Sox decided it was time to cash in on Kaat, who was turning 37. December 10, 1975, will be known for two developments. One, American League owners had approved the sale of the White Sox to Bill Veeck, who was making his grand return to baseball. Two, Kaat was traded that day to the Phillies for three prospects. Kaat ended up on Phillies teams that won 101, 101 and 90 games in successive seasons—and he was back with Allen, who was traded there in 1974. Kaat left Philadelphia at age 40 and was mostly a reliever by then, but he pitched until he was 44 with the Yankees, then the Cardinals. But in his career as a starter, he was embraced by three different fan bases. Although Kaat spent 15 seasons with the Twins, he was also claimed by White Sox and Phillies fans as one of their own. Kaat, in August of 2023, was part of an alumni gathering in Philadelphia—during a series against the Twins, ironically. And Kaat threw out the first pitch before an August 11 game, to his old teammate Bob Boone.

While Kaat pitched for my favorite team, most of his career was spent with the Twins. When the Washington Senators were allowed to move to the Twin Cities for the 1961 season, the *Minneapolis Star* ran pictures of some of the key players who were coming with the team. Harmon Killebrew, Earl Battey, Bob Allison and Camilo Pascual were among the players shown. They all would be loved by Twins fans, with Killebrew arguably the greatest Twin of them all. Kaat wasn't among them, as he was headed into his age-22 season and had appeared in just 16 games with the Senators over the previous two seasons. Twins fans would find out just what the redheaded lefty was all about. By the time his distinguished career was over, he was the Twins' career leader in wins (189), losses (152), starts (422), innings pitched (2,959⅓) and walks (694)—records that stood 50 years after his final game with the Twins. He also might have been the best-fielding pitcher of all time, collecting 16 consecutive Gold Glove awards during his career. He hit 16 home runs in his career and is the last Twins pitcher to homer in a game, on June 11, 1972, at Cleveland.

His durability and reliability made him one of the most popular Twins of all time as well as their best left-handed starter. His 25 years of distinguished play eventually earned him entrance into baseball's Hall of Fame in 2022, voted in by the Golden Days Era committee.

Kaat was born in 1938 in Zeeland, Michigan, a community founded by Dutch settlers in the 1840s. Zeeland is not far from

Holland, Michigan, which is known for its famous windmill. Kaat was seven years old when his father took him to a Detroit–Boston doubleheader in 1946. Kaat became a baseball fan that day as he looked out on the field and saw Red Sox legends like Ted Williams in their prime. Little did Kaat know then that he would one day face Williams during his debut season of 1959. Kaat collected baseball cards and listened to games on the radio. Zeeland was in range of Chicago, Milwaukee and Detroit, so he could listen to Cubs, White Sox, Brewers or Tigers games as he liked. He was pitching for tiny Hope College, located in Holland, when a scout for the Washington Senators spotted him. The Senators offered Kaat $4,000 to sign with them. The White Sox, however, offered $25,000. John Kaat, Jim's father, told his son to take the $4,000 offer.

At the time, any player who received a bonus over $4,000 had to spend two seasons on the major league roster. That kept big-spending teams from outbidding other clubs for young talent and stockpiling them in the minors. John Kaat wanted his son to learn the game, which he could not do sitting in the White Sox bullpen. Jim Kaat has told this story a few times. His father made $72 a week, so he gave up more than six times his weekly salary so his son could learn the game the right way. And it would happen.

In 1957, Kaat threw 73 innings for Superior, Nebraska. The next year, he was at Missoula, Montana, where he played for Jack McKeon. "Kid, you're going to pitch in the big leagues," McKeon told him. "You're pitching for me every four days. Might pitch a little in relief between."

McKeon, a player-manager at the time, was a catcher. So he worked closely with his young prospect. Kaat took the ball that year and threw a lot. He learned what worked and what didn't. He learned how to problem solve. He learned how to pitch and be a professional. McKeon, who would manage for 16 years in the majors and win a World Series with the Marlins in 2003, gave Kaat support that he needed as a young pro—teaching him lessons he would not have learned while idling in the bullpen in the majors as a bonus baby.

Kaat debuted with the Senators in 1959, getting his head handed to him during his three appearances. He went 1–5 with a 5.58 ERA over 13 games in 1960. Then he was part of the Twins' inaugural season in 1961.

"When we moved from Washington in 1961, the expectations were not that high because we were a last-place team," Kaat said. "We were excited to be going to a new city. The early '60s, we made a pretty good run."

Kaat was just 9–17 in 1961, his first full season in the majors. But his ERA came down from the stratosphere, to 3.90, and he gave up only 12 home runs in just over 200 innings. Then he went 18–14 with a 3.14 ERA in 1962. Kitty had arrived. He threw a decent fastball that he could place anywhere he wanted. He threw a hard curve that some would call a slider today, a higher-arching curveball and a changeup. But Kaat would mix and match, add and subtract through the years as he tried to stay a step ahead of the hitters. He even threw a screwball for a while. His walk rate dropped after his big-league baptism years and he became one of the best left-handers of his generation, with some arguing that he was one of the better lefties of all time.

As Kaat improved, so did the rest of the team. The 1962 Twins won 91 games, a 21-game improvement from the previous season. Harmon Killebrew smashed 48 home runs and drove in 126 runs. Bob Allison added 29 home runs. Camilo Pascual went 20–11. That was the beginning of a run in which the Twins won at least 90 games in six of nine seasons. The 1964 season saw the team dip to 79 wins, but Kaat went 17–11 with a 3.22 ERA. But there was a new kid on the block in outfielder Tony Oliva, who led the league in batting average, runs, hits, doubles and total bases. He was voted AL Rookie of the Year and finished fourth in MVP voting. The Twins led the AL in scoring that season, so something was brewing.

Three months into the 1965 season, Kaat had a very nice 2.09 ERA but was only 6–7, as he was locked into several tight contests and offense had scored a total of nine runs in his seven losses. The Twins, however, were just one-half game out of first place. Kaat went 3–1 in July but, more importantly, the Twins won seven of his eight starts and ended July with a six-game lead. The New York Yankees had won the previous five AL pennants and nine of the last 10. Signs of decline were evident in 1965, leaving a handful of teams in the mix to assume division supremacy. It would be the Twins who moved into first place for good in early July.

Kaat went 9–3 the rest of the way to finish 18–11 on the season. And he scattered eight hits while giving up an unearned run on September 26 when the Twins clinched the pennant with a 2–1 victory over Washington. Kaat struck out Don Zimmer for the final out. The Twins won 102 games that season despite missing Harmon Killebrew for seven weeks with a dislocated elbow and Camilo Pascual for five weeks because of back surgery.

But the 1965 Twins were years in the making and finally putting it all together. In addition to Killebrew and Pascual, there was the catcher, Earl Battey. Kaat was a young pitcher then and put a lot of faith in Battey. "He would come out sometimes if I was getting roughed up a little bit." Kaat said. "He would have that little wry smile and say, 'Are you even trying today?'"

There was the underrated Bob Allison in left field, who formed a dangerous power-hitting partnership with Killebrew.

"When they came up together, they were No. 3 and No. 4, like Ruth and Gehrig," Kaat said. "Bob really was a good all-around player. He was Rookie of the Year [in 1959]. He was a guy that probably as prepared to play every game as hard as he could. He, along with Frank Robinson, [was] probably feared by second basemen and shortstops the most because he went into second base on a mission."

There was shortstop Zoilo Versalles, who won the AL MVP award that season after batting .273 with 19 home runs, 77 RBI, 126 runs scored, 45 doubles, 12 triples and 308 total bases. "Zoilo had done things that shortstops hadn't done before, with home runs and stolen bases," Kaat said. "And he had that unbelievable range where he could fly down the left field line and make these catches in short left field that we hadn't seen other shortstops do."

Tony Oliva hit .321 and led the team with 98 RBI. Jimmie Hall hit 20 homers and 86 RBI. The Twins were a well-balanced team. Kaat formed an effective pairing with right-hander Mudcat Grant. Right-hander Jim Perry was in his prime as well.

The Dodgers were led by the indomitable duo of Sandy Koufax and Don Drysdale, who combined to go 49–20 during the regular season. The offense was eighth out of 10 NL teams in runs scored, as no one hit over 12 home runs. So it looked like the first team to score would win.

Koufax should have started Game 1 but did not pitch because the game fell on the holy day of Yom Kippur, and he was Jewish. That put Koufax in line to pitch Game 2—opposite Jim Kaat.

"We didn't have interleague play then," Kaat said. "And we only had that Game of the Week [on television]. So I had never seen Koufax pitch in person. He didn't pitch Game 1 because of the Jewish holiday. So I'm warming up next to him in the bullpen. And I thought, 'Wow, I mean, you can just hear the ball come out of his hand.' And I remember he looked at me and said, 'You guys play in this weather?' It was kind of gray and overcast day. I was like, 'Wow, this might be the best chance we have.'"

The game was scoreless—and hitless—through three innings. Each starter had walked a batter. Kaat was in awe watching Koufax work over Twins batters. "I said to [pitching coach] Johnny Sain on the bench, 'If I give up a run, this game's over. Nobody can hit this guy.'" The Twins broke the scoreless tie in the sixth with two runs and would go on to win Game 2 by a 5–1 score. The final two runs were driven in by a Kaat single following an intentional walk, which he took great pride in sticking to the Dodgers for putting a man on to get to him. Kaat hit 16 homers in his career and batted .247 in 1965. Good thing ESPN wasn't around then. The Twins were up 2–0 in the series after whipping the Dodgers 8–2 in Game 1. Drysdale was knocked out in the third inning. "When Walter Alston came out to take the ball, Drysdale gave him the ball and said, 'I bet you wish I was Jewish!'"

The tables were turned when the scene shifted to Chavez Ravine. The Twins lost all three games while scoring a total of two runs in the City of Angels. Koufax outclassed Kaat in Game 5, going the distance and striking out 10 in a 7–0 romp. The Twins won Game 6 to force a winner-take-all Game 7—and Koufax–Kaat III. Kaat faltered in the fourth inning, giving up a home run to Lou Johnson and an RBI single by Wes Parker. Koufax pitched another complete game shutout, striking out another 10 Twins, to win the World Series.

The 1966 Twins slumped to 89 wins, finishing nine games behind Baltimore. But Kaat carried the starting rotation with the best season of his career. He was at the height of his powers, throwing with pinpoint control while piling up innings. He pitched at least eight innings 24 times. From June 27 through the remainder of the season, Kaat got a decision in all 25 of his outings. Kaat pitched in 1965 with a slight shoulder problem that caused his arm to tire around the sixth inning. He was fully healthy in 1966. The difference: after throwing just seven complete games in 1965, he threw a league-leading 19 in 1966. Other numbers sparkled: A 25–13 record, 41 starts, 304⅔ innings, 1.6 walks per nine innings. All those led the league. There was only one Cy Young Award given at time—separate awards for the American League and National League were given out beginning in 1967—and it went to Sandy Koufax, who was 27–9 with a 1.73 ERA.

"I just got in a nice groove." Kaat said. "And if I gave up four or five runs, we would win 8–5. So it was a combination of winning the close ones and then [getting run support]. It was one of those years where you had everything together. It's like golf or any other game. You can rent it for a short period of time, but you never own it for your whole career."

Things can change quickly during a career. Injuries, players coming and going. And mentors being taken away from you. That's what Kaat went through following his great 1966 season. Pitching coach Johnny Sain, who had a profound effect on Kaat's career, was fired after the season. Sain was having differences of opinion with manager Sam Mele, and Mele asked to have him fired after the season. Kaat did not take this development quietly, issuing a lengthy statement in support of Sain that ran in the local papers at the time. "Allowing him to leave our ball club is like the Green Bay Packers allowing Vince Lombardi to leave them," Kaat wrote. It didn't go over well with Mele or coach Billy Martin. And Kaat had to meet with owner Calvin Griffith to clear the air. If Kaat had gone 13–25 in 1966, he might have been looking for work too.

Did Sain make a difference? Mele was fired after starting 25–25. The Twins had a team ERA of over 4.00 in April and June. It was 3.14 during the 1965 season. Cal Ermer took over, and the Twins embarked on the great pennant race of 1967. On August 1, the Twins were five games back and behind the White Sox, Red Sox and Tigers. By August 18, they were one and a half games ahead in first place. Kaat posted a 2.98 ERA in August to help the cause. In September, he was 7–0 with a 1.51 ERA. The Twins spent September between one game ahead and one game behind—an entire month of intense, battling baseball. Kaat pitched the Twins to a 7–3 win over California to take a one-game lead over Boston with three games left to play. They lost all three, including the final two games at Boston, as they fell apart at the end of the Great Pennant Race.

The Twins crashed to a seventh-place finish in 1968, but Kaat was a respectable 14–12 with a 2.94 ERA. The 1969 and 1970 teams both reached the postseason. Down 2–0 to Baltimore in the 1968 ALCS, the Twins had Kaat fresh and ready to go in Game 3, but manager Billy Martin elected to go with Bob Miller instead. Miller was knocked out in the second inning and the bullpen could not fill the breach in an 11–2 loss that knocked them from the playoffs. Owner Calvin Griffith had directed Martin to start Kaat in the game, but Martin had sided with manager Sam Mele during Mele's differences with pitching coach Johnny Sain. And he believed Kaat had something to do with Mele getting fired during the 1967 season.

This was one of several issues that led to Martin being fired after just one season as manager. Bill Rigney took over in 1970, and the Twins returned to the postseason. They were swept again by the Orioles, who averaged nine runs a game in the series. Kaat got a chance to pitch in this series but dropped Game 3 to Jim Palmer. The Twins would not reach the postseason again until their World Series–winning season of 1987.

At this point, Kaat was beginning to distance himself from that magical 25–13 season in 1966. He had remained an above-.500 pitcher until 1971, when he slipped to 13–14, but none of the seasons were like '66, when he was a horse. His 1972 season started out as a flashback to his greatest season, when he raced out to a 10–2 record and 2.06 ERA in 15 starts. He piled up the innings, including a May 24 game against the Royals when he went 11 innings to win 1–0.

"Marv Grissom was Bill Rigney's pitching coach," Kaat said. "Marv was a right-hander that threw a screwball. Not many righties did. He taught me the screwball, and that's when I got off to a really good start in 1972. Phil Roof was my catcher. I threw fastball, screwball, curveball. I didn't throw any sliders. And, lo and behold, I slid into second base and broke a bone in my left wrist. So I was done for the year."

Kaat had the best winning percentage in the American League when he slid into second base to break up a double play against the White Sox and suffered a hairline fracture of his left wrist. The next season, he was a different pitcher.

In 1973, owner Calvin Griffith felt Kaat, 11–12 with a 4.41 ERA at the time, was past his prime. Kaat maintained that he was still recovering from his injury. "I never really got the feel for that screwball that I had in 1972," Kaat said. "I was not pitching well in 1973, but my arm was starting to come back. Bob Rodgers was our bullpen coach, and I had heard that they were going to put me on waivers. I said, 'I can't blame them for doing that. My record [is] not that good. But my arm is coming back. I'm not done yet.'"

Kaat, indeed, was put on waivers, where he was claimed by the White Sox. Kaat had the right to veto the claim, since he had 10 years in the major leagues and five with the same team. Kaat decided to move on. He was worn out by years of contract squabbles with Griffith. In his book, *Good as Gold*, Kaat revealed that in 15 years of getting contract offers from Griffith, seven of them began with a salary cut. This despite him going 190–159 with the Twins over 15 seasons, winning at least 16 games five times. He was on his way to becoming the winningest active pitcher in the game. Also, Johnny Sain, who was the Twins' pitching coach until he was dumped after the 1966 season, was the White Sox pitching coach. Kaat felt that Sain would be the perfect fit for him, as Kaat believed his arm was still bouncing back from injury. On top of it all, White Sox general manager Roland Hemond offered Kaat a $10,000 raise to sign with the White Sox. The anti-Calvin! Kaat started packing for Chicago—where he would begin the next phase of a career that had 10 more seasons to go. Kaat was 93–78 after leaving the Twins, including two 20-win seasons. He also won a World Series in 1982 with the St. Louis Cardinals. The 17-year gap between World Series appearances was a record.

Kaat retired following the 1983 season. He coached for a couple of seasons before settling into a rewarding second career. What would Kaat do if he weren't in uniform? Let's see. He commands attention when he enters a room with his trademark strut. He's a charismatic, opinionated, thought-provoking storyteller. Television! In 1986, Kaat began broadcasting Yankees games. The 2022 season was his final year in the booth. He had won seven Emmy Awards for sports broadcasting by then.

One honor eluded him. Kaat appeared on the writers' Hall of Fame ballot in 1989, receiving 19.5 percent of the vote. Over the next 15 years, Kaat never received more than 29.6 percent of the vote, well below the 75 percent needed for election. It was during a time when wins mattered more than other revealing stats. And the fact that Kaat won 283 games—falling short of the 300-win mark that was considered a requirement for the Hall, in most cases—meant he couldn't get enough votes. His case was turned over to the Veterans Committee, where he languished for several seasons. He received 10 of 16 votes in 2011, finishing second. He received 10 again in 2014, one behind two of his former teammates, Tony Oliva and Dick Allen.

The Veterans Committee was reorganized in 2016, so Kaat wasn't up for election until 2021 as part of the new Golden Days era of candidates. By then, attitudes about pitchers needing 300 wins had changed. Former Twins teammate Bert Blyleven, with 287 career wins, was voted into the Hall in 2011. And Kaat would experience the same thrill in December 2021, when he received the call that he was headed to Cooperstown, New York, as well. Better yet, his induction class included Tony Oliva, whose candidacy lasted 45 years. "I really didn't think this day would ever come," Kaat said after getting the call from Jane Forbes Clark, chair of the board of directors of the National Baseball Hall of Fame and Museum. "I mean, I know I'm not in the same class with Sandy [Koufax], and Juan Marichal, and Gibby [Bob Gibson], and [Tom] Seaver and on and on. But I'm grateful they recognized the accomplishments over a long period of time."

Kaat arrived in Minnesota a baby Twin trying to survive in a league during the Golden Era of the game. He grew up as Twins fans experienced Major League Baseball in their state for the first time. Once the new-car smell wore off the new franchise, he was a part of a Twins team that reached the World Series and was just a game away from a championship. He then became the top left-hander in the game. Kaat will be remembered for being not just one of the first Twins, but one of the very best.

PART 3

THE STADIUMS

8
Metropolitan Stadium

ONE OF THE BIGGEST BASEBALL FANS IN THE TWIN CITIES is local lobbyist and entrepreneur Julian Loscalzo. Loscalzo lobbied on behalf of the Saints as they pushed to have their stadium, CHS Field, built in downtown St. Paul and opened in 2015. He operated a bicycle-taxi business. He now operates Ballpark Tours, which organizes an annual trip that includes stops at major and minor league stadiums. Ballpark Tours was a derivative of an effort called Save the Met, which saw a group of local die-hard baseball fans plead for outdoor baseball while the Twins prepared to move indoors to play in the Metrodome in the 1980s. The goal of the annual trip was to watch baseball outdoors, not at some antiseptic outpost that was shared with a football team and held monster truck rallies.

As Ballpark Tours' website stated, their group consisted of "purveyors of outdoor baseball." Their Save the Met T-shirts are no longer produced and have become a collector's item among hardcore Twin Cities baseball fans—or fans of Loscalzo.

Loscalzo also was a beer vendor at Metropolitan Stadium in his younger days, which forged his love of fresh, green grass and a sport that incorporated the elements. He brought his young son to games, sat him in a section, asked a few fans to look after him, hoisted his case of beer and went to work, checking back every couple of innings.

"I remember some nights you could go to the back and watch the moon rise in the cornfields while the sun was setting over the west," Loscalzo said. "It was really picturesque. Just cool."

By then, the Twin Cities of Minneapolis and St. Paul had become cool. In 1961, the area was home to a Major League Baseball team, the Twins, and a National Football League team, the Vikings.

As far as baseball went, it was the tie that bound the five-state region, as fans from around Minnesota, North and South Dakota, Wisconsin and Iowa traveled to watch games at the Erector Set nicknamed the Met. It resembled an Erector Set because it was first built for the minor league baseball team, expanded for the Twins, then expanded more for the Vikings—who then expanded on that.

Loscalzo worked there. Kent Hrbek was the local product from Bloomington who one day would be inducted into the Twins Hall of Fame and have his No. 14 retired. As a six-year-old kid, he wore No. 6 for his T-ball team because Tony Oliva was his favorite Twin. Hrbek rode his bicycle to the Met on under-16 discount nights to watch Tony O. and the Twins before eventually breaking into the majors while the team still played at the Met.

Although Metropolitan Stadium quickly became outdated and behind the times, it was Minnesota's first professional sports stadium, rising from the cornfields in Bloomington. It was unforgettable.

Longtime Twins president Dave St. Peter, as a youth, climbed into his parents' Town and Country station wagon and rode in from Bismarck, North Dakota, to attend games. His father, Dominic, was a Yankees fan, so they would drive in when New York was in town. That answers a question many have had whenever they turn on a Twins game against the Yankees and wonder why there are as many Yankees fans as Twins fans at times: It began all the way back in the early years of the franchise. From 1947 to 1964, the New York Yankees won 10 World Series and lost in the series five other times. Yankees great Roger Maris was born in Hibbing, Minnesota, before moving to Grand Forks, North Dakota, then Fargo, as a child. Maris' first professional season was with the Fargo-Moorhead Twins of the Northern League in 1953. If you were going to drive in from North Dakota for a baseball game, it was going to be to see the opponent with national pull and who had a local guy on the team.

"My vivid memories are sitting in the upper deck, right behind the Twins' dugout on the first base side," St. Peter said. "Splendid memories. I remember my brother trying to get autographs. We got one from Tony O. Just the whole experience of going to a game was pretty cool."

This is how the region felt about Major League Baseball coming to town. The St. Peters would also visit Valleyfair, a longtime amusement park, or have dinner at popular steakhouses like Murray's. It was a brand that reached hundreds of miles in each direction. In later years, the five-state region—Minnesota, Wisconsin, Iowa, and North and South Dakota—came to be known as Twins Territory. The Met was the first big conference room for committee meetings.

The construction of the Met made the Twin Cities a big-league town while activating a fan base throughout the Upper Midwest. It was the place to go from 1961, when it was considered a state-of-the-art sports venue, until 1981, when it had become out-of-date while the desire to build a multipurpose stadium downtown grew.

Metropolitan Stadium was built on 164-acre swath of farmland bordered by 78th and 82nd Streets to the north and south and 24th Avenue and Cedar Avenue to the east and west. It opened in 1956, when the Minneapolis Millers of the American Association played there while representatives courted Major League Baseball for a team. But this process began back in 1952, when three men met for lunch: Gerald Moore, who became president of the Minneapolis Chamber of Commerce; Norm McGrew, who represented the Chamber of Commerce at the time; and Charles O. Johnson, sports editor and columnist for the *Minneapolis Star Tribune*. Soon after that, a committee was assembled to look into landing a team here.

Earlier in this book, we covered how the committee was a jilted lover a few times before finally getting the Washington Senators to move into Metropolitan Stadium before the 1961 season—nine years after that first meeting in Minneapolis. The process of getting funding for the Twin Cities' first major league ballpark involved its own moments of drama, but the challenge brought together the business community and fans eager for big-league baseball.

The original estimate placed the cost to build Metropolitan Stadium at around $4.5 million. This would end up being a woefully short estimate, as the final cost of the Met before the Twins moved in for the 1961 season was more like $8.5 million. Note to cities (and taxpayers): most estimates are wrong. Some are too high. Many end up too low. Cities have tried to proceed with caution in recent years.

To pay for the stadium, the City of Minneapolis was given approval in July of 1954 to issue $2 million in bonds. These bonds were purchased by individuals and businesses for a little as $500 each with a rate of return of 2 percent. The bonds would be paid off through stadium revenue. Once the $2 million was secured, then the remaining $2.5 million would be sold to investment houses across the country. Those who purchased bonds also received priority seating and reserved parking. This might have been the precursor to personal seat licenses, a revenue-generating tool used today in which fans pay thousands of dollars to reserve a seat in the club section of a stadium—and still must pay for season tickets each year.

By early 1955, $1 million in bonds had been sold. Keep in mind that $500 in 1955—the lowest cost for a bond then—is more than $5,600 today. Friends and co-workers were splitting the cost of bonds like a few folks going in together on pull tabs today. The public wanted to be part of the movement and put up its dollars.

The challenge of selling these bonds was accepted by a civic-minded group called the Minute Men, who contacted business and individuals to have a hand—and their wallets—in the stadium drive. More than 200 Minute Men went to work on selling bonds, with a goal of $800,000. There were 16 teams of sellers, with at least nine members per team, challenged to sell $50,000 in bonds per team. The teams took on names of major league teams. The person who headed up the Cardinals wrote a letter to the St. Louis team, explained what they aimed to accomplish and received a box of Cardinals caps for team members to wear.

Local papers covered the push like it was a playoff race. There were updates when someone well-known joined one of the bond-selling teams. The *Minneapolis Star* ran standings of how much each team had raised in bond sales. The Yankees team grabbed an early lead only to be taken over by the Indians.

On April 1, it was announced that the Minute Men had exceeded their goal by $412,000. The community's hunger for Major League Baseball fueled a collaborative effort to secure the funding. But Metropolitan Stadium was going to be much more than that. Professional football, professional soccer and other special events were coming to Bloomington. What special events? For instance: On April 27, 1955, an application was received from the Lutheran World Federation to use the stadium—more than two years away.

Investment companies were to sell the remaining bonds. Groundbreaking took place on June 20. It looked like the Twin Cities was on its way to building a stadium that would attract a Major League Baseball team. But there was a problem. The investment companies fell short of what was expected of them. A holiday drive to sell $1.2 million of A-2 bonds was needed while Metropolitan Stadium was two weeks ahead of schedule—although the roof was scratched from the plans and less blacktopping of the parking lot was ordered to cut costs. By Christmas Eve, the public had stepped up again, purchasing nearly all the $1.2 million, with the rest selling over the next several days. These pushes to sell bonds were covered breathlessly by local media. The focus returned to the construction project.

Except for one setback, when a portable heater exploded, igniting other heaters and tanks and causing $250,000 of damage, the stadium opened on April 24 when the Minneapolis

Millers played host to Wichita in the first regular season game in the stadium. It would be announced later that year that the official name of the facility would be Metropolitan Stadium. It was quickly shortened to the Met by locals.

The *Star Tribune* produced a special section to mark the opening of the ballpark. The section was well-supported by advertisers—including the Lutheran World Federation, whose event was 16 months away.

It was a state-of-the-art, yet flawed, park. The decks were cantilevered, meaning no large posts in the middle of sections would obstruct views of the field. When it opened in 1956, capacity was around 18,000. When the Twins arrived in 1961, a section was added to increase capacity to just over 30,000. That section, however, was not connected to the main concourse. Fans had to leave the park to get to concessions. And, by the way, a renovation was needed to expand the stadium for the Twins' arrival from Washington. The cost: $9 million. The roof was never added. But the facility did include a Twins Room where scribes, if they chose to do so, could wet their whistles following games.

On April 21, 1961, the Twins played their first regular season game at the Met—a 5–3 loss to the new Washington Senators. Washington's Marty Keough led off the game with a single against Twins right-hander Camilo Pascual. Three batters later, Dale Long hit the first homer in the park's history, a two-run blast. The game was tied 3–3 before the Senators pushed him two runs in the ninth to spoil the opener in front of an announced crowd of 24,606. The 1961 Twins went 70–90–1. Cookie Lavagetto was the first manager in club history but was fired after a 23–36 start and replaced by Sam Mele. Harmon Killebrew hit .288 with 46 homers and 122 RBI to pace the offense. Pascual was 15–16 on the mound.

By the mid-1960s, the capacity had increased to accommodate more than 45,000 spectators. The park was built for a slugger like Harmon Killebrew. The left field foul pole was 343 feet away and the left-center field wall was 365 feet away. Even center field was just 402 feet from home. Right in Killer's wheelhouse. Of Killebrew's 573 career home runs, 246 were hit at the Met. Bob Allison, Don Mincher and Jimmie Hall also found the confines friendly to their power strokes.

The young talent that owner Calvin Griffith brought with him from Washington began to positively impact the club's fortunes. The Twins won 91 games in 1962 and 1963. The 1965 team won 102 games before losing the World Series in seven games to the Dodgers—despite the Twins holding home field advantage. The Twins also celebrated division titles in 1969 and 1970—getting swept in three games each time by the Baltimore Orioles. Overall, the Twins were 3–4 in playoff games at the Met.

The Twins also hosted the All-Star Game there in 1965, back when the game was taken a little more seriously than it is today. Players played while banged up. Starting pitchers went longer than an inning if reasonable. American League manager Al López was more interested in trying to get every player on his team in the game. Gene Mauch, the National League skipper, said he was managing to win. "After I put a guy like Willie Mays in the starting lineup, why should I replace him?" Mauch said. "He's one of the best and he told me this morning he wanted to play despite a hip bruise. Mays is like Mickey Mantle. Both could limp into the Hall of Fame."

In front of a crowd of 46,706, Mays led off the game with a home run off Milt Pappas. Joe Torre added a two-run homer later in the inning and the National League led 3–0 before adding two more runs in the second. Five home runs were hit in the game, but Ron Santo's infield single in the seventh allowed Mays to score the winning run in the NL's 6–5 victory in the Midsummer Classic. San Francisco Giants right-hander Juan Marichal, who pitched three innings, was named Most Valuable Player. Six Twins players were named to the team, with catcher Earl Battey and first baseman Harmon Killebrew in the starting lineup. Killebrew thrilled fans by blasting a home run in the fifth. Local fans were able to watch 20 future Hall of Famers in the game, which was the biggest event held at the stadium to that point.

There were other special moments held at the park. On June 3, 1967, Killebrew hit a home run off Lew Burdette of the Angels. The announced distance was 430 feet where it hit the stands, which was met with derision from fans and Twins staffers. The home run was later amended to 520 feet, then 522. Killebrew, noting that he'd hit a ball completely out of Tiger Stadium in Detroit, wasn't sure if the blast at the Met was the longest of his career.

There is a stadium seat attached to a wall of the Mall of America—which was built on the site of the stadium in 1992— to mark the spot where Killebrew's home run landed. Next to the seat is a sign that reads, HARMON KILLEBREW, THANK YOU FOR THE MEMORIES. It's not the actual seat the ball struck, only a seat from the stadium placed on the wall to mark the spot. Killer's homer landed in the bleachers, where there were rows of bench seats. The seat at the MOA is a from a box seat. A group of fans took the section of seating where Killebrew's home run landed and donated it to the Hall of Fame.

The seat at the Mall of America can be found in the middle of the mall, in an indoor amusement park called Nickelodeon Universe. The first sign that marked the landing spot of Killebrew's prodigious blast was stolen. Sometime after that,

Clyde Doepner, a dedicated memorabilia collector, was contacted and offered the sign in exchange for $1,000. "That was back when $1,000 was really a lot of money," said Doepner, who became the Twins' curator.

The home plate from Metropolitan Stadium is marked by a plaque at its actual spot from where the stadium's infield was, making it an attraction for baseball fans who visit the venue.

There was one not-so-special moment at the Met. On August 25, 1970, a bomb threat was called in during a Twins game against Boston. The call came in around 8:30 PM. A week earlier, a bomb had gone off at the Old Federal Building in Minneapolis, so officials weren't going to take any chances. At 9:15 PM—during the fourth inning—legendary Twins public address announcer Bob Casey made the following announcement:

"The Twins have been advised by the Bloomington police that there will be an explosion here at the Met at 9:30. Please leave the stadium in an orderly fashion," Casey said, according to the Minneapolis Tribune.

The announced crowd of 17,697 was asked to move to the parking lots. The problem was that Twins and Red Sox players were asked to stand in the middle of the field and away from any explosion. While many fans did go to the parking lot, many other fans saw the players milling about on the field and saw opportunity. About 1,000 fans went onto the field to talk to players and get autographs. A picture in the Minneapolis Tribune showed a smiling Tony Oliva chatting with fans on the field. Boston star Carl Yastrzemski also attracted attention. Vendors entered the field and sold beer and other refreshments.

A young Twins fan named Tim Laudner, then 12 years old, was in the stands with his father that night. The Laudners went to the parking lot while the bomb threat was investigated.

Laudner went on to star at Park Center Senior High School, located in nearby Brooklyn Park, and the University of Missouri before being drafted by the Twins and being part of their 1987 World Series championship team. "We were in the upper deck, and we went out the parking lot and sat in the car and then they got the all clear," Laudner said. "I told my dad, 'I'm not going back to the upper deck. I don't want to die.' I think we managed to find our way into the main level and watch some more of the ball game."

The game was delayed for 43 minutes but resumed around 10:00 PM after police checked the stadium and found no bomb. The bomb threat was traced to a pay phone on the first deck of the ballpark, one of more than a dozen threats called in around town that night.

The real excitement that night was on the field. Boston's Tony Conigliaro blasted a home run off Tom Hall in the eighth for the only run of the game.

As for other memories from the Met, you just might be able to walk into a room full of Twin Cities baseball fans and find a couple who removed a seat or other part from the stadium when it closed at the end of the 1981 season. The stadium that was built thanks to the pocketbooks of individuals and businesses had run its course. The Twins and Vikings were vacating the stadium for the shiny new Hubert H. Humphrey Metrodome. And there were some souvenirs to be had.

"We came in semi-prepared with a few wrenches," Loscalzo said. "We would take a back off of one seat and look to see if anyone [was] coming. We would run up to the top and [throw] it off the end. We had a couple buddies down there who would just take them. We had a pickup truck and would stick them on the pickup truck. We probably got 8 to 10 sections of the seats."

The final Twins game at Metropolitan Stadium was played on September 30, 1981, a 5–2 loss to the Royals. Roy Smalley popped out for the final out. That team finished 41–68–1 in a season that was shortened due to labor battles between owners and players. Roy Smalley batted .263 and led the team with seven home runs. Right-hander Pete Redfern was 9–8. And the managerial situation was the same as in the first season at the Met. Johnny Goryl started the season going 11–25–1 but was replaced by Billy Gardner, who went 30–43.

Things were worse for the final Vikings game on December 20, 1981, as the second half of their contest against the Chiefs was played among a cacophony of wrenches and saws removing seats. Some fans just stomped on chairs until they broke off. The American flag was taken down during the fourth quarter. Fans climbed the scoreboard and began pulling out wires and bulbs, to the point that the clock stopped at precisely 3:10 PM.

Fans stormed the field at the end of the Vikings' 10–6 loss, tearing down the goalposts to cap a violent end to the Met's existence.

Metropolitan Stadium served its purpose as a multi-use facility, working better for baseball than football. It was a special events venue as well. The Beatles, The Eagles and The Allman Brothers all held concerts there. Several wrestling matches were held there, with Dick the Bruiser, Vern Gagne and Mad Dog Vachon among the headliners.

The Minnesota Kicks of the North American Soccer League played there from 1976 until they folded in 1981. A North American Soccer League–record 46,164 fans attended a game against Pelé and the New Cosmos. They drew more than 49,000 for a playoff game against San Jose that season. The early success, many locals theorized, was that most of the fun was in the Met's parking lots for tailgating, with fans eventually wandering in to catch parts of the games. The early attendance boom the Kicks enjoyed led to them always making the first lists of potential expansion sites once Major League Soccer came online in the 1990s.

The Met was a legitimate sports and entertainment hub, but it wasn't maintained well and lacked its luster from the mid-1950s. The Vikings paid for 6,000 seats before the 1965 season that pushed capacity to 47,900. They received a more reasonable lease deal out of their investment.

But it wasn't enough. Owners, both football and baseball, recognized the need to enhance their revenue streams. Playing in front of 48,000 would not be enough for the Vikings. Baseball's economics were changing, too. St. Louis outfielder Curt Flood challenged baseball's antitrust exemption, which had allowed it to operate as a monopoly. Because of the reserve clause, players were attached to teams for life, unless they were traded. Flood and players' union head Marvin Miller filed suit, demanding that he be declared a free agent. The Supreme Court ruled in favor of Major League Baseball but, a few years later, the reserve clause would be struck down, ushering in free agency.

The Twins were playing in a stadium that was behind the times and not maintained properly. Attendance had fallen below 1 million in eight of the previous 10 seasons. Free agency was coming, and a fiercely frugal Griffith already had several publicized contract squabbles with players. Twins officials had hoped a renovated Met that included some sort of cover or retractable roof was feasible. But the movement to build a downtown domed stadium gained steam.

It didn't take long, in terms of stadium life, for leaders to begin discussing what a domed replacement stadium would look like. Hints were dropped as early as 1970. The Vikings enjoyed a home field advantage when opposing teams visited in November and December and were hit with cold, snowy weather. Imagine what opposing teams thought when they saw flame throwers being used to break through the ice and snow! But this was before advancements in thermal wear. The fans froze their keisters off. For football, its best capacity was 49,000 in the early 1970s, and cities were building larger arenas. There was infrastructure, suite needs and availability problems—the Lutherans couldn't gather there in January, for instance.

Griffith, it has been written, was torn. He had hoped to remain in Bloomington. His lease deal for any dome called for him to receive a smaller percentage of concession revenue than at the Met.

After 20 years, both the Twins and the Vikings moved downtown to the Metrodome before the 1982 season. Minneapolis leaders got what they wanted—a downtown stadium that brought people to the city in a period during which families and corporations were moving to the suburbs. The Vikings received a better lease deal than they had at the Met. Griffith agreed to move but wasn't sure if it would be enough for him to withstand the winds of economic change that blew in his face.

The Met sat untouched and died a slow, painful death as it fell into dilapidation until it was bulldozed in 1985 to make way for the Mall of America. The Met was gone, but it brought major league sports to the region, raised generations of fans and will never be forgotten.

But it was like my 1976 Oldsmobile Cutlass. Lots of fun memories of driving it around. But when the rusty bumper is falling off the frame, it's time to move on. The Twin Cites said goodbye to the Met and moved on to a more up-to-date ballpark. Or so they hoped.

9

The Metrodome

IT WAS BLAND. IT WAS BLUE. IT WAS QUIRKY. IT WAS BASEBALL inside a warehouse.

The Hubert H. Humphrey Metrodome was made to keep its sports teams protected from the volatile weather that threatened the Twins in April and the Vikings in November and December. It was not built to win awards or be worthy of snapshots. It was constructed in the era of multipurpose stadiums springing up around the country, like Riverfront Stadium in Cincinnati, Three Rivers Stadium in Pittsburgh, Fulton County Stadium in Atlanta and others. Kansas City had a unique setup with its Truman Sports Complex, which placed stadiums for the Royals and Chiefs in the same area, separated by a parking lot. Original plans for that complex included a roof on tracks that would cover each stadium when needed.

The Dome opened in 1982, which was before baseball's architectural craze in building charming ballparks that were nestled near city cores and provided picturesque backdrops for spectators. It was before fancy luxury boxes were the rage, before retail space was a priority and before players showered and dressed in country-club-level facilities.

The best part of the Dome was that it was reliable. The Twins didn't worry about postponing games because of rain, cold or snow. Twins fans from North Dakota could drive into town without worrying about cancellation. You realized that when you entered the Dome before a game, you weren't going to see the sun for a while. Driving to the park during a glorious afternoon could be tough because you were headed inside. You could enjoy baseball but not the great outdoors.

At least you knew a game was going to be played.

That's what the Dome was asked to be. Reliable. It was built without frills. You walked into the Dome and saw AstroTurf, then the blue seats. Then concrete, then the retractable seats in right field that were covered with what looked like a plastic bag. That's why that section of the park—er, stadium—was nicknamed "the Baggie." The seats retracted for baseball games, but the design still provided seating for more than 46,000 fans, with the ability to be expanded to more than 55,000. For football games, the capacity was over 64,000. To prepare it for baseball, a whole section of seats would collapse up against a wall in right field. To prepare it for football, the seats would be pulled out and a forklift would come out, hoist the pitcher's mound into the air and carry it to storage.

But the Metrodome was configured better for football than baseball. Baseball viewers sat in seats that provided great views of a football field. But fans sitting along the third base line had to turn their heads to the right to see home plate for baseball games. It was a different way to experience baseball, which led to mockery through the years. Before the Twins faced the

Tigers in the 1987 playoffs, Ed Sherman of the *Chicago Tribune* wrote, "Comparing Tiger Stadium to the Metrodome is like comparing a vintage Rolls and a Pacer. There is no comparison." John Schuerholz, the general manager of the Kansas City Royals in the 1980s, had a suggestion about how to improve the Dome: "Nuke it."

Just protect the players and fans from the elements and, hopefully, there would be entertainment along the way. And, from 1982 to 2009, the Dome did its job. It just did it unlike any park in America.

Kent Hrbek grew up in Bloomington, Minnesota. He starred at Bloomington Kennedy High School. As a youth, he rode his bicycle to Metropolitan Stadium to watch Twins games. He was signed by the Twins out of high school, worked his way up the minor league ladder and debuted in 1981, the final year at the Met. He played 12 games in his hometown stadium. The next season, the Twins moved to the Metrodome.

Hrbek and his teammates thought it was neat to break in a new ballpark and enjoy the modern amenities it provided. But...

"Reality sank in pretty quickly," he said.

When I refer to the Dome as "reliable," I mean to praise. Fans make ballparks. Great moments make ballparks. Great food and great views of a skyline should be accoutrements to a sports viewing experience. The Metrodome has provided everlasting memories to a generation of Twins fans, with World Series titles in 1987 and 1991 at the top of the list.

Even if bland, the Dome provided other things. When you enter Fenway Park in Boston, you can hear the ghosts whispering. When you enter Wrigley Field, you wonder if an outfielder is going to lose a ball in the ivy. When you enter Dodger Stadium, you wonder which movie stars will be in the stands that night.

When you walked into the Dome, you wondered how its quirks were going to impact the game that day.

As Hrbek and friends found out, the artificial turf, called SuperTurf, was harder than they anticipated. In the coming years, it would be replaced by AstroTurf in 1987 and FieldTurf in 2004. But SuperTurf was bouncy. That was home field advantage No. 1. Twins players learned the importance of running hard when they hit routine singles to the outfield. If the fielder wasn't familiar with the turf, he could run in too fast to get to the ball and see it bounce over his head. Twins players began yelling "Bounce!" when routine hits headed for the outfield. The turf also was advantage No. 2. A ground single could turn into a triple if someone like Cristian Guzmán slapped a hard grounder to the gap and it split the defense.

"They had the baggie [in right field] and they had the turf really hard," infielder Roy Smalley said. "I mean, they basically put the living room carpet down on the cement. We traded bad hops and wind in the Met for really big hops inside the Dome."

Then there was the roof—advantage No. 3. The roof had two layers. The outer layer was Teflon-coated fiberglass, while the inner layer was acoustical fabric. The result was a ceiling with the color of a well-worn baseball, and outfielders frequently lost balls against the ceiling while tracking them. There also was a blind spot down the left field line, due to the way lighting was angled. Outfielders sometimes had to trust their tracking skills and run to where they thought the ball was headed until it would suddenly appear again. The Twins learned how to deal with these things. If a rookie outfielder was called up to the majors, Twins manager Tom Kelly would have him take fly balls in left field *after* games to simulate game conditions. From 1985 to '94, the left field wall was topped with a six-foot plexiglass screen, which kept some well-struck balls in the park.

Between the turf, the blind spot, the baggie in right and the speaker in play, there were things that happened in the Metrodome that didn't happen in any other major league ballpark.

For proof, ask Daryl Boston. "That was my nightmare stadium," he said.

Boston, a prep standout from Cincinnati, was the first-round pick of the White Sox in 1981. Hyped as a multi-tool player, Boston reached the majors as a 21-year-old in 1984 and expected to be a core player for Chicago for years to come.

If I were in a courtroom putting the Metrodome on trial for crimes against opposing players, Boston would be my first witness.

On October 4, 1986, Boston was the starting center fielder for Chicago against the Twins at the Dome. In the second inning, Greg Gagne lifted a fly ball to straightaway center. Boston took a few steps in and immediately flung his arms out to each side. He had lost the ball in the ceiling. The ball bounced several feet behind him and rolled to the wall. Right fielder Steve Lyons raced over to retrieve the ball, but it was too late to catch Gagne, who legged out an inside-the-park home run.

The Dome wasn't done with Daryl. In the fourth inning, with two runners on base, Gagne slapped a single to center field. Boston saw this ball just fine—for a moment. Boston ran in to field the ball and possibly throw home because Billy Beane, the runner on second, was fast. The ball hit the Metrodome turf and bounced over Boston's head. He reached up for the ball, but it ticked off his glove and rolled to the wall once again. Gagne had a second inside-the-park homer, the first time since 1972 that a player had two inside-the-park home runs in the same game. And that time was Dick Allen of the White Sox against the Twins at the Met. Official scorer Bob Beebe ruled that it was a hit. When asked by the *Minneapolis Star and Tribune*, Bebee replied, "It took a Dome bounce over his head."

That was the park in a nutshell. Dome dogs were served in the stands and there were Dome bounces and Dome doubles on the field. Gagne completed a splendid day at the Dome by tripling in the sixth.

In 2023, when he was a coach with the same White Sox, Boston was asked about playing in the Dome. "I've been charged with outfield play, and I have to tell my players how bad I was at the Dome," Boston said. "The roof. The baggie. When it got dark it was tougher at night than it was in the day. It was a mess, for me."

The inflated bubble was real. And it wasn't just weird. It was really weird. Because the roof was supported by air, speakers hung from the roof. If there was a storm outside, the speakers would eerily sway. But compared to the bouncy turf, Teflon roof and baggie in right field, you didn't think that much of it. Until it came into play. If a batted ball hit a speaker, which was quite a distance from home plate, it would generally be ruled a home run. But there were exceptions. Tigers first baseman Carlos Peña was awarded a double in 2003 on a ball that hit a speaker. Chili Davis, while with the Twins, hit a speaker in 1992 and was called out. The Angels' Mo Vaughn thought he had hit a long home run in 2000, but the ball struck a speaker in right center and fell for a single.

The Dome giveth. And the Dome taketh. Players thanked the baseball gods when quirky plays worked their way and pleaded for forgiveness when things went against them. And some just felt the forces inside the Dome were applied against them.

Texas manager Bobby Valentine would put tape on the large ventilation shafts behind home plate to see if the fans were turned on and off to benefit the Twins. Players were asked about using the fans to their advantage. Executive vice president/ general manager Andy MacPhail overheard Al Newman tell a reporter, "That's exactly what we do." MacPhail knew Newman was kidding but liked the response. "Put it in their heads," MacPhail said. "You know, it clearly was a home advantage."

The Detroit Tigers felt that way in 2004 following a 6–5 loss to the Twins. Manager Alan Trammell and bench coach Kirk Gibson were convinced that the Twins had manipulated the airflow in the Dome for their own benefit, blowing air in from the outfield when the Tigers batted but not when the Twins were at the plate. Trammell argued that a drive by Rondell White in the ninth should have been a lead-changing home run. Instead it was blown back into the playing field.

"It seemed like the air conditioning was blowing in our faces in the ninth inning," Trammell said after the game. "No question there was some air in the ninth."

Gibson was a little more descriptive: "That POW flag [in left field] looked like it was in a thunderstorm. They had that thing cranked."

The Twins explained that air is pumped into the stadium during the late innings to offset the air that escapes when fans walk through the exits. And fans were regularly blown out of the doors when leaving the building with the escaping air.

Detroit's claims didn't lead to an investigation by the league, so the whole thing eventually blew over. The Dome had enough quirks of its own and did not need any man-made shenanigans. So the game will be remembered for more than Detroit spewing hot air. The winning runs were scored on a home run by Joe Mauer—the first of his storied career.

There was nothing man-made about the goofiest event in the Twins' history in the Metrodome. No one saw it coming. Well, maybe a few Twins did. The Teflon roof was pocked with holes that acted as a drainage system that would keep the roof from caving in because of snow. I know. We'll get to that later. In 1984, the Oakland A's were in town and had Dave Kingman on their roster. Kingman was one of the game's feast-or-famine home run hitters. He slugged 442 home runs in his career, few of them cheapies. He also struck out more than 100 times in 14 different seasons. That was before strikeouts became more acceptable in the game.

On May 4 of that season, Kingman stepped to the plate against Frank Viola and took a mighty swing. The result was a high pop-up that headed for the roof. Twins first baseman Mickey Hatcher, filling in for an injured Kent Hrbek, waited for the ball to descend. And waited. And waited. The ball had gone through one of the drainage holes in the roof, never to return to the field of play.

"After it didn't come down for a few seconds, I was covering up," Viola said at the time. "I didn't know when it was coming down."

Hatcher, one of the game's great characters, grabbed a ball out of the umpire's bag and pretended that it had come down and he had grabbed it. The umpires weren't falling for that one. After a consultation—a baseball going through the roof wasn't covered in the ground-rules meetings before the game—they awarded Kingman a double.

Hatcher joked afterward that he spent the rest of the game looking up at the roof with his hands held out, because "you knew it was going to come down and hit you in the head sometime."

Before the next day's game, a worker went up to the roof, got the ball and dropped it as Hatcher stood below and tried, unsuccessfully, to catch it.

In 2004, the Twins brought Kingman to town to celebrate the 20th anniversary of the play. The Angels were the opponent, and Hatcher was their hitting coach. So the Twins held a re-en-actment. Hatcher dressed up in catcher's gear and went out between first and second base. A Dome staffer went to the roof and dropped a ball through the now-legendary hole. Hatcher stumbled and fell as the ball bounced off him as the crowd laughed. There were only 10,155 fans at that 1984 game, but many more than that likely have claimed to have been there to witness a once-in-a-lifetime event.

The route the Twin Cities took toward building Metropolitan Stadium made for a good story about a little city growing up and wanting professional sports. The path city leaders took to building the Metrodome would have made you reach for the Maalox.

The first talk of building a dome goes as far back as 1970—just nine years after the Twins and Vikings moved into the Met. The Vikings were playing in a stadium more suited for base-ball and its capacity was the smallest in the National Football League. The upkeep of the Met was less than desired, it was already losing its luster and owner Calvin Griffith watched fans stay home in April because of the weather. By that time, architect Robert Cerny had floated the idea of a domed stadium in downtown Minneapolis. Soon, another 10-plus years of sta-dium debate was about to launch. And, once again, it got off to a poor start, as an initial plan in the early 1970s placed too much responsibility on taxpayers to build.

Both teams' leases were up in 1975, as the sports fans' dilemma returned once again. Local fans loved baseball. And there were fears the Vikings would move if a new stadium wasn't built. But help wealthy owners pay for a stadium? That was tough to swallow. There was a plan to expand the sta-dium to more than 58,000 for $10.1 million and add a dome for $21.2 million. A 65,000-seat stadium would cost around

$51 million. Minneapolis mayor Charles Stenvig, claiming tax-payer fatigue, preferred renovation. Over the next year, ideas were floated without financial backing. Build a football-soccer stadium next to the Met. Build a dome by the Seven Corners area near the University of Minnesota campus. That way the Gophers could leave Memorial Stadium, which, apparently, was obsolete the day it opened.

Every idea had a detractor. Over the next several years, locations in Bloomington, Blaine, Coon Rapids, Eagan, downtown Minneapolis and the Midway area of St. Paul were proposed as sites. The plans either didn't gain traction or faced too much pushback from politicians.

The stadium wars had arrived, as two teams looked for a better stadium situation.

A deal was struck in December 1978 to fund a $55 million downtown domed stadium, with one of the components being a liquor tax. In April, the liquor tax was repealed, leading to reports that Bloomington wanted to jump back in as a contender. Some wanted to revisit the possibility of building a stadium by the University of Minnesota. Nothing has come easy when trying to build professional sports stadiums in Minnesota. The deal was back on in May, as the liquor tax was changed to include a hotel-motel tax, 30-year bonds, donations from the business community and a special tax district created near the stadium site. Ground broke on December 20, 1979, and the stadium was ready for Opening Day 1982. The nation's fifth domed stadium—following the Astrodome in Houston, Texas; Silverdome in Pontiac, Michigan; Kingdome in Seattle, Washington; and Louisiana Superdome—was completed in time and for a total of $62 million, with the final $7 million coming privately to meet finishing costs. The Twins lost 11–7 to Seattle in the first regular season game ever played there. Dave Engle had the first hit—a home run—in the bottom of the first inning. Gary Gaetti went 4-for-4. Pete Redfern took the loss for the Twins in front of an announced crowd of 52,279. Domeball was apparent right away, as Engle got stuck in the turf while attempting a sliding catch of a sinking drive. The ball got by him for a double.

As the game was played, a group of about 75 lovers of outdoor baseball gathered in a parking lot at Metropolitan Stadium for another goodbye. They wore thick coats and ski caps. They lit fires, drank from a keg of beer and listened to the game on the radio. Car horns blared when Engle hit his home run. The gathering included members of the Save the Met group that opposed moving indoors to watch baseball.

The 1982 Twins went on to lose 102 games, so the only buzz that year was generated by the new stadium. It wasn't enough, as only 5,213 showed up the next night.

There was one thing missing from the Dome that season: air conditioning. There were no plans for it. In 1976, a local architect told legislators that movement of air in Dome to keep the roof inflated would be enough to keep fans cool and lower costs even more. As the summer months rolled around, that ended up being poppycock. I wasn't around in 1982, but I remember a conversation with former Twins media relations man Tom Mee, who described it as such: "Oppressive was an understatement." Owner Calvin Griffith said at the time, "It's uncomfortable right now for our fans. They are sitting here in 85 degrees, and they are not getting a sunburn."

Air conditioning was installed by June of 1983, turning the Sweatrodome back into the Metrodome. Owner Calvin Griffith had a couple clauses inserted into his lease agreement. One was an escape clause if attendance dipped below 1.4 million— or below the average American League attendance—for three consecutive years. The other was that air conditioning had to be installed if attendance was being affected by the lack of it.

That wasn't the only glitch with the new stadium. "We also quickly learned that the roof had a few faults, like caving," Kent Hrbek wrote in his book *Tales from the Minnesota Twins Dugout*. The roof "officially" tore five times, although there were rumors of a sixth that were never verified. It twice affected the Twins during series against the Angels. An April 14, 1983, game against them was postponed because heavy snow tore the roof. On April 26, 1986, a storm with high winds hit during a game and caused a small tear over right field. The game was delayed for nine minutes but eventually resumed. The Twins led 6–1 in the bottom of the eighth before the tear. Once play resumed, the Angels scored six runs in the ninth to win 7–6.

It had its quirks, but it was Minnesota's stadium. Decibel records were broken during the runs to the World Series in 1987 and 1991, as fans screamed while under a blizzard of Homer Hankies. During those times, the Metrodome was called the Thunderdome because of the moments when audiences were at full throat. Fans make stadiums, and the Dome was as unstoppable as the great moments during the title-winning seasons were abundant. Bert Blyleven and Frank Viola fueling the 1987 team—a team that had grown immeasurably following a 102-loss season in 1982. Kirby Puckett's Game 6 performance in 1991, setting the stage for Jack Morris' heroic 10-inning Game 7 outing, perhaps the greatest World Series game ever played.

Of course, there were many more great moments under that bubble. The Dome was the only stadium to have three different players collect their 3,000th hit in the stadium—Dave Winfield in 1993, Eddie Murray in 1995 and Cal Ripken Jr. in 2000. Brad Radke won his 20th game in 1997 there. It's where Frank Thomas hit the 500th home run of his career. Bert Blyleven collected the 3,000[th] strikeout of his career in 1986 at the Dome. It's where Kent Hrbek hit a 480-foot homer off Charlie Hough in 1984. Tom Kelly won his 1,000[th] game there. Scott Erickson (1994) and Eric Milton (1999) threw no-hitters there, with Milton's coming in a game with a 12:00 PM first pitch because the Gophers had a football game against Louisiana-Monroe that evening.

It was home of the 1985 All-Star Game. Tom Brunansky represented the Twins. Dave Parker won the first-ever Home Run Derby there. Jack Morris, born in St. Paul, took the loss in a 6–1 National League win. The Metrodome would gain the distinction of being the only stadium to host a World Series, Super Bowl, NCAA Final Four and All-Star Game.

In 1988, the Twins drew 3,030,672 fans, becoming the first American League team to draw more than 3 million fans in a season.

The Dome was the site for the end of the incredible 2006 season, with Joe Mauer clinching the batting title, Johan Santana wrapping up a Cy Young season, Justin Morneau putting the finishing touches on an MVP season, and the team, trailing Detroit by 1½ games entering the final week, clinching the division title. Twins players came on the field to join fans watching the Tigers lose to the Royals on the big screen at the Dome. Fans erupted and players took a celebratory lap around the field when Detroit made the final out in a 10–8, 12-inning loss to Kansas City.

The Dome allowed high school, college and amateur baseball teams an option to play while there was still snow on the ground. Many of these games followed weekend Twins games. One Sunday, we learned that Cretin-Derham Hall High School was playing after a Twins game. They had a pretty good prospect named Joe Mauer on the team. We kept one eye on the field while writing up the Twins game that day. Mauer, on cue, homered over the baggie during his first at-bat. Mauer wound up hitting 36 of his 143 major league home runs at the Dome. That day was just a preview of what was coming.

The Dome of course, didn't just serve the Twins and Vikings. It was the home of monster truck rallies, concerts, prep football games, college basketball games and NBA games. The Rolling Stones played the Dome three times. Michael Jordan scored 45 points in the first Timberwolves game ever played in the Dome. Citizens could rollerblade around the concourse during the winter. The Dome was the setting for the movie *Little Big League*.

The Metrodome hosted events that served the entire region but in particular gave fans two World Series championships. Since then, only the Minnesota Lynx of the WNBA has won a professional sports title among local teams.

"The Metrodome should, in my opinion, go down as one of the greatest public investments the state of Minnesota ever made," Twins president Dave St. Peter said. "When you consider the fact that it was it was probably the last of its generation multipurpose facility built in kind of the end of that cycle. So it didn't have the staying power of other facilities. But when you consider, in my opinion, the finances, the financial payback on that facility, it was an efficient building to build, relatively speaking, and it was operated in a fiscally responsible way. And when you think of the portfolio of events that took place in that building, World Series championships, a Super Bowl, two Final Fours, to all the prep championships. The Timberwolves' opening season. The role for high school and college baseball, Special Olympics. It wasn't a great baseball stadium, but there was a lot of great baseball played at the Metrodome."

The Dome was not aesthetically pleasing and was called a lot of names because of it. One thing that was true about the Hubert H. Humphrey Metrodome: it did its job.

10

Target Field

AFTER AN OFFSEASON IN WHICH THE TWINS SEEMED TO BE on the brink of being contracted, the club began a 2002 campaign that would end with them winning their first division title since 1991. Off the field, the Twins continued to push for a new stadium. Owner Carl Pohlad, in 1994, referred to the Metrodome as "economically obsolete." Yet his efforts to get a stadium were batted back time and time again. Along the way, his approach—threatening to leave, volunteering for contraction—rankled fans and lawmakers.

In 1992, it was time to try something else. Pohlad put the team up for sale in February after being told by officials that he was an impediment to a stadium deal getting done. The sale would come with the stipulation that the team remain in Minnesota. Several months passed without an offer. That was problematic, because a new owner would likely be asked to contribute to any stadium construction. There would be an acquisition cost as well as construction costs. It didn't seem realistic that someone would write $250 million in checks in 2002. Meanwhile, the sentiment toward passing a stadium bill was changing in the Twins' favor. Where there was resistance to subsidizing a stadium for a billionaire owner like Pohlad, there appeared to be more of a big-picture approach toward keeping Major League Baseball in the Twin Cities.

Donald Watkins, the Alabama businessman-attorney who claimed he was worth $1.5 billion—although he wasn't listed on the Forbes 400 list of the wealthiest individuals—was still sniffing around the team. But the Twins and Major League Baseball officials were skeptical that Watkins actually had the money he claimed he had. If he was, indeed, worth $1.5 billion, he would be the wealthiest Black man in America. Watkins claimed to hold energy rights, but no one was sure.

After his Twins offer of around $125–$150 million failed to gain traction—due to the skepticism—he approached the Anaheim Angels about a purchase and produced a $150 million letter of credit. That effort failed to expedite a deal as well. By the end of 2002, Watkins' interest in owning the Twins was a distant memory. And his bid to purchase the Angels would experience the same fate.

Governor Jesse Ventura, a former wrestling and movie star who shockingly won election in 1998, signed a stadium bill in May that included $330 million in funding at a site to be determined. While the contraction train was knocked off the tracks for 2002, there was still concern that it could roll again in a year or two. That forced lawmakers to act, and the result was a deal the Twins had hoped for. It wasn't perfect—the Twins would have to contribute $120 million—but it was a deal that would keep them in Minnesota. The next step was to find a site.

St. Paul believed it had a chance to move the team to the capital city. Talks didn't get very far when Pohlad was reluctant to promise they would play there, even if voters approved funding. Minneapolis couldn't get involved unless there was a referendum to approve taxpayer contribution. No one wanted any part of a referendum. About the same time, the Twins deemed that the St. Paul site was not suitable to their needs due to potential infrastructure costs. So no shovels in the dirt. As the Twins clinched the division title in September, their future was in doubt once again. Players and owners agreed to a deal in which contraction could not happen until 2007. This gave local politicians time to sort out stadium options, which were getting more nuanced because other sports teams wanted new facilities.

There had been rumblings about building stadiums for the Twins, the Vikings and the University of Minnesota football team. The Vikings balked at any thought of renovating the Metrodome for them, to the point where owner Billy Joe "Red" McCombs threatened to sell the team. If the Twins were getting a new stadium, the Vikings wanted one too. Building stadiums for all three teams would cost well over $1 billion. The Twins were the most urgent case, while the Vikings and Gophers had leases that expired in 2011.

So let's start the stadium wars again. It was a series that had more sequels than *Star Wars*. In 2003, newly elected Governor Tim Pawlenty named a stadium screening committee to sift through proposals and recommend where new homes for the Twins, Vikings and Gophers would be. Sounds like a great idea, right? It was the *eighth* committee appointed to tackle the issue since 1995. Other communities in the metropolitan area had expressed interest by that point. Eden Prairie, for instance, was prepared to offer land for the Twins and Vikings to have neighboring stadiums. Minneapolis made its intentions clear in December of that year, approving a site in the Warehouse District—right near Target Center—in an area called Rapid Park. Target Center was the home of the Minnesota Timberwolves and Minnesota Lynx, so a baseball stadium nearby would create a sports complex of sorts. The site was wedged between a highway, parking ramps, railroad tracks and the Hennepin Energy Recovery Center—a fancy name for the city incinerator.

When the calendar turned to 2004, it marked 10 years since Carl Pohlad had mentioned a new stadium to the Metropolitan Sports Facilities Commission, a request that was met with setback after setback. Through the years, Minneapolis battled St. Paul to be the team's home. The Vikings and, eventually, the Gophers made sure they weren't forgotten. Stadium debates are part of Minnesota's heritage. Because of the now-larger scope of the deal, there was no stadium solution in 2004. In 2005, the Twins and Hennepin County thought they had a plan in place for a $478 million stadium in the Warehouse District. The Twins would contribute $125 million while the public would be on the hook for 75 percent of the costs. There was initial blowback, claiming it was too sweet of a deal for the Pohlads. And opponents wanted a referendum. This deal ended up dying on the shelf as the state dealt with a budget crunch and focused on other issues. Governor Pawlenty became determined to have another deal in place by the March 2006 legislative session. An important development took place before that. A judge ruled that the Twins were not bound to play in the Metrodome beyond 2006. Now lawmakers, once again, had to consider the possibility of the Twins moving.

A revised plan for a $522 million stadium was approved by Hennepin County in April. Meanwhile, the Vikings suggested to lawmakers that a *three*-stadium solution—for the Twins, Vikings and Gophers—was the best approach to end the stadium debate. *Star Tribune* columnist Sid Hartman wrote that Las Vegas was looming as a relocation option for the Twins.

On May 21, at approximately 5:00 AM, the stadium bill was passed by the legislature at the end of a marathon session. Twins president Dave St. Peter, watching the proceedings in the Senate chamber, flashed a thumbs-up to Jerry Bell, president of Twins Sports Inc. The 12-year stadium push was over. Minnesota was getting outdoor baseball. The University of Minnesota, a day earlier, received funding for an open-air football stadium. Nearly $1 billion was earmarked for sports stadiums. And the path was cleared for the Vikings to get a stadium deal down the road. After years of blockage, the funding floodgates opened.

"Once that shovel goes into that ground, that's when I'll start getting excited," catcher Joe Mauer said. Bell, the Twins' lead negotiator, had suffered from fatigue as he attended countless meetings about potential stadium deals and spent countless hours at the state capitol in St. Paul trying to find a solution. He spent that Saturday night pacing around the capitol. After the bill was passed, he couldn't sleep. "You work on something to 10 years and now it's finally over, its finally happened. How can you sleep?"

It was quite a fight. In the end, Minnesota got it right. In 2010, the Twins moved back into an outdoor stadium named Target Field. Located in the Warehouse District just north of Target Center, the park ushered in a new era of Major League Baseball in the Twin Cities.

Target Field was the culmination of 12 years of work by the Pohlad family to unite with legislators to solve the stadium issue in the Twin Cities. Fans of outdoor baseball could come back out to the ballpark and watch a fly ball head toward sunshine. Sure, it was going to be cold and possibly snowy in April and chilly in September. Warming areas with radiant heat were placed around the ballpark. But if you live here, you see people bike through snowstorms, use frozen lakes as shortcuts or huddle by outdoor rinks in the winter to watch their kids play hockey. Minnesotans adapt. They layer up, grab hand warmers, zip up their Gore-Tex jackets and head outdoors.

Groundbreaking was scheduled for August 2. But the day before, during rush hour and as fans headed downtown for the Twins game against the Royals, tragedy struck. The I-35 bridge over the Mississippi River—less than a mile from the Metrodome—was full of traffic when it began to creak, rattle and sway before collapsing into the river. More than 100 vehicles—including a school bus with 50 children returning from a day camp swimming outing—plunged down toward the river. The school bus miraculously landed on all four wheels on a parkway, missing the water. A design flaw, investigators said, likely led to its collapse. The horrific accident killed 13 people and injured 145.

The Twins were in their clubhouse preparing for a game against the Royals when word of the collapse shook up the team. The Dome was filling up for the game—the announced attendance was 24,880 that night—but everyone was calling to check on friends and loved ones who might have been on the bridge. It reached the point where cell phone service occasionally crashed from the volume of calls. Management had a decision to make—to play the game or postpone it. After speaking with Minneapolis mayor R.T. Rybak, the decision was made to play the game.

"There was a conference room in the upper level of the Twins' offices where I would office and where [general manager] Terry Ryan would office as well," Twins president Dave St. Peter said. "We gathered there shortly after we had gotten word and turned on the television. The first thing that we started to hear was concern from our clubhouse about family members that were on their way to the game. Ron Gardenhire and I think players were concerned. We had some discussion with the mayor, R.T. Rybak. There was a flurry of phone calls. I don't remember the exact timing, but this all happened within a very compressed timeline. And we decided to play, and the reason we decided to play was we thought the worst thing we could do would be to put those people back out on the streets and back out on the roads at a time when people were asked not to drive through the area. Therefore, we decided to play, and I don't think it was probably a popular decision inside of our clubhouse. But the reason we decided to do it is we didn't want to create a further challenge to the recovery effort."

The following night's game with Kansas City was postponed because of the tragedy. Groundbreaking took place on August 30, during which 5,000 fans showed up and sat in makeshift stands. Fireworks filled the air as a group of lawmakers, Twins officials, and players Joe Mauer and Michael Cuddyer each held a shovel—fitted with bats for handles—for the ceremony.

A few dissenting fans stood on an overpass above the ceremony holding signs. One read: BRIDGES, NOT BALLPARKS.

Major League Baseball commissioner Bud Selig, who had discussed contracting the Twins a few years earlier, drew some boos when he appeared at the ceremony. But he was full of praise for the Twins on this day. "All stadium situations are a struggle, but it was the perseverance of everyone involved that eventually carried the day." he said. "Your patience was rewarded, and your loyalty has been great...the future is now secure for the next two to three generations of Twins fans."

The groundbreaking took place as a dispute over the price of the land ensued. But the sides reached an agreement, and the project went on as planned. The next challenge was building a stadium on 8.5 acres of land. That was similar in acreage to Fenway Park, which opened in 1912. That meant it was below modern ballpark standards. This was solved by purchasing air rights over nearby railroad tracks and building over them to make 8.5 acres look more like 10.5 acres. Populous, the architectural firm that designed the ballpark, was just starting to cook. A potential eyesore just right of center field, Parking Ramp B, loomed as a threat to the aesthetic wonders of the stadium. That issue was solved by using an enormous wind veil that covered one side of the ramp. A section of right field seats—that invoked memories of the stands in the old Metropolitan Stadium—rises high enough to cover the other side of the ramp. This was one example of the nods to history that are visible around the ballpark. The section of right field seats near the foul pole cantilevers a bit over the playing field. Metropolitan Stadium was one of the first stadiums to feature such an approach to designing grandstands.

But don't be mistaken. It's not fair to call Target Field a retro ballpark. It's also not fair to tab it as a purely modern design, although it has plenty of modern amenities. The compromise between these two styles created a ballpark that seamlessly blends with downtown. The home plate area is located on the southwest side of the ballpark, so right field opens to connect with downtown Minneapolis, creating the grand entrance to the stadium while welcoming the Minneapolis skyline.

Fans were kept in mind as other parts of the stadium were designed. One thing the Twins lamented about the Metrodome was that fans could not see the field from the concourse. Another was that carts and garbage containers had to be pushed on that same concourse, creating an eyesore. The Twins corrected that by including a service level in which all that wheeled traffic could take place away from pedestrians. Fans can see the field from most of the concourse. A place like Oracle Park in San Francisco, for example, does not allow for views from the concourse and carts and bins roll around with the fans. And that repugnant smell of garlic fries—unless you like the smell of garlic fries—permeates the concourse,.

Target Field also screamed, "This is Minnesota!" in two distinct ways. The stadium was dressed in Kasota Stone, a limestone trucked in from Mankato, Minnesota. And 14 black spruce trees were planted on an incline behind the center field wall. The trees created controversy, though. More on that later.

Twins history is reflected in several ways at Target Field. A celebration sign of Minnie and Paul shaking hands over the Mississippi—a classic logo from the 1960s—rises 46 feet in the air in center field. The sign lights up when the Twins score a run and after victories. The original flagpole from Metropolitan Stadium is positioned behind the right field seats (it had to be shortened). In one of the dining areas of the stadium, the Town Ball Tavern, part of the floor from the old Minneapolis armory was installed. That's the floor the Minneapolis Lakers played on before moving to Los Angeles. The premier restaurant at the stadium was called the Metropolitan Club (it has since been renamed). Instead of fans entering through Gate A, B or C or Gate 1, 2 or 3, they enter through Gates 3, 6, 14, 29 and 34. Those are the uniform numbers of Twins Hall of Famers Harmon Killebrew, Tony Oliva, Kent Hrbek, Rod Carew and Kirby Puckett.

Target Field also included all the bells and whistles of modern stadiums. The video board was 57 feet high and 101 feet wide (it would be expanded to 178 feet wide in 2023). There were

401 women's bathroom fixtures and 266 for men. Expanded concourses, meeting rooms, 59 suites, radiant heat for those chilly games, waiting rooms for players' families, hot and cold tubs in the training area, expanded dressing rooms for umpires. Yes, the umpires received upgraded quarters.

The Twins incessantly pursued excellence as they designed the various rooms and levels of the ballpark. Here's a couple of examples. Major league umpire Tim Tschida, a native of St. Paul, was driving back to the Twin Cities after working a series in Milwaukee. He had reached Eau Claire, Wisconsin, when his phone rang. It was Bill Smith, the assistant general manager at the time, who later became general manager. Smith told him that team was going to build a new ballpark and it was going to be the best in baseball. And he wanted Tschida's help with designing the umpires' room. Tschida told Smith that space was more important to umpires than amenities. Space so media could enter rooms if interviews were needed. Space so families could meet them after games. And a separate private area where they could shower and dress. He asked for a separate tunnel to the field, so they didn't have to bicker with teams on the way off the field if there were any problems during games. And he asked that the groundskeeper's office was nearby so they could communicate easily about potential weather delays. "They did everything I suggested, and it turned out really well," Tschida said.

Smith pointed out that, in the final design, two auxiliary dressing rooms were placed across the hall from the umpires' room. One of them serves as the drug testing room/barber's room. But something else was in mind. "The concept for those was that we're eventually going to have female umpires in the big leagues," Smith said. "and the concept was that female umpires would have a locker room right across."

For the first time since 1961, this was the Twins' chance to chase perfection. They sent representatives to every stadium in the league to cull ideas they would use to make the perfect ballpark. They asked clubhouse attendants about the design of the visiting clubhouse. They met with local media to ask what they wanted in the press box. We asked for a dedicated elevator to the clubhouse level, and the Twins obliged.

Every detail was sweated over. Owner Jim Pohlad didn't like that the roof canopy that covers most of the stadium had an exposed underside. So he agreed to pay extra to have it finished. And there was a disagreement over the flooring in the bathrooms on the suite level. Many in the group were comfortable with stained concrete. Then Laura Day, who would be named executive vice president and chief business officer—and who was the only woman in the room that day—spoke up. "Laura Day said, 'Gentlemen, this is our suite level. We are not having concrete floors in the men's and women's room. We're having tile.'" Smith said. "And everybody looked around and said, 'Okay.'"

New restaurants often hold "soft openings" before their grand opening. It's a posh way of saying, "We need to have a practice run so we don't fall flat on our faces on opening night and chase people away." The Twins did the same with Target Field by staging a few games to practice crowd entry, critique food service, see how the field played, etc. The first official event at Target Field was a college baseball game between Minnesota and Louisiana Tech on March 27, 2010. The Twins treated it as a daylong open house, charging fans $2 and allowing them to roam the stadium from when the gates opened at 9:00 AM until 5:00 PM—with the baseball game scheduled for 1:00 PM. The Twins capped the crowd at 25,000 but were willing to sell as many as 35,000 tickets if enough of the 9:00 AM crowd left the building early. At least, that was the plan.

The Gophers baseball team met at the Metrodome before taking light rail to the Target Field stop. They got dressed and went onto the field. Then the grounds crew had to repair the divots on the field that were made by the Gophers' jaws dropping. "When I walked out there, that was about the coolest thing I had ever seen," shortstop A.J. Pettersen told the *Minneapolis Star Tribune* that day. The Gophers lost 9–1, but few remember that. As for the 25,000 cap on attendance, 37,757 showed up for the soft opening. "We've been trying to find the worst seat—what we think would be bad—to sit there and see if it is bad," Twins fan Meredith Lind said that day. "Haven't found one yet."

It was the Twins' turn the next week, as they played two exhibition games against St. Louis before heading for road games against the Angels and White Sox.

The Twins officially returned to outdoor baseball at home on April 12, 2010, in front of a sold-out crowd of 38,145 as Carl Pavano pitched them to a 5–2 victory over the Boston Red Sox. Boston's Marco Scutaro got the first hit, a single off Pavano in the first inning. The first home run was blasted by Jason Kubel, off Scott Atchison in the seventh. The ball landed in the right field bleachers, where 13-year-old A.J. Nitzschke—whose brother, Kirby, was named after Kirby Puckett—grabbed the ball and fought off attempts from other fans to dislodge it. After the game, the Nitzschkes—who had driven up from Lawton, Iowa, for the game—were brought to the bowels of Target Field. In exchange for the ball, A.J. received an autographed Joe Mauer jersey.

There were 39,715 on hand for the opener because the Twins gave away tickets to former players and Target Field construction workers. Among the humans and non-humans in the crowd were umpires Tschida, from St. Paul; Mark Wegner, also from St. Paul; and Jeff Nelson, from Cottage Grove, Minnesota. They were pulled off other umpiring crews so they could work the opening game in their home state. They had some of the best seats in the house. The next-best seat was in the first row of the Champions Club section directly behind home plate. Among spectators in that row was Bullseye, a bull terrier and official mascot of the Target Corporation.

They all watched the first home win by a Twins team that won the American League Central division with a 94–68 record. It was a highly anticipated season for the club as well as the stadium. Mauer was coming off an MVP year and, three weeks earlier, had signed an eight-year, $184 million contract extension. The club had added shortstop J. J. Hardy, second baseman Orlando Hudson and future Hall of Famer Jim Thome to boost the offense. The team looked tough to beat on paper, and they were until they were swept by the Yankees in the first round of the postseason.

There was also a casualty of the first season at Target Field. The black spruce trees were fired after the season after proving to be a distraction. Hitters like a clear batting eye, and the fluttering branches of the trees, hitters said, could interfere with their tracking of pitches. It was an issue from day one, as Ron Gardenhire and Michael Cuddyer expressed concern. "We've got chainsaws," Gardenhire joked after the game. "Minnesota's got plenty of chainsaws. If we don't like it, we'll just come here late night and whack them." More hitters offered the same opinion of the trees, which were never made available to comment. "When you're hitting during the day and see the wind blowing stuff around and the tips of the trees [moving], it was just distracting," said Justin Morneau, who had won the 2006

American League MVP with the Twins. "You want a batter's eye to be simple." Despite the trees, Morneau got off to a blistering start to the season, batting .345 with 18 homers and 56 RBI through 81 games before suffering a concussion when he took a knee to the head while sliding into second in Toronto and missed the remainder of the season.

Cuddyer, in a 2023 interview, admitted that he was concerned about the trees. But Cuddyer, a first-round pick in 1997 who enjoyed a 15-year career despite being deaf in one ear, always looked at things differently. He performed magic tricks. He wanted to open a bar called Fuel where folks could swipe a credit card and fill their glasses with beer pouring out of a gas pump. He took a cribbage board and expanded it so a game could be played in different directions at once. He called it "extreme cribbage". And he also saw some positives in playing in the Metrodome. One, he knew there would be a game every day. Two, the cramped clubhouse and trainer's room forced camaraderie. He didn't like the trees but offered a workable solution.

"I never said take the trees out," Cuddyer said. "I said add more trees. The gaps between the trees are too big. That was the issue. If you're a right-handed hitter facing a right-handed pitcher, the ball would go from no tree to tree back to no tree. You've got fractions of a second to make a decision. But in that fraction of a second it literally would go to two different backdrops. So what I said was making more trees and then they ended up taking the trees and I got blamed for it, which—that was an improvement, but I also knew that those trees meant something.

"I played three years in Colorado. It was a damn forest out there."

The St. Paul Saints, an independent league team at the time, couldn't resist needling the big brother. The Saints soon planted trees behind their center field wall and continue to do so. And they became a Twins affiliate in 2021.

In 2012, Target Field was ranked first by ESPN in terms of fan experience. The sightlines, the design, the attention to detail, the concession choices, the heated field and warming stations around the park made it a smash hit right off the bat. "I love it. I love that everyone is right on top of you, the fans," said right-hander Kyle Gibson, who pitched for the Twins from 2013 to '19. "The natural elements to it that are from Minnesota. The colored windows that spell out 'Twins.' They thought of everything." Was it the best ballpark in the league? Definitely in the top 10. If you take out the ballparks that double as cathedrals to the game—Fenway Park in Boston, Wrigley Field in Chicago and Dodger Stadium in Los Angeles—a case could be made that Target Field was one of the top five ballparks in the league over its first dozen years. And the Twins, through 2023, had put upwards of $50 million in improvements into the park to keep it up to date.

Building Target Field came with the reward of hosting the 2014 All-Star Game. The Twins' Brian Dozier was tabbed to participate in the Home Run Derby but was eliminated in the first round. The American League prevailed in the game 5–3, with Twins closer Glen Perkins pitching the ninth to teammate Kurt Suzuki.

That would not be the only special event at Target Field, as it became one of the most versatile venues in the Twin Cities. In addition to hosting college and high school baseball games, three college football games were held there, including a matchup between local rivals St. John's and St. Thomas that drew a then record crowd of 37,355 for a Division III football game. As of 2023, around 20 concerts have been held at the stadium, including Paul McCartney, Kenny Chesney, The Eagles,

Billy Joel, Luke Bryan and The Killers. Even the State of Hockey has had its moment at Target Field, as the Wild played host to St. Louis on January 1, 2022, in the NHL's Winter Classic. The temperature at puck drop was below zero, but a crowd of 38,619 took in the game. And they cursed in the frigid air as the Wild lost 6–4.

So Target Field has shown it can do nearly everything the Metrodome did. Just better and without a roof.

PART 4

THE CRADLE OF GREATNESS

11

Dave Winfield

TWINS EXECUTIVE ANDY MACPHAIL KNOCKED ONE OUT OF the park in 1991 when he signed right-hander Jack Morris to an innovative three-year contract, one that included an opt-out clause after each of the first two years, and watched Morris lead the Twins to the second World Series in franchise history. It was Morris who provided one of the greatest moments in World Series history when he told manager Tom Kelly that he wanted to pitch the 10th after shutting out the Braves for nine innings. Morris pitched a scoreless 10th, and the Twins won the championship in the bottom of the inning. Morris' homecoming could not have gone any better, even if it was just for one season.

MacPhail brought another local hero back home before the 1993 season as he tried to plug a hole in the lineup the way he'd plugged a hole in the 1991 rotation. This one sort of fell into his lap.

Dave Winfield could not come to a contract agreement with the Toronto Blue Jays, for whom he had driven in the World Series–clinching run in Game 6 with a two-run double in the 11th inning. The victim that game: Atlanta left-hander Charlie Leibrandt, who had given up a game-winning home run to Kirby Puckett in Game 6 of the 1991 World Series—also in the 11th inning. Winfield was a free agent, but MacPhail sensed that it would be a financial stretch to sign the St. Paul native and former Minnesota Golden Gopher. MacPhail's mind would be changed when he picked up the phone in his office in December of 1992 and discovered Winfield was on the other end. "Do you still have an opening on your team for a good player?" Winfield said at the time. Money wasn't the main objective. And things escalated from there.

While MacPhail conferred with owner Carl Pohlad, who eventually gave his blessing, the clubhouse recruitment push began. Manager Tom Kelly spoke with Winfield about how he would be used. Kirby Puckett, who had recently signed a $30 million contract that made him one of the game's highest-paid players, called Winfield and talked up the team he would be playing with. MacPhail then worked out the details of the contract—two years, $5.2 million, with incentives that would push it over $6 million. And with that, the Twins had brought back one of the greatest athletes in Minnesota sports history. "I'm not here to hang around and hang on," Winfield said the day he signed with the Twins. "I'm here to kick butt. It's a new challenge, but I think it is going to be fun and there's going to be a lot of excitement." Winfield could have played elsewhere for more money, but felt it was the right time to come home.

By the time he joined the Twins, Winfield was 41 years old, well traveled, highly decorated, multidimensional and a future Hall of Famer. He was back to where it all began.

Winfield was born in St. Paul and grew up in the city's Rondo neighborhood, a residential, cultural and economic hub for St. Paul's Black community. Baseball players Toni Stone, one of a few women to play in the Negro Leagues, and Hall of Fame catcher Roy Campanella, who played for the St. Paul Saints of the Brooklyn Dodgers farm system, lived in Rondo. The area fell victim to gentrification as homes and businesses were demolished to make room for the construction of Interstate 94 between 1956 and '68. The Winfields were one of many families forced to relocate for what was considered progress. They relocated to the Midway area, settling in at a row house less than a mile from the Oxford Playground, which later became the Jimmy Lee Recreation Center, where they dominated in youth sports. Winfield played on the Attucks-Brooks American Legion team during the summer. It was led by Bill Peterson, an ex-marine who would have a hand in developing many young ballplayers. Winfield landed on scouts' radars following his sophomore year in high school, when he opened eyes during a tournament in Omaha. That put him on track to be drafted in the first round in 1973.

After starring at St. Paul Central High School, Winfield moved on to the University of Minnesota, where he played baseball and basketball. In basketball, he was a reliable player and good rebounder who helped the Gophers reach the Sweet 16 round of the NCAA basketball tournament in 1972, but also was known for his role in the giant brawl with Ohio State on January 25, 1972, during which he landed several blows on Buckeyes player Mark Minor. He avoided discipline, while other players were suspended for the remainder of the season. There was no such pugilism on the baseball diamond, where Winfield was a two-time All-American and three-time All–Big Ten selection who was known for his pitching as much as his hitting.

Winfield's college exploits led to him being drafted by four teams in three sports. The Padres drafted him with the fourth overall pick; the NBA's Atlanta Hawks made him a fifth-round pick; the ABA's Utah Stars made him a sixth-round pick; and the Minnesota Vikings took him as a tight end in the 17th round of the NFL draft. Winfield never played college football. He chose baseball, but the Padres offered him just a $15,000 signing bonus. "I told the Padres I wouldn't sign for that and go to the minors, even though their Triple-A team was in Hawaii," Winfield said, with a laugh. San Diego brought him straight to the majors as an outfielder, and he hit .277 in 56 games as a 21-year-old. By 25, he was an All-Star. By 27, he had career highs with 34 homers and 118 RBI.

Winfield's swing went against conventional hitting. He would hold the bat almost at shoulder level, then drop his hands down to his waist before ripping at the ball. Few hitters have been able to prosper with a hitch in their swing, but Winfield made it look good. Winfield's website includes a silhouette of him preparing to hit a ball, which shows how much he dropped his hands. But he did so much damage that way. The 6'6" Winfield filled up the batter's box. Opponents who tried to place pitches on the outside corner of the plate were only allowing Winfield to extend his arms and pulverize them. "When he was young, they said he was never gonna be able to hit because he had too big of a hitch," Molitor said. "So it kind of shows you that there's more than one way to hit."

Winfield moved to the Yankees for the 1981 season. In eight years, he batted .291 with 203 homers and 812 RBI. He could run, throw and do it all. But he could not make owner George Steinbrenner happy. Things got off to a rough start when Steinbrenner signed him to what he believed was a 10-year, $16 million contract. But there was a cost-of-living adjustment clause in the deal that lifted it to $23 million, angering the Boss. Winfield proved he was one of the best all-around players in the game, but Steinbrenner criticized him for his lack of production in the 1981 World Series, referring to him as "Mr. May." The owner was suspicious about how Winfield's foundation spent its money, to the point where he hired known gambler Howard Spira to dig up dirt on Winfield to discredit him. Steinbrenner served a two-year suspension for that scheme.

While his excellence on the field was obvious, Winfield needed thick skin off it. He missed the entire 1989 season before Steinbrenner attempted, once again, to trade him. Only when Angels owner Gene Autry stepped in with a contract extension did Winfield, who had veto rights because he was a 10-year veteran who had spent at least five seasons with the Yankees, agree to the deal. It was the jolt to his career that he needed, as he won the Comeback Player of the Year award in 1990 for batting .267 with 21 home runs and 78 RBI. After two years in California, Winfield signed with the Blue Jays and led them to the World Series title.

So Winfield had been through it all by the time he signed with the Twins. He had played in small markets like San Diego and one of the largest media centers in the world in New York— and thrived in both. He had endured controversies—not just with Steinbrenner, but with the Canadian animal rights community. In 1983 he was arrested by Toronto police for unnecessary suffering of an animal when his final warmup throw before the fifth inning killed a seagull at Exhibition Stadium. "The first time all year he's hit the cutoff man!" manager Billy Martin yelled as police arrived at the clubhouse. Winfield posted bond and was released, and the charges were dropped after it was determined that the throw was not intentional.

But Winfield was more than a baseball player by then. He bought tickets for disadvantaged children while in San Diego. He began a foundation that provided free medical checkups for families. He funded the Dave Winfield Nutrition Counseling of Hackensack Medical Center. He opined about race relations. He created a scholarship fund for student athletes in St. Paul. He had rounded out his life to include business and philanthropy. He was well-spoken and carried himself with class. Kirby Puckett referred to Winfield as the "Ambassador of Baseball."

"I played a lot of years in the National League," Winfield said when he signed with the Twins. "I went to New York, and that will shape you in a whole different way. They try to bend you and break you and throw you away. All of those things shape your life."

Winfield's task was to help shape a Twins team that believed it could compete in 1993. Winfield landed in a lineup with Kent Hrbek, Chuck Knoblauch, Shane Mack and Brian Harper. Most importantly, it had Kirby Puckett, one of the best players in the game. The two first met during Puckett's rookie year of 1984, when Winfield was in his fourth year with the Yankees. Winfield was running out to play defense while Puckett was coming in from the outfield. He yelled at Puckett and told him he was taking him to dinner after the game. Winfield proceeded to advise Puckett on how to have a long career in the game. Now they weren't just friends; they were teammates.

The season was practically over in April. The Twins were 8–6 at one point before losing eight straight games and falling under .500 for good. The offense fell off from the previous season, but it was the pitching staff that blew up in their faces. Scott Erickson fell to 8–19 with a 5.19 ERA. No starter had an ERA under 4.00. Winfield hit .230 with four home runs in April. He had a strong 42-game run from late June through mid-August when he batted .358. He finished with a .271 batting average, 21 homers and 76 RBI, frequently batting behind Puckett in the order.

Thanks to a .355 month of July, Winfield was in line to join an exclusive club by the end of the season. On September 16, Winfield grounded a single through the hole at short off Oakland's Dennis Eckersley to become the 19th player to collect 3,000 hits. Once at first base, he tipped his helmet to the crowd while receiving a standing ovation. Among the announced crowd of 14,654 were Toronto's Jack Morris and Paul Molitor—fellow St. Paul natives who wanted to watch Winfield make history. "The Blue Jays had flown into town," Molitor said. "And it was Devon White, Dave Stewart and myself were having dinner at J.D. Hoyt's. And we're saying that if Dave gets a hit, we're going over to the Metrodome because he needed two hits to get to 3,000. So he gets his first hit, and we get the check and head over to the Metrodome. We were in the stands to watch Dave poke one through to left field off Eckersley. So that was pretty cool."

Besides the milestone, Winfield was disappointed in his season. He played in 143 games that season but had only 76 RBI, and that is unacceptable for a run producer. Reaching the milestone at home, in front of family and friends and where the electricity was near playoff levels, meant a lot to him. For the Twins, it was a highlight of a dismal 71–91 season. They also stumbled onto something. Moments after Winfield became Mr. 3,000, fans began snapping up tickets for collectibles. The Twins didn't turn down the unexpected revenue, and a secondary market was born. There were many fewer people in attendance than 14,654 that day, as the number was inflated by fans seeking memorabilia. The Twins would go on to sell unused tickets for Cal Ripken's 2,000th consecutive game played in 1994 and 3,000[th] hit in 2000, Eddie Murray's 3,000[th] hit in 1995, Eric Milton's no-hitter in 1999 and Frank Thomas' 500th home run in 2007.

In 1994, Winfield got off to a somewhat slow start but posted an .801 OPS in May and batted .316 in July. The Twins sputtered again with a pitching staff that might have been worse than the previous season. With no chance at the postseason, the Twins decided to trade Winfield to a team that had a chance at the playoffs. Cleveland was in a fight with the White Sox for AL Central supremacy and took on Winfield for cash considerations. Winfield never played an inning that season for the Indians because of the players' strike in August, which wiped out the remainder of the regular season and postseason.

There were reports that, because no games were played after the trade was made, Cleveland took the Twins out to dinner at the GM meetings during the offseason as "cash considerations." It ended up being a story fueled by a comment made in jest between Twins GM Andy MacPhail and Cleveland GM John Hart. Winfield never played for the Indians that year—although he signed with them for the 1995 season, which would be his last. Winfield batted .191 that season with only two home runs while battling rotator cuff soreness in his left shoulder. One of Winfield's final murderous swings came on Memorial Day that season, when he went deep off White Sox left-hander Wilson Álvarez to fuel a comeback victory and set up Cleveland's run to the division title. He had offseason surgery on his shoulder but decided to retire at age 44. He compiled 3,110 hits, 465 home runs and 1,833 RBI during a 22-year career that included 12 consecutive All-Star Game appointments and one World Series title. He was the fifth player to collect 3,000 hits and hit 450 home runs. He faced Bob Gibson in the 1970s and Roger Clemens in the 1990s. Winfield was a disciplined eater and trainer, keeping his large frame in top shape while averaging 135 games played over a 22-year career.

"I think it's amazing even that he's playing every day," Eckersley said as Winfield approached 3,000 hits. "I have the same birthday as Dave, and I'm three years younger, and I find the game grueling. I can't imagine playing every day, through the bumps and bruises, and attacking the game the way he does. He makes me feel old."

Winfield continued his charitable endeavors following his playing career, wrote three books and spoke about bettering the game. A Hall of Fame announcement seemed perfunctory because the numbers and reputation were there. And Winfield reached the Hall of Fame on his first try, getting 84.5 percent of the vote. Kirby Puckett, his onetime protege then longtime friend, was second with 82.1 percent of the vote. That year's ballot also included Jim Kaat, Bert Blyleven and Jack Morris—three future Hall of Famers. Winfield's induction gave Minnesota its second Hall of Famer and first since Charles "Chief" Bender in 1953. More would follow, as the St. Paul express was just warming up. Paul Molitor and Jack Morris weren't that far off. And many felt that another St. Paul prep star, Joe Mauer, could join them.

But Winfield was the first car of that train. He came from humble beginnings to become one of the best athletes in Big Ten history before embarking on a Hall of Fame career during which he performed on the biggest stage and attained his greatest achievements. And he continued to thrive in business and community service following his playing career. He was a local hero who became a national attraction. "I always had confidence and desire," he said. "I wanted to spread out. I had a vision that wasn't linked to where I grew up. I did a lot of reading. I wanted to travel and meet people. I could always see myself going places and doing things."

12

Jack Morris

St. Paul knows the formula. Develop a system of playground and recreation centers. Identify coaches who are dedicated and principled. Make sure the kids are occupied and having fun. And you will develop Hall of Famers.

It's not that easy. St. Paul just made it seem that way as a cradle of baseball greatness in the 1950s. Three players were born and had their careers molded on the fields and in the gyms that populated the Capital City. St. Paul was known as the birthplace of F. Scott Fitzgerald, Warren Burger and a couple of Andersons—Louie and Loni. A sports wing eventually opened, one that includes three legendary baseball players— Dave Winfield, Jack Morris and Paul Molitor.

"St. Paul has always been a town known for its neighborhoods and playgrounds, whether it was Rice Street, Oxford, Linwood, Frogtown or Highland Park," Molitor said. "We had a sense of commitment to sports and the luxury of being taught the proper way to play from some great coaches, peers and families."

Winfield, Morris and Molitor were not drafted nor developed by the Twins and did not have lengthy careers with their hometown team. Morris played one year. Winfield nearly two years. And Molitor for three years as a player, several as a coach and four as manager of the Twins. But the history of the Twins can't be told without including their careers. Because, at some point, they all returned home, where they were known and loved and provided memorable moments for Twins fans.

St. Paul was the place where this phenomenon occurred, a city with its own farm system for churning out future stars. The Oxford Playground, later named the Jimmy Lee Recreation Center, was where Winfield and Molitor played as children. A few blocks away, there was Toni Stone Field near St. Paul Central High School, where Winfield starred in high school. It also was where Winfield, Molitor and Morris played American Legion ball. When Molitor was six through eight years old, he played at the Linwood Recreation Center, which was not far from Jimmy Lee. Morris' teenage hangout was the Edgcumbe Recreation Center, not far from the other three facilities. Morris attended Highland Park High School, which also was in the area. But then there was Cretin-Derham Hall High School, located just south of Edgcumbe. Molitor went to school there, but it was also the place where future NFL players Chris Weinke, Matt Birk, Corbin Lacina, Michael Floyd, Steve Walsh and Seantrel Henderson played. It was even home of future MLB umpires Tim Tschida and Mark Wegner. This success spanned generations, as another St. Paul baseball legend, Joe Mauer, was born in 1983. He also played at Jimmie Lee and went on to be the best catcher of his era during a 15-year career. And, in 2024, he was voted into the Hall of Fame, joining Winfield, Morris and Molitor.

The St. Paul sports machine was working perfectly, churning out future professional athletes for decades. It was this pipeline that produced some of the most memorable moments in Twins history. And it started with Morris, the winningest major league pitcher in the 1980s, World Series hero and Hall of Famer.

Morris was the son of Arvid, who worked for Minnesota Mining and Manufacturing, which later became corporate behemoth 3M. His mother, Dona, was a housewife. When Morris was around 13, his family moved from Mendota Heights to Highland Park, mainly because of the youth baseball options it offered. Morris and his brother, Tom, a left-handed pitcher, inherited the competitive gene from their father. They hated losing. Jack Morris once cried after a poor youth baseball appearance. The family eventually had to discuss the dangers of obsessing over defeats. "If my brother and I went out and had a bad [basketball] game, it almost got to be no fun coming out," Morris said early in his career. "But I think Dad grew up during those years too, because after a while our whole family sat down and talked about how ridiculous it was that sports controlled our lives so much that it affected everything else in our lives."

The Morris brothers learned to channel their competitiveness better. And they were good. Tom was the pitcher for Highland Park, while Jack played third base. Jack had a strong arm, but he didn't know where the ball was going. "He could throw hard enough to knock down the backstop in high school," said Bill Lorenz, the former Highland Park coach, in 1987. "He just couldn't hit the backstop." Lorenz felt Morris could thrive as a hitter and possibly reach the majors. Morris accepted a scholarship offer to attend Brigham Young University in Provo, Utah, which offered a longer schedule than the local University of Minnesota, where it was cold and snowy into April. When the coaching staff at Brigham Young laid eyes on him, they saw a pitcher. Vernon Law, who won the 1960 Cy Young Award, worked with Morris and the other BYU pitchers there. Morris made the switch from position player to pitcher but struggled with the lifestyle. If he had a poor outing, he sulked over the next few days before he could start again. "And I was an ornery son of a gun," he said. This was evident after he was selected by the Tigers in the fifth round of the 1976 draft and reached the majors the next year. During the early years of his career, he earned the nickname "Mt. Morris" for his eruptions. He handled his emotions better with age, but his competitive fire continued to run hot. Morris has admitted to being a young player with a temper. When that was channeled properly, he was one of the best pitchers of his era. And he would use it well in Game 7 of the 1991 World Series.

But first, Morris needed to develop. His talent was obvious when he went 17–7 in 1979. A significant development occurred in 1983, when he went into a bullpen session and teammate Milt Wilcox showed him how to throw a forkball. A lightbulb went off when Morris saw the pitch drop as if it were falling off a table. Eureka! "Two starts later, I threw it in a game, "he said. "I felt like I was cheating."

Morris went 20–13 that year and won at least 18 games over four of the next five seasons. "Once he came up with this thing," Hall of Famer George Brett said while making the forkball drip with his hand, "he became a different pitcher."

Morris won his first World Series with Detroit in 1984, going 19–11 that season. The Tigers surged to a remarkable 35–5 start that season. Morris no-hit the White Sox on April 7. As a young fan growing up in Chicago, I remember Ron Kittle striking out on that damned forkball to end the game and feeling a strong dislike for the opposing pitcher. His mustache made him look like a villain from a Western movie. After a 10–1 start, Morris went 4–7 over the next 12 outings. The Tigers were on their way to a special season, but fans felt Morris was ruining their procession to the World Series. Media scrutinized him. Teammates griped about how difficult he could be to deal with. This was "Mount Morris," the steamy side of him that rankled those nearby. Fellow Hall of Famer Alan Trammell remembered a game in which Tigers manager Sparky Anderson went to the mound to remove Morris from a game. His routine was to clap his hands twice before asking for the ball. "Well, Jack being the competitor he was, he didn't realize what he did, but he was so hot he didn't want to come out of the game he slammed the ball in Sparky's hand and broke some blood vessels," Trammell said. Anderson would later explain to Morris the proper procedure for leaving a game. "And it kind of woke Jack up. Oftentimes, you know, Jack was really remorseful after the fact. But his hot blood.... That stuff was there, it was real."

All of this was headed to the Twins before the 1991 season. Morris was in a contract squabble with the Tigers and began considering his options. The Twins, he felt, were becoming harder to beat. He took the loss to the Twins in Game 2 of the 1987 American League Championship Series as Minnesota went on to win the championship. Morris and his agent, Dick Moss, had negotiated with the Twins about joining them following the 1986 season, raising hopes among local fans about an earlier homecoming. But talks broke down, with Morris wondering if he was a victim of collusion. Things were different following the 1990 season. He signed a three-year deal for $7 million that included bonuses that could push the deal to $11 million. Morris wanted to one day pitch in his hometown, and this was his opportunity.

"I grew up in Minnesota," he said after the deal was hammered out. "It's a small-town state, and I'm basically a small-town person." The Twins' pitching staff included some experienced arms, like right-handed starters Kevin Tapani and Allan Anderson and relievers Rick Aguilera, Steve Bedrosian, Carl Willis and Terry Leach. There were a couple youngsters too, like Scott Erickson and Paul Abbott. The Twins depended on Morris to front the rotation and be the arm to push them over the top. There were some doubts that, at age 36, the winningest pitcher in the 1980s still had it in him to handle the role. Oh, yes, he did.

He started out 3–5 with a 5.34 ERA before heating up. Morris went 10–1 with a 2.13 ERA from mid-May to mid-June, reminding everyone of the frontline pitcher he was with Detroit. Fortunately for him, he had time to find his form because Scott Erickson won 12 consecutive decisions during the first half of the season on his way to a 20–8 record. Tapani had strong months in May, July and August. This pitching triumvirate carried the Twins through the regular season. Morris had mellowed some by this point of his career. The outbursts had subsided. But his desire to compete and win never left him. "To this day I call him Black Jack," said Al Newman, a popular utility player on the 1991 team, "because the day he was pitching it was if he was mad at everybody. It's a term of endearment. He was all business on game day. To me, he was a big help to Scott Erickson being as dominant as he was. I just think Erickson took on that persona that year from watching Jack."

Morris won both his starts in the 1991 ALCS against Toronto, as the Twins moved on to the World Series. Morris made three starts in the World Series against Atlanta, winning two while posting a 1.17 ERA. He was emotional before his Game 1 start as he thought about pitching the biggest game of his life in front of his hometown fans. Battling a lingering chest cold, Morris didn't have his best velocity or control in Game 1 but was effective enough to pitch seven innings in the Twins' 5–2 victory. Greg Gagne and Kent Hrbek hit homers to pace the Twins. Morris pitched into the eighth inning but walked the first two batters before being replaced by Mark Guthrie. "I know I can pitch better," he said afterward. "It's no secret. This wasn't one of my best games."

He pitched better in Game 4, holding the Braves to one run over six innings. But he was removed for a pinch hitter in the seventh inning with a 2–1 lead, which didn't sit well with him. Mike Pagliarulo's home run earlier in the inning gave the Twins the one-run lead. Morris' spot in the batting order was up with two outs, and Twins manager Tom Kelly sent up pinch hitter Gene Larkin. Morris was ready to pitch the eighth inning—and beyond—but lamented National League rules. What made matters worse was that Carl Willis entered and gave up the game-tying home run to Lonnie Smith. Then the Braves got a sacrifice fly by Jerry Willard with one out in the ninth to win the game. Afterward, Morris expressed his disdain for National League rules. When asked if he was upset, he replied, "We didn't win the game, did we? Should I be happy? Thank you." Then he ended the session.

After taking a 2–0 lead in the series, the Twins lost all three games in Atlanta and faced elimination in Game 6. Morris lobbied to start the biggest game of the year, but Kelly went with Erickson. If the 1991 World Series was one of the best ever, Game 6 is one of the greatest World Series games ever. Erickson gave up three runs over six innings but was chased from the game in the seventh following Mark Lemke's leadoff single. That run eventually scored to tie things at 3–3. But this was the Kirby Puckett game, when the future Hall of Famer stole a Ron Grant drive headed for the plexiglass in left-center then blasted a walk-off home run in the 11th to force Game 7. Morris, with the latest Game of the Year in his hands, played Marvin Gaye's "Let's Get It On" in the clubhouse afterward. Those were his thoughts in the moments following Puckett's home run.

The series already was one for the ages. "Somebody's got the storybook," Kelly said. "I wish somebody would let us in on the ending." The Twins had their big-game pitcher, Morris, ready to work. He received a standing ovation as he walked out to the bullpen to warm up for his matchup against John Smoltz. Morris had his good fastball from the beginning. He also threw a slider, forkball and changeup. But when he was right, he could be deceptive. That's what made him a Hall of Famer. Smoltz, in Game 7, was right there with him. Explosive fastball. Filthy slider. Both pitchers shoved that night—a nicer way of saying they stuck up the hitters' keisters. Morris stranded two runners in the third and two more in the fifth. He pumped his first after striking out Ron Gant to end the fifth, saying later he did it after home plate umpire Don Denkinger finally called a borderline pitch a strike.

Morris wiggled out of a dangerous spot in the eighth with the bases loaded and one out. Lonnie Smith led off with a single before Terry Pendleton doubled to left center to put runners on third. Smith should have scored but all kinds of shenanigans were in play. Shortstop Greg Gagne and second baseman Chuck Knoblauch acted like they had the ball and pretended to start a double play. Left fielder Dan Gladden pretended he was going to catch the ball. Who knows if one of these attempts to deke Smith worked? Morris' theory was that Smith lost the ball and slowed down. Ron Gant grounded out, then David Justice was intentionally walked. That brought up Sid Bream, who hit into a first-to-home-to-first double play to end a crazy, yet scoreless, half inning.

Smoltz was pulled in the eighth, but Morris kept pitching. He had thrown 118 pitches when the game headed to extra innings. Did Morris have another inning in him? "He's pitching the game of his life here," Kelly said. "Do you want to take him out? No. Do you want him to lose? No." Morris wanted to pitch the 10th. Pitching coach Dick Such felt Morris could do it. So Morris went back out. Eight pitches later, Morris walked off the mound to deafening cheers after pitching 10 scoreless innings in Game 7. Gladden led off the bottom of the 10th with a double; Knoblauch bunted him to second. Intentional walks to Puckett and Hrbek. Then Gene Larkin's pinch hit single to win the World Series. The Twins had their second title. Morris had his dream season—and the World Series MVP Award.

"You gotta be a man to do that kind of stuff," Winfield said of his fellow St. Paul product. "Heart. And he did it at home to win for a home team. If there is a defining point in his life, you've got to remember that."

Winfield followed Morris to Minnesota, signing with the Twins before the 1993 season and collecting his 3,000th hit that year. Molitor followed Winfield in the homecoming tour, signing with the Twins before the 1996 season then collecting *his* 3,000th. But Morris had to follow both to Cooperstown. Winfield was a first-ballot electee in 2001. Molitor joined Winfield in the Hall of Fame in 2004.

After opting out of his contract with the Twins the day following Game 7 in 1991, Morris signed with Toronto, went 21–6 and won a second consecutive ring. After a 7–12 season in 1993, Morris went 10–6 with Cleveland before calling it a career. He finished 254–186 with a 3.90 ERA. Morris spent 15 years on the Baseball Writers Association of American ballot, failing to receive the necessary 75 percent of the votes for induction. The 300-win plateau was still an unofficial requirement for enshrinement. Although attitudes about looking beyond wins were changing—Bert Blyleven was inducted in 2011 with 287 wins—voters weren't ready to go there with Morris, who had 33 fewer wins. And his career ERA would have been the highest for any Hall of Famer. Supporters argued that Morris was a horse, in terms of workload, who saved bullpens and pitched to game situations better than anyone. And his Game 7 triumph should be a testament to how he pitched and competed.

Morris' case was kicked upstairs to the Modern Baseball Era committee. That committee included known Morris supporters in Winfield, Rod Carew, Toronto executive Paul Beeston and Atlanta executive John Schuerholz. On December 10, 2017, Morris was elected by the committee for induction into the Hall of Fame, receiving 14 of 16 votes.

Morris had been stung by rejection so many times that he hadn't considered how to react if he was voted in. His voice cracked and he fought to remain composed during a press conference the following day. That revealed how much the honor meant to him. "I don't know Jack personally," said Hall of Famer Robin Yount, who also was on the committee, "but that's not the guy I knew on the mound, snorting and sniffing and crap coming out of his face and literally was out there for blood and to get you out. He has a soft side!"

13

Paul Molitor

LISTENING TO AND WATCHING TWINS GAMES PROVIDED THE soundtrack to Paul Molitor's childhood.

He was five years old when the franchise moved from Washington, D.C., in 1961, and he was old enough to enjoy the 1965 team that reached the World Series before losing to the Dodgers in seven games.

He remembers Harmon Killebrew's killer clouts and Tony Oliva's lethal left-handed swing. He was also a big fan of strapping outfielder Bob Allison, whose No. 4 Molitor would wear once he arrived in the major leagues. "The games weren't all televised back then," Molitor said. "My dad got me a transistor radio and would let me listen to games if I got my homework done. I followed the 1965 run. I remember watching the World Series in school [St. Luke's Catholic School]. They rolled in a little TV into the classroom because they were all day games."

Molitor took batting practice while wearing a Killebrew T-shirt. He would go out to the backyard of his home with his father, Richard, who would throw balls high enough by the fence that his son could turn into Allison, jump up and catch them. He sat in the upper deck in left field at Metropolitan Stadium, watching his heroes.

The franchise was new. Minnesota finally had Major League Baseball after nine years of dreaming, and Molitor was part of that first generation of fans who were captivated by big-league baseball. Molitor was heartbroken in 1967 when Jim Kaat injured his elbow in the third inning of the second-to-last game of the season at Boston—the end of the Great Pennant Race. He was forced from the game with a 1–0 lead. Boston scored in the middle innings to win the game, won again the next day and captured the pennant. "There were a lot of those things," Molitor said of his childhood fandom.

Twins catching great Earl Battey lived in St. Paul, in the Rondo neighborhood, and Molitor was thrilled about running into him occasionally at a local drug store. After injuring his elbow while pitching in the eighth grade, Molitor was examined by Twins team physician Dr. Harvey O'Phelan. When he entered the waiting room for his checkup, Twins pitcher Luis Tiant was there. "We both had the same injury," Molitor said. "We both had a stress fracture of the scapula. And I thought it was kind of cool. I was disappointed about being hurt, but..."

Along with Dave Winfield, Jack Morris and Joe Mauer, Paul Leo Molitor was one of St. Paul's favorite sons. He starred in baseball, basketball and soccer at Cretin High School (before it merged with Derham Hall in 1987), then was an instant impact player for the University of Minnesota before being drafted by the Brewers and making a difference right away there, too. He spent 15 seasons with the Brewers, three seasons with Toronto, then three seasons with the hometown Twins.

Like Winfield and Morris, Molitor also returned to play for the local team. All three grew up within a five-mile radius of each other in St. Paul, making you wonder what was in the water back then. Molitor lived just five blocks from Winfield in the Midway area, and their careers were just as approximate. They both played for the same American Legion team during the summer, Attucks-Brooks Post 606, although Molitor was still in grade school and just part of a reserve squad while the older Winfield was a star shortstop and pitcher. They both attended the University of Minnesota, where they became All-American players. They were both first-round draft picks, as Winfield was selected by the Padres with the fourth overall pick in 1973 and Molitor with the third overall pick in 1977. Both were All-Stars—with Morris—when the Midsummer Classic was played at the Metrodome in 1985. Both signed as free agents with Toronto, with Molitor replacing Winfield as the Blue Jays' designated hitter in 1993. Both won World Series titles with the Blue Jays. Even their 3,000[th] hits occurred with the Twins on the same date, Winfield's coming on September 16, 1993, at the Metrodome and Molitor's on September 16, 1996, in Kansas City. It needs to be mentioned, too, that Morris also left the Twins to sign with the Blue Jays, where he shared that World Series moment with Winfield. Non–Upper Midwesterners joke that Minnesota is in Canada, so perhaps it was appropriate that three St. Paul guys ended up on a Canadian team.

While Winfield was a tremendous athlete who did it all— throw, hit, hit for power and run—Molitor might have been one of the most cerebral players of his time. Molitor knew the angles. He could envision things before they happened. That's not to undervalue his other talents, because they were immense.

At the plate, Molitor didn't have a hitch in his swing and didn't have a leg kick. He figured out how to transfer weight from his back leg to front leg without a stride. He was quiet in the batter's box, eyes level from the moment the pitcher released the ball to when Molitor had whacked it between fielders. He had quick wrists and ran well. His approach was developed over the first handful of seasons in the majors, and it was trial by fire.

Molitor spent one season in the minors, batting .347 in 64 games at Class A Burlington in 1977. Despite a strong spring training in 1978, Molitor was cut from camp and slated to start that season at Class AAA Spokane. He was waiting for teammate Jim Gantner to give him a ride to the minor league camp when he received a call from the club and was told not to leave. Shortstop Robin Yount was considering retiring and taking up professional golf just four years into his career. He was beat up and tired of losing. A foot injury suffered while riding a motorcycle in the California sand dunes during the offseason likely played a part, too.

Molitor became the greatest fallback option ever, as manager George Bamberger penciled him in as the Opening Day starting shortstop—and leadoff hitter. Molitor, inexperienced hitting in that spot, grounded out in his first at-bat but delivered an RBI single off Mike Flanagan on his next trip to the plate. He had three hits in each of his next two games and was on his way. He moved to second base when Yount rejoined the team in May and finished with a .273 batting average. Molitor finished second to Detroit's Lou Whitaker in Rookie of the Year voting. Molitor ended up with the nickname "The Ignitor," but he was learning on the job in 1978, honing an approach that would lead him to 3,319 career hits. Like most young players, he was chasing bad pitches and sought a way to put the ball in play more.

"The quieter I was, the longer I could see [pitches] and recognize [them], the less I chased," he said. "So I incorporated it as a two-strike approach, originally. Just spread out [my stance] a little bit and just kind of picked my foot up and put it back down. Eventually, I started to realize I could do that from the beginning of a count. Maybe put a little bit more into the torque, into the load, so you could still drive the ball with before you got to the two-strike situation. But I didn't do that originally. It was something that just evolved out of what I thought was necessary to become a better hitter."

The 1979 season was the first of 12 in which Molitor hit over .300. He was an All-Star at age 23 and led the league in runs scored at age 25. Except for big-time power, Molitor was one of the most complete offensive players in the game. And pity on the pitchers who threw that bowlegged man a first-pitch fastball, for it was going out faster than it came in.

On the bases, he was a moving clinic. He knew when to take an extra base and when to advance from first to third on hits to left field, and he could pick out the right pitch to steal a base on. He was so smooth on the bases that the Twins had him teach baserunning during spring training years after he was done playing and managing. "I was coached to be aggressive," he said. "Levels of instinct vary, for sure. However, a player's baserunning ability can improve through better circumstantial awareness and anticipating things that might happen before they do."

Molitor saw the game on a different level than most.

There are ups and downs through every career, and it is dangerous to play the "what if?" game. But as robust as Molitor's production was, the early years of his career were noted for a series of injuries that kept him off the field. He estimated that he's had at least 50 shots of cortisone—which relives inflammation and pain—in his career. Although he was named to the All-Star team in 1980, he could not play because he was recovering from a pulled rib cage muscle that limited him to 111 games that season. In 1981, he played in just 64 of 109 games in that strike-shortened season because of an ankle injury. He played the 1983 season with a sore wrist, batting just .270. Tommy John surgery, when a tendon is harvested from elsewhere in the body to replace a torn ligament, limited him to 13 games in 1984. Two hamstring injuries in 1986 limited him to 105 games. By that point, Molitor was a .291 career hitter with a .766 on base-plus-slugging percentage and coming off a few down seasons. And he was just a handful of seasons removed from his wild and crazy days in the early 1980s, when he was one of many major league players to use cocaine. Molitor started because of peer pressure and used cocaine to cope with his injuries.

By the mid-1980s Molitor, and most of baseball, had cleaned up their act. In 1987, Molitor ripped off a 39-game hitting streak—the seventh-longest of all time—while batting .353 and finishing fifth in MVP voting. Baseball was captivated as Molitor made a run at Joe DiMaggio's record 56-game hitting streak. Alas, the streak ended on August 26 with a hitless game against Cleveland. He was in the on-deck circle when Rick Manning singled to drive in the game-winning run in the 10th. Manning was booed by fans who wanted to see Molitor get a crack at extending his streak. But at age 31, Molitor turned back the clock. It was the start of a 10-year run during which he batted .300 eight times for three different teams—and .341 twice. Molitor was baseball's version of Benjamin Button, the movie character who aged in reverse. Molitor flourished as he entered his mid-thirties, when most players experience a decline. Sixty-five percent of Molitor's 3,319 hits came after he turned 30. He believed the injuries he suffered early in his career made him appreciate the game more, so he did more to stay on the field and get the most out of his talent. "I had that ritual the last multiple years of my career when I'd go out and run my sprints at 6:47 PM, then come back sit on the top steps of the dugout and made sure I took it in," Molitor said. "It's one thing to get there [the majors] and another to play when you're 40. That might have been part of the longevity thing. Plus, you know that your ability to maintain skill is God-given more than anything you do. I tried to maximize it as long as I could."

A player can do more to shorten a career than lengthen it, apparently. "I did some of those things, too." Molitor said.

Molitor thought he would spend his entire career in Milwaukee. Playing for the hometown Twins was a dream, but Molitor was entrenched in Sudsville, was productive and had fans enthralled with his brilliance. Molitor hit .320 in 1992 but was at the end of a three-year, $9.1 million contract. Sal Bando, Molitor's former teammate, had just been appointed general manager. And he was about to show Molitor that loyalty meant nothing when payroll needed to be slashed. Molitor expressed his desire to stay with the only organization he'd known, but Bando botched things from a communication standpoint. More than a month had passed since the end of the 1992 season without a contract offer, so Molitor became willing to listen to offers from elsewhere. Bando, meanwhile, traded for Kevin Reimer to be the team's designated hitter. What gives? Molitor was supposed to serve that role.

Bando made two offers that reflected a significant pay cut from 1992, when Molitor made $3.4 million. They weren't going to offer arbitration, where Molitor would likely have been granted a raise to over $4 million. Brewers fans erupted when Molitor signed with Toronto for three years and $13 million.

He joined fellow St. Paul native Jack Morris on the team while replacing the other St. Paul native, Dave Winfield, as the designated hitter. Winfield, who helped the Blue Jays win the World Series in 1992, signed with the Twins. And the Brewers went on to win 69 games in 1993 while Molitor, wearing No. 19 in honor of buddy Robin Yount, had one of the best seasons of his career, batting .332 with a career-high 22 homers and 111 RBI and helping Toronto repeat as champions. Molitor batted .458 in the World Series, earning MVP honors.

The Blue Jays weren't as successful the next two seasons, and Molitor had another decision to make when his contract expired. Five teams expressed interest despite Ponce de Leon approaching 40. Morris was 35 when he signed with the Twins in 1991. Winfield was 41 when he signed with the Twins in 1992. Molitor was 39 when he signed in 1995. His suitors included Cleveland, where he would have landed in a good lineup. Baltimore, where his general manager in Toronto, Pat Gillick, had moved, was also interested. Milwaukee, desperate to bring him back after its blunder in in 1992, approached him as well. But Molitor followed his heart and went back home. He signed a one-year, $2 million contract with a $2 million player option for 1997 with the Twins. Molitor thought for years that if he ever left Milwaukee, the destination would be Minnesota. He just detoured through Toronto to get there.

"I was gonna turn 40 that upcoming season and Tom Kelly had reached out and we met in the wintertime, and he painted a pretty rosy scenario. The second half the team had had in '95 [was encouraging], and there was just a lot of things that made it attractive. I thought the time had passed me by for me to have an opportunity to come home. But yeah, it just kind of came later on than I ever would have expected."

The 1996 Twins scored 877 runs, slightly above the league average. Five players with at least 100 games had an OPS over .800, which is above average. Marty Cordova hit .309 with 16 homers and 111 RBI. Rich Becker batted .291. A couple of supporting players, Roberto Kelly and Ron Coomer, hit .323 and .296, respectively. Chuck Knoblauch had a fantastic season, batting .341 with 14 triples, 13 home runs and 45 stolen bases. But the hitter who energized the team was Molitor.

Molitor batted .386 in April, hitting his way on in his first eight games as a Twin. He ended the month with a nine-game hitting streak. In fact, Molitor failed to get a hit in just three games that month. His only "slump" was in May, when he checked in with a .269 average. After that, it was vintage Molitor, turning 40 while turning heads and leading the league with 225 hits. And he matched Knoblauch's .341 batting average.

When Molitor signed with the Twins, it was believed that he would need two seasons to get the 211 hits he needed for 3,000. But by the middle of the 1996 season, he was on pace to reach the mark by mid-September. "Ask [golfer] Greg Norman about pace," Molitor said in June. He kept hitting, batting at least .310 every month other than May and a blistering .388 in August. The countdown was on in September. The *Minneapolis Star Tribune* dedicated a corner of the front page of its sports section for updates as Molitor neared the milestone. The Twins came off road games in Toronto, Milwaukee—what a coincidence—and Texas before coming home to a nine-game homestand with Molitor just 13 hits away. Molitor had 11 hits before the final game of the homestand but was hitless in four plate appearances against Seattle. On to Kansas City. Molitor singled to right field in his first at-bat against Royals left-hander Jose Rosado for hit No. 2,999. He flied out to right in his second at bat before coming to the plate with one out in the fifth. Rosado was a rookie with much promise in 1996 and would go on to be named to two All-Star teams. On this night, he threw a high fastball that Molitor got to, and No. 4 sent a drive to right center that split center fielder Rod Myers and right fielder Jon Nunnally by a hair. Molitor flew around second and charged into third with a headfirst slide. Molitor became the 21st player with 3,000 career hits—and the first to do it with a triple. "It's probably fitting," he said. "I spent a lot of time in the dirt and the grass, rolling around, in my career."

The Twins' bench emptied and mobbed him with salutations. Manager Tom Kelly, who had remained near the dugout as the Twins celebrated World Series titles in 1987 and 1991, even came out to third to hug and congratulate Molitor. The Royals played a video on their scoreboard saluting Molitor for his achievement as "Born to Run," the hit song by Bruce Springsteen—and friend of Molitor—played in the background. Robin Yount joined George Brett in the stands to witness the moment. After the inning ended, video tributes from Brett, Yount and Rod Carew were played. With that triple, Molitor and Dave Winfield were the first players from the same town to reach 3,000 hits.

Molitor's first season with the Twins was nearly perfect. He was one of the oldest players in the league but hit .341. He reached 3,000 hits. He proved he was still a dangerous hitter at age 40. Two things kept it from being perfect. One, the Twins finished 78–84. Two, Kirby Puckett woke up during spring training that year and noticed a dot blocking his vision in his right eye. Tests revealed that he suffered from glaucoma, a devastating blow to a franchise and fan base that loved the roly-poly right-handed hitter. It was supposed to be the Paul and Puck Show, as the two had become good friends over the years. Playing the "What if?" game once again, many believed that Puckett would have driven in 130 runs while blindfolded in the middle of that lineup. Puckett held a press conference during the season to announce that his condition meant the end of his career. "As far as what he had meant to that team, the fact that the reality was starting to sink in that he had seen his last game was overwhelming for a lot of people, including myself," Molitor said. What would have been? Molitor speculated that the Twins might have been closer to a playoff spot with Puckett in the lineup, which could have encouraged the front office to bolster the pitching staff for a playoff push. But that's the danger when you go down the "What if?" road.

Molitor had signed a one-year deal with an option when he joined the Twins in 1996. But, declining his player option, he signed on for another two seasons. He hit .305 in 1997, his 12th season batting at least .300. He batted .281 in 1998, poor by his standards, and decided to end his playing career at the end the season. His three seasons were a gift to the Twins. They were able to see him at his best and were able to absorb how he articulated the game. "He was the smartest baseball man I ever played with," said outfielder Matt Lawton, who was teammates with Molitor for all three seasons he was with the Twins. "He knew everything about the pitchers. He had all the baserunning tips. He walked up to me one day and asked me what kind of hitter I wanted to be. And it got me thinking. Do I want to be a hitter for average? Do I want to hit home runs? I think I could have hit for a higher average."

Some 25 years later, Molitor has never used the word "retire" to mark the end of his career. Maybe he wanted to include time as a coach and manager. Within two years, Molitor was on Kelly's staff as a coach, the start of 17 years during which Molitor helped on the major and minor league levels. He served two stints as a coach on the major league staff. During his first stint, in 2001, he was ejected from a game in Cleveland for arguing against Mike Fichter's tight strike zone. After his ejection, he threw a batting tee onto the field to illustrate his point that Fichter was forcing pitchers to put the ball over the fat part of the plate. Everyone expected Molitor to one day become a manager. He was offered a front office role with the Brewers and the Blue Jays were willing to let him be a player-manager before 1998. Molitor decided to stay home and not uproot his family to move to Canada. Plus, he loomed as Tom Kelly's replacement. When Kelly stepped aside following the 2001 season, Molitor and Ron Gardenhire were considered as the leading candidates to replace him. Molitor, concerned about the possibility of the Twins being contracted, took his name out of the running, and the job went to Gardenhire.

Molitor's induction to the Hall of Fame was a foregone conclusion. His 3,319 career hits, 605 doubles, seven All-Star Game appointments, four 200-hit seasons and a World Series MVP in 1993 were enough evidence. He was the fifth player ever with 3,000 hits and 500 stolen bases and the third player ever with 3,000 hits, 600 doubles and 500 steals. He received 85.2 percent of the votes, comfortably over the 75 percent threshold required for induction. The ceremony was an emotional one, as both inductees—Molitor and Dennis Eckersley—revealed personal struggles. For the first time, Molitor publicly acknowledged his son Joshua, who was born outside of marriage in Toronto. Eckersley spoke of his battle with alcohol and struggling marriages. When the two posed with their Hall of Fame plaques, tears flowed from Molitor's eyes. "I've been through divorce in the last three years," he said. "I had problems with drugs early in my career. I know how tough this could be for families. You have to try to make something out of it, try to persevere through it."

Is life a lesson to be learned, or an experience to be lived? Molitor could answer yes to both questions. The game has given him much more than it has cost him, but it doesn't lessen the pain caused by his mistakes. And that moment in Cooperstown was as cathartic as it was ceremonial.

When Molitor was on a field, everything was clear, simpler and more manageable. Molitor didn't just manage, however—he excelled. After his playing career was over, he was expected to run a team someday. While he spent 17 seasons waiting for that opportunity while helping the Twins out in various roles, he did sneak away one year as the hitting coach in Seattle. Eddie Guardado, one of his best friends in baseball, was pitching there. And Pat Gillick, who brought him to Toronto, had taken the role in Seattle. Molitor agreed to the position, which came with one request: get Ichiro Suzuki to walk more.

Suzuki came to the majors in 2001 from Japan as the most heralded player from that country at the age of 27. He christened his major league career by winning the batting title with a .350 average. He was one of the greatest contact hitters in the history of the game, but relied on his ability to adjust to pitches rather than lay off ones off the plate. The Mariners wanted Ichiro to rely less on his superior bat-to-ball skills and more on being selective to draw more walks. Seattle was smart in having Molitor approach him with the plan instead of some career minor league player who had worked his way to the majors as a coach. Molitor's credentials spoke for themselves. Ichiro was all ears and was willing to try a more patient approach. It was a disaster. Ichiro was batting .255 after the first month of the 2004 season when Molitor said to him, "Remember that talk we had in spring training? Forget everything we said. Go back to being who you were." Suzuki hit .392 the rest of the way and set the record for hits in a season with 262. Over the last three months of the season, Suzuki batted .423.

"I don't think I had a month in the major leagues where I had 50 hits," Molitor said. "He had four that season." So Molitor was the hitting coach during Ichiro's record-breaking season. But the Mariners' attempt to fix something that wasn't broken kept Suzuki from making a run at 300 hits.

The big managing opportunity came when the Twins let Ron Gardenhire go following the 2014 season. Gardenhire had won six division titles in the 2000s but had just posted his fourth consecutive losing season when the Twins sought to make a change. Molitor made his intentions clear. "I'm here to win," he said. His roster had some players who weren't established; Joe Mauer, who had moved to first following his concussion and wasn't the same hitter; the rotation lacked frontline starters; and Torii Hunter, who was 39 and in his final season. Molitor improved the team by 13 wins from the previous season. That was followed by the crash of 2016, when the Twins lost 103 games and longtime GM Terry Ryan was let go in July. A young core—which included Jorge Polanco, Miguel Sanó, Eddie Rosario, Max Kepler, Byron Buxton and José Berríos—took its lumps. There was a regime change following the season, as Derek Falvey, 33, was brought in from Cleveland to run baseball operations, while the highly respected Thad Levine was hired from Texas for the GM role. The Twins were going to embrace analytics like never before while building out their research department. But owner Jim Pohlad made it clear that Molitor had to remain as manager for at least a season.

The 2017 Twins went 85–77 while finishing second in the division and qualifying for the postseason. Several of the younger players took a step forward. The Twins were eliminated by the Yankees in the wild card game, but Molitor was voted AL Manager of the Year. Even if Falvey wanted to bring in his own manager, he couldn't do it to someone who had led the team back to the postseason while winning an award. To the contrary, Molitor landed a three-year contract extension following the season.

Unfortunately for Molitor, the 2018 Twins regressed to 78–84. Sanó and Buxton dealt with injuries. There was a lack of depth in the rotation. Polanco served an 80-game suspension for using performance-enhancing drugs. And the Twins scored 77 fewer runs than the previous season, which was cause for alarm. How much was Molitor at fault? It's never easy to tell. In many cases, good players make coaches and managers look like geniuses. But if the message out of the skipper's office isn't being received well, that becomes an issue. Molitor was an old-school player but was willing to adapt to the hip and with-it analytics surge. When he was on Gardenhire's coaching staff in 2014, he researched data on shifting. Gardenhire was a little nervous about totally embracing it, and Twins pitchers had to be sold on getting used to not seeing defenders being used traditionally. But it eventually was implemented. Molitor was willing to embrace it, pointing out that analytics in his final season was dramatically different than his first.

"Actually," he said with a chuckle, "I had to post, outside of the reporters' view, back in my locker area all the new statistical categories with definitions. Someone would ask me about weighted runs created or of wOBA [weighted on-base average] or FIP [fielding-independent pitching] or whatever, and I pretended like I knew what I was talking about. But a lot of times I had to go check and see what the heck was going on. But a lot of it was good. It made me work harder and, hopefully, a little smarter."

Molitor's coaching staff was a mix of new-school and old-school minds. Jeff Pickler would make data-based presentations to Molitor and the other coaches. Eddie Guardado was old school. He pitched for 17 seasons, trusting his stuff and throwing his guts out. That's how he preferred to impact players. There was a feeling that Molitor could have done a better job at playing traffic cop with the two groups. When a team with a young core doesn't progress as much as a front office believes it should, details like how information is disseminated to players are scrutinized more. "We just think a change in voice and potential style with some of these younger players could be of benefit to us," Falvey said the day Molitor's firing was announced. A lot of things went wrong in 2018. In addition to Polanco's drug suspension, Ervin Santana needed finger surgery. Sanó reported to camp out of shape, approaching 300 pounds. Some of the veteran mercenaries Falvey and Levine brought in—Logan Morrison, Addison Reed and Lance Lynn—fell short of the desired impact. But you go to the source to fix a short circuit. In this case, it was the manager's office. Molitor received the news shortly after the season ended. He quickly rushed to his son's elementary school to break the news to him before he learned online or on social media.

Molitor, 305–343 in four seasons as manager, has remained in the Twin Cities and is content with not being in a big-league dugout. And he continues to assist the club in a variety of duties. As late as 2023, Molitor served as a special instructor during spring training and served as a radio analyst during a road trip to Texas and Cleveland. Minnesota sports teams have a way of maintaining relationships with people they fire. Molitor and Ron Gardenhire stop by Target Field for special events and represent the organization at other functions.

The terrific triumvirate of Molitor, Dave Winfield and Jack Morris reflects St. Paul's love for baseball and the investments in youth participation. Their passion and talent were forged on St. Paul's youth baseball fields and led them to big-league stardom. And some of those fields still exist some 50 years later. And there was some secret sauce left over as a fourth St. Paul native became a Hall of Famer in 2024, when Joe Mauer was voted in on his first year on the ballot. Mauer played on the same fields as Molitor and Winfield and went on to give a masterclass in catching for the 10 years he was behind the plate. Molitor played against Joe's father, Jake, in grade school and high school. And Molitor was the manager for the final four years of Mauer's career.

"We like the way that St. Paul has been represented the way it has been in baseball lore in our state," Molitor said in a 2023 interview, "and with Joe potentially getting in here, hopefully sooner than later, there will be four players. At the All-Star Game in 1985 when Jack and Dave and I were able to don the American League uniforms and do it in the Twin Cities, that was just a cool moment. It wasn't prideful. It was something that doesn't happen every day."

14

Joe Mauer

As a 10-year-old, Joe Mauer liked whatever sport was in season. In the fall, it was football. In the winter, it was basketball. After that, baseball took over.

"If I had to pick one," Mauer said, "it probably would have been basketball then."

Mauer grew up playing at the Jimmy Lee Recreational Center as well as the Griggs Playground, both in St. Paul. He was often the youngest on the court. "He would more than hold his own," Jake, one of his two older brothers, said. "In pickup games, Joe was the first kid picked probably 95 percent of the time." By all accounts, he wasn't too shabby. He competed hard, had quick feet and had little shake to his game. He ended up being an All-State basketball player, averaging 20 points and 6 rebounds a game as a junior then 19.4 points and 7.8 rebounds as a senior.

Yes, this is Joe Mauer, the sweet-swinging, ground-breaking Hall of Fame catcher. The first catcher to win three batting titles and the only American League catcher to lead the league in hitting. He was the AL's Most Valuable Player in 2009, batting .365 with 28 home runs. This guy? A basketball player?

This guy was an even better football player. He took up that sport in fifth grade, when a coach approached his father, Jake Mauer Jr., and said, "I've seen Joe throw a baseball. Now I want to see him throw a football." Mauer went to a practice, recognized several of his buddies and joined in. Football turned out . . . just OK. As a sophomore quarterback for Cretin-Derham Hall High School in St. Paul, he threw for 373 yards in a game against Bloomington Kenndy. His junior season, he threw for 2,507 yards and 32 touchdowns. As a senior, he threw for 3,022 yards and 41 touchdowns and was named Gatorade National High School Football Player of the Year. He went 25–2 as a starter and received a scholarship to play for Bobby Bowden at Florida State, the college where former Cretin-Derham Hall great Chris Weinke played.

Baseball eventually won out, thank goodness.

Mauer's father, Jake Jr.; grandfather, Jake; and brothers, Jake III and Bill, all played baseball, which was a reference point for the youngest Mauer. The game was in their blood. There is video of Mauer swinging a bat at age three, a swing that resembles the stroke that led to 2,123 major league hits. By age four, he was banned from T-ball games at Griggs Playground because he hit the ball too hard. As he got older, his swing was honed with the help of a device his father made from PVC pipe wide enough to slide a baseball through. A ball is dropped through one end of the tube, from about eye level. The ball rolls down through the tube and falls from about waist high. That's when the batter must time his swing to meet the ball. Hours of drills with the device produced a smooth, fluid yet fast swing. The family would later produce and market the contraption as the Joe Mauer Quickswing.

But it would be an insult to point to a man-made series of tubes as the reason why Mauer was such a talented hitter. If true, there would be a Quickswing in every backyard in America and more left-handed-hitting catchers would roam the Earth. It's not the arrow, it's the archer. Mauer's gift to baseball was to use his sharp batting eye, excellent coordination, brilliant anticipation and robot-like mechanics to drive balls all over the field. You would hear about players battling with their mechanics holding their bats too high or too low, struggling with their timing, opening their stance to get to inside pitches more. These subjects rarely came up with Joe Mauer. He might have adjusted his stance a little bit over the years. But the trigger, getting his hands through the strike zone and the follow-through were largely the same throughout his 15-year career.

So baseball was the sport that made the most sense for Mauer to pursue, even as accolades piled up in basketball and football. It also helped that scouts were calling him a future first-round pick as early as his sophomore season.

"Over the summer of my sophomore year, I got to go play for Team USA at the Pan Am Games," Mauer said. "That's kind of when the baseball thing was like, 'Hey, I've got a pretty good shot at doing this, if I continue to do the right things and keep improving. I could have a chance.' That was kind of the lightbulb moment, I guess."

The first time Joe Mauer's name appeared in the *Minneapolis Star Tribune* was in a basketball roundup on February 24, 1999. "Raiders sophomore forward Joe Mauer scored 9 of his 20 points in the fourth quarter," it read. We had no idea what was to come. No idea that Joe Mauer was going to dominate the Twin Cites prep scene over the next few years. Mauer entered

Cretin-Derham Hall as a 5'8" freshman but grew to 6'3" by the end of his sophomore year. All the skills—there were athletes on both sides of his family—blossomed.

Two months later, Mauer was in the *Star Tribune* as part of a spring sports preview story—having not played a single game as a sophomore yet. He ended up hitting .576 that season and landing on the All-Metro team. That fall, he was touted as Cretin-Derham Hall's "next superstar quarterback," behind Weinke and Steve Walsh. Mauermania was at full throttle by then.

While he was leading the football team to state title games, scouts were flocking to his baseball games. Mauer batted .588 with 4 homers and 28 RBI as a junior. Scholarship offers in both sports poured in. He had a list of schools if he decided to play football. "It's a good problem to have," he said at the time. "I'm not sitting around and thinking about it. I want to have a successful, fun senior year and not worry about other things."

Meanwhile, the Metrodome often had high school or college baseball games following Twins day games. Following one Sunday game, reporters noticed that Cretin-Derham Hall took the field to warm up for a game. "Good," I said loud enough for the other reporters in the press box to hear. "We get to see what all the fuss about Joe Mauer is about." Any skepticism was abated in the first inning after Mauer planted a pitch over the baggie in right field.

As Mauer's senior year began, the Twins were finishing up a 69–93 season, one that would guarantee them the first-round pick in the 2001 draft. Mauer's draft stock had rocketed from first round to possibly a top-five selection. Mauer continued to do Mauer things. He led the football team to the state championship game before losing to Eden Prairie. He helped the basketball team go 28–2 and reach the state semifinals. And he batted .625 with 14 homers and 48 RBI while leading the baseball team to a state championship. Mauer batted .575 in his high school career—and struck out just once in 222 at-bats. That occurred on June 16, 2000, against Elk River in a state tournament game at the home of the Minnesota Golden Gophers. Paul Feiner had given up a homer and a single to Mauer during his first two plate appearances. On the third, Feiner threw a 2–2 curveball—the 12-to-6 kind—that Mauer swung at and missed. There was Feiner's 15 seconds of fame.

Legendary Twins scout Mike Radcliff first saw Mauer play when he was 15 years old. Over the next few years, dozens of Twins officials would watch Mauer play various sports at Cretin-Derham Hall. Terry Ryan, the Twins' general manager at the time, was in the stands to watch Mauer play baseball, football and basketball. Ryan, a scout to the core, had top grades for Mauer. Baseball doesn't have a scale of 1 to 10. The scouting scale is 2 to 8. Ryan rarely gave out 8s to prospects. He did so for Alex Rodriguez coming out of Westminster Christian School in 1993. And he did it with Bo Jackson coming out of Auburn University in 1986. Mauer, who was a good but not great runner as a catcher, was close. "His accuracy was an 8. His receiving was an 8," Ryan said. "His hands were an 8. His makeup was a 12. You can fudge numbers as you go through evaluation of this amateur stuff. If you have makeup and you can hit, hitters play. If you can hit, you are going to play in the majors."

The consensus as the draft neared was that there were four players worthy of the first overall pick: Mauer; Mark Teixeira, a third baseman out of Georgia Tech; Mark Prior, a right-hander from USC; and Dewon Brazelton, a right-hander from Middle Tennessee State. Prior was considered one of the best college pitchers ever. For a Twins team that historically struggled to get an ace starter for its rotation, it was an opportunity to grab a player many believed could go straight to the majors.

A little background is needed here. One decision can change a franchise's fortunes. Prior to the 1990 draft, the Twins scouted Stanford right-hander Mike Mussina multiple times. And, multiple times, Mussina didn't pitch like a top prospect with the Twins in attendance. On draft day, the Twins decided to select Todd Ritchie with their first-round pick. Despite being the 12th overall pick in the first round, the Twins even gave Ritchie the sixth-highest bonus that round, $252,500. Mussina went to Baltimore with the 20th overall pick and became a Hall of Famer. Ritchie was released after two seasons with the Twins and ended up 43–54 in his career. That decision cost the franchise. Mussina could have helped sustain the Twins' success following the 1991 World Series title.

So there was a chance for the Twins to land their long-sought-after rotation anchor in Prior. The 2001 Twins got off to a fast start and were 50–31 at the halfway point. There were thoughts that Prior was good enough to assist in the playoff chase by the end of the season. The scouting staff did its due diligence before the draft with all four picks. But it came down to either Prior or Mauer. The Twins knew that Mauer, who grew up just seven miles from the Metrodome, wanted to play baseball and was willing to sign. They also engaged Prior about a signing bonus, which led to a couple of tense exchanges with Prior's father, Jerry. The father felt he was getting the "good cop, bad cop" routine from Ryan and his assistant general manager Wayne Krivsky. Prior's bonus demands were now headed toward $15 million, which would have been a record at the time. There was one heated conversation prior to the draft that took place as Ryan and Krivsky conferred at Ryan's home in Eagan, Minnesota.

"That happened right in that office right there," Ryan said while pointing from his dining room. "I was talking to Mr. Prior and Wayne says, 'Do you mind if I talk to him?' I said, 'Go ahead, Wayne.' Well, he didn't last long."

Only four times had a catcher been selected with the first overall pick, the last being Danny Goodwin in 1975.

Pitching is the most important aspect of baseball. So if a team has a chance to draft a difference-maker at the position, it should take it. But the Twins could not resist the hometown product who was a legitimate top prospect and who was more signable than Prior. On Tuesday, June 5, the Twins made Mauer the first overall selection of the draft. He joined Dave Winfield and Paul Molitor as St. Paul natives who were selected within the first five picks of the draft.

Mark Prior was selected by the Cubs with the second overall pick. By then, the Prior family was relieved the Twins hadn't drafted their son because of the combative conversations Jerry Prior had with the Twins in the days leading to the draft. Jerry Prior had suggested that the contract Drew Henson signed with the Yankees in 1998, six years and $17 million, should be a guide for his son's deal. The Twins balked.

"Whenever I think of Minnesota," Jerry Prior said. "I'll think of [then governor] Jesse Ventura and Terry Ryan."

Mauer signed for a bonus of $5.15 million. Prior signed with the Cubs for a record $10.5 million. "I don't think he wanted him to play for the Twins," Ryan said. Prior made his major league debut in 2002. A year later, he won 18 games while being named to the All-Star Game. Then injuries derailed his promising career, as he pitched his final major league game in 2006. Mauer debuted in 2004 and would play 15 seasons. His 55.2 WAR (wins above replacement) was the highest of all the first-round picks in 2001.

About a month after being drafted, Mauer signed and began his professional career with the Twins' rookie league team in

Elizabethton, Tennessee. His brother, Jake, was a 23rd-round pick of the Twins in the same draft out of the University of St. Thomas, located in St. Paul. Joe Mauer went 2-for-4 with a walk in his pro debut. And despite being one of the youngest players on the team, Mauer led the team with a .400 batting average over the 32 games he played.

It would not take long for Mauer to reach the majors. Mauer batted .302 with four home runs and 62 RBI the next season at Low-A Quad Cities. In 2003, Mauer batted .335 over 62 games at High-A Fort Myers and .341 in 73 games at Class AA New Britain. Once you prove you can hit on the Class AA level, you're likely a future major leaguer. The Twins determined during that offseason that Mauer was ready for the majors. As for how long, refer to Ryan's comment about Mauer's makeup.

The day Mauer was drafted, a local reporter approached Twins starting catcher A.J. Pierzynski about his job security. It seemed like an odd question to ask a baseball player when it takes years of development before a draft pick reaches the major. But two and a half years later, the Twins were ready to move forward with Mauer. In November of 2003, the Twins traded Pierzynski and cash considerations to San Francisco for left-hander Francisco Liriano and right-handers Joe Nathan and Boof Bonser. It was one of the great fleece jobs in Twins history, as Nathan became one of the best closers in club history and was inducted into the Twins Hall of Fame. Liriano became an All-Star and would have piled up more honors if not for a career-altering elbow injury in 2006. Bonser pitched only four seasons but did start a playoff game for the Twins. And the tradeoff of Pierzynski for Mauer makes it even more lopsided.

Mauer made his major league debut on April 5, 2004, at the Metrodome against Cleveland, collecting two singles and two walks while scoring two runs. He singled in his first at-bat the next night. Two singles moved him to third before he needed to come out because of a sore left knee. The Twins discovered that Mauer strained his left meniscus when his cleat got stuck on the rubber warning track behind home plate as he chased a pop-up. Two days later, he had part of his meniscus removed. The Twins announced that Mauer would miss around three to four weeks. He ended up missing nearly two months. He returned June 2. On June 6, he broke a 3–3 tie with a three-run homer off Detroit's Esteban Yan—his first major league homer. He played until the All-Star break while still battling knee problems. He pinch hit in the first game following the break, then landed back on the disabled list with recurring knee problems. Part of the problem was a change in medication, which was expected. He spent the rest of July, all of August and part of September rehabilitating his knee, to the point where the Twins felt they could use him as a pinch hitter or designated hitter in the second round of the postseason. The Twins never got there, losing two extra-inning games to the Yankees on the way to dropping the AL Division Series in four games. It was the beginning of a run of 18 consecutive postseason game losses that lasted into 2023, which was the longest playoff losing streak in North American professional sports at the time.

Mauer's rookie season was limited to 35 games, but he showed plenty of promise, batting .308 with 6 homers and 17 RBI. His on base-plus-slugging percentage of .939 was fantastic for a rookie. The Twins didn't wait to cash in on their local hero, giving away Mauer baseball cards and Mauer bobbleheads and selling ticket packages that came with a Mauer coffee mug. He was just 21 but being marketed as if he were a perennial All-Star. Twins fans couldn't get enough of Mauer. He was polite and likeable, signed autographs and was from a large, popular family in St. Paul. Everyone knew a Mauer. There was a hockey-playing side of the family as well as a baseball-playing side. An uncle, Ken, was an NBA referee—after playing with Paul Molitor for the Gophers baseball team. Most of Joe Mauer's sentences began with, "That's the thing," or "It's kinda funny." And his damn sideburns were perfect.

His rookie season would also be the harbinger of things to come, as the knee injury he dealt with would not be the only physical setback of his career. As a matter of fact, Mauer went on to miss more than 350 games in his career due to various ailments—and that doesn't count the days off he had for in-season maintenance. The Twins also had trouble, at times, determining how much time Mauer would miss because of them. But that was just a slight detraction from an otherwise marvelous career in which Mauer dominated the catching position—at the plate and behind it.

Mauer once said his swing "doesn't have a lot of stuff going on." The résumé he built, however, did. In 2005, he batted "just" .294 with 9 homers and 55 RBI. Things began to click in 2006. The Twins were terrible at the start of the season before June 8. Everything was great after June 8, as they finished 96–66. Mauer ended up in a batting race with the Yankees' Derek Jeter and Robinson Canó while the Twins were tied with Detroit heading into the final weekend of the regular season. It was still tied through 161 games. Mauer went 2-for-4 with a double to finish at .347, ahead of Jeter by four points. The Twins won 5–1 as Detroit lost in extra innings, at home, to Kansas City. That allowed the Twins to win the division for the second time in three seasons.

It was the first of three batting titles for Mauer, the only catcher to do so. He hit .328 in 2008 for this second title and .365 in 2009 for his third. By then, opponents just shook their heads at how calm yet dangerous he was at the plate. His pregame routine was in place. Watching Mauer take batting practice was like watching him water his lawn. He would begin by hitting several balls to left field, then several to center and then several to right. He sprayed balls wherever he wanted. Once that part of the field was saturated, he'd move on to the next part.

Except for the 2009 season, Mauer didn't hit for much power during his career. It was his choosing. He knew where his sweet spot was: on pitches up and on the inner half of the plate. But he largely stuck to what made him a batting champion. He wore out the opposite field with singles, mastering the ability to go the other way on inside pitches while other hitters would get jammed. He also didn't like to swing at first pitches, despite having a career batting average of .353 when he did. He preferred to track the movement of the first pitch, gaining information on what that pitcher had that day. Later in his career, managers began making pitching changes more frequently. Mauer pointed out that he might see four different pitchers in one game. Opponents seemed to pick up on this and frequently piped strike one down the middle of the zone, which irritated some observers who thought Mauer was too passive.

The pitcher, in these moments, often was sealing his own fate. With two strikes, Mauer slightly widened his stance and worked on staying short to the ball. He seemed calmer at the plate with two strikes on him than when the count was 0–0. He had a career .249 average with two strikes. Derek Jeter's was .228. Alex Rodriguez's was .213. Albert Pujols' was .232. "Joe Mauer's two-strike approach was the best I've ever seen," Twins manager Ron Gardenhire said.

The 2009 season was when everything fell into place for the St. Paul product—after he recovered from another injury. This time, it was a sore sacroiliac joint, which connects the lower spine to the pelvis. The inflammation spiked during spring training games, forcing Mauer to see a specialist at Johns Hopkins University for a second opinion.

Mauer missed the first 22 games of the regular season. On May 1, Mauer made his season debut against Kansas City at the Metrodome. On his first swing of the season, Mauer planted a pitch over the left-center field fence for a home run. He added a double, a walk and three runs scored in a 7–5 Twins win. Mauer belted 11 homers and batted .414 in May. The month also included one of his signature defensive plays. In the ninth inning of a game at Yankee Stadium, with one out and the fast Brett Gardner at second, Francisco Cervelli hit a ball up the middle that deflected off left-hander Jose Mijares' glove and back toward home plate. Mauer scrambled to grab the ball. Gardner rounded third and never stopped. Mauer turned to first, faked a throw, spun toward home, dived and tagged Gardner before he reached the plate. "That's one of the best plays I've ever seen," backup catcher Mike Redmond said after the game. "Instinct-wise, that play was off the charts. I told him I don't know how he did it."

Mauer batted .407 as late as June 21 before falling below the elusive .400 mark for good. That month included one of his signature hitting performances, in the first game of a series against the Cubs at Wrigley Field. As soon as the 2009 sched-ule was released, Teresa Mauer began making phone calls to arrange a trip to the landmark ballpark to watch her son play. By the time the series rolled around, Teresa Mauer had about 150 friends and family members on the trip.

The Twins had flown in the night before following four games in Oakland. In the hours before the series opener against the Cubs, I walked down the tunnel to the visitors' dugout at Wrigley. Around a corner, I heard someone coughing and hacking up a storm. I turned the corner and saw Joe Mauer by the bat rack.

"My goodness, you sound terrible," I said.

"Yeah, I picked up something when we were in California," Mauer said.

"Are you going to be able to play?" I asked.

While coughing, he replied: "I have to. My mother is here, and she has nearly 200 people in the stands."

The Cubs estimated that about 15,000 Twins fans showed up for each of the first two games of the series, so there was a roar when Mauer lined a single to right in his first at-bat. "Let's go Twins!" chants bounced off the rafters of the venerable stadium. The chants grew louder when Mauer batted in the third inning and homered over the ivy-covered wall in left-center field. By the late innings, "Let's go Twins!" had morphed into "Let's go Mauer!"

Mauer went 3-for-3 on July 1 to push his batting average to .392. To show you the challenge of maintaining such a hitting pace, Mauer batted .309 that month but saw his average drop to .359. A .400 season was impossible, but a career year wasn't. Mauer batted .391 in August and .358 in September. Then he was 6-for-25 in five October games. His final average of .365 was the second-highest ever by a catcher in a single season. And it was a remarkable power year for him, as he blasted 28 home runs. There were supposed to be four games in October, but the Twins finished the regular season tied with the Tigers for first place in the AL Central. The Tigers were headed to the Dome for a Game 163. The Twins were moving into Target Field next season, so there was a ceremony following game No. 162 to bid farewell to a building that was given one more night. "I wrote this speech thinking that this was going to be it, but it's not it," Twins legend Kent Hrbek told a crowd of 51,155.

"You guys went and screwed up my whole speech. We've got to come back here on Tuesday and drink more beer!" Mauer went 2-for-4 with a double—Game 163 stats counted—as the Twins won in 12 innings to win the division.

So let's add it all up. Mauer led the league with a .365 batting average, .444 on-base percentage and .587 slugging percentage—the modern triple crown. It is easily one of the top five offensive seasons by a catcher. He also won his second Gold Glove. And the batting title was his third. All before he turned 27. He batted .345 against left-handed pitchers. He batted .536 against Cleveland.

Mauer was the favorite to win the AL Most Valuable Player Award, with Derek Jeter and Mark Teixeira of the Yankees and Miguel Cabrera of the Tigers in the running. Around 12:50 PM on November 24, 2009, Jake Mauer received a text from his son.

"Press conference at the Dome at 3 PM," it read. "And I'm wearing a suit."

Dad replied, "I will be there. And I will NOT wear a hat."

Mauer received 27 of 28 first-place votes, easily winning the MVP as Teixeira finished second. He joined Zoilo Versalles, Harmon Killebrew, Rod Carew and Justin Morneau as Twins to win the award. And Mauer ended up as the only St. Paul native—not Dave Winfield, Jack Morris or Paul Molitor—to win an MVP award.

Endorsement deals followed. Gatorade, Kemps, MLB: The Show, Head and Shoulders and other companies signed him up through the years as a spokesman. But the big deal was fast approaching. Mauer was scheduled to make $12.5 million in the final year of a four-year, $33 million contract. So he was going to be a free agent after the 2010 season. There were rumblings that the Yankees were willing to pay him $25 million to $30 million a year. And the Red Sox would likely get in the sweepstakes too.

Mauer would have challenged Earl Webb's record of 67 doubles if he played 81 games a year in Fenway Park.

The Twins put an end to all the concern in March of 2010 when they inked Mauer to a franchise-record eight-year, $184 million contract. "I'm just thrilled to do this for the rest of my career," Mauer said. "I've told everyone here that I'm going to give you everything I've got."

While the Twins stepped up to retain their hometown hero, there was plenty of reaction from around the league. Tampa Bay manager Joe Maddon expressed relief, noting that Mauer would have likely signed with division rivals Boston or New York if he had become a free agent.

White Sox manager Ozzie Guillen was despondent over Mauer *not* leaving the division. "I wish they didn't sign him so he can go somewhere else, and I don't have to face him 19 times," Guillen said. "But it's great for him and great for baseball. God bless his mom and enjoy the money. If you don't know where to spend it, I send you my number."

Joe was emotional during his press conference that day. But one question came from the back of the interview room that seemed innocuous at the time. It would focus on a future that Mauer had no idea he was headed for, but that defined his path. "Joe, how long do you think you will remain a catcher?" Mauer replied, "I haven't really thought about that. I just want to focus on helping the Twins win."

In four years, that question would be answered.

Mauer hit .327 in 2010 with nine home runs and 75 RBI. Then came 2011, the first year of his eight-year, $184 million contract. Mauer entered the season following December surgery on his left knee, the same one he injured in 2004. He spent most of spring training rehabilitating the knee rather than preparing for the long season. He didn't bat in a game until

March 16. Rushing into the season only made matter worse. On April 14, during a series at Tampa Bay, he came down with a viral infection. But the Twins announced that Mauer was going on the 15-day disabled list with bilateral leg weakness. Typing "bilateral leg weakness" into an online search returns many possibilities, some of them very serious. Speculation swirled that Mauer might have a crippling disease. All Mauer knew was that he lost 15–20 pounds because of the viral infection. "When bilateral leg weakness came out, I really don't know where that came from," he said. Mauer missed 58 games, returning on June 17. With Justin Morneau out with neck surgery, Mauer filled in some at first base. The ailments kept coming. A sore neck in August forced him to miss a week. An upper respiratory infection the first week of September knocked him out for two games. Then pneumonia on September 16 knocked him out for the rest of the season. Mauer played in just 82 games in 2011, batting .287 with three home runs and 30 RBI. He didn't hit his first home run until July 27. With Mauer and Morneau ailing, the Twins crashed to a 63–99 record.

The 2012 season was vastly different, as a fit Mauer finished fourth in the AL batting race with a .319 average and led with a .416 on-base percentage. He did so as a catcher, first baseman and designated hitter. Everything pointed to a duplicate season in 2013 when a foul tip off Ike Davis' bat socked Mauer right in the mask during a game against the Mets. Mauer, months earlier, had remarked how he had taken more foul tips off his mask than he could remember. It turned out that Davis' was a doozy. Mauer felt fine on the flight to Detroit but had to take himself out of the lineup the next day when he experienced dizziness during pregame work.

"I saw him taking ground balls and he said he felt a little off," teammate and close friend Justin Morneau said. "He missed a couple ground balls and he's usually pretty solid over there." Morneau understood what Mauer was going through. Morneau was batting .345 with 18 home runs through 81 games in 2010 when he suffered a concussion after taking a knee to the head while sliding into second base in Toronto. He would miss the rest of the season while dealing with lingering fogginess and headaches. It lingered into 2011 and he was never the same player. He did win a batting title in 2014 with Colorado but was not the power threat or run producer that made him the AL MVP in 2006.

Mauer was placed on the seven-day concussion disabled list. He wasn't ready to be activated after a week. Then two weeks. Then a month. Mauer would make progress, then suffer setbacks that kept him sidelined. It cost him the rest of the regular season—one in which he batted .324—and lingered into the offseason. He was sensitive to light and had to leave the room when one of his six-month-old twin daughters began to cry. He battled with symptoms for three months following the blow to his mask. By the time he arrived at spring training to prepare for the 2014 season, the decision had been made to move him to first base. He had suffered a major concussion and was a risk for a reoccurrence if he took more blows to the face mask.

It's unfortunate that Mauer was moved to first base. There was a vacancy there—the team had traded Justin Morneau in August—which made it a convenient move. And Mauer had filled in at first base 56 times over the previous three seasons. But Mauer was a good athlete with a strong arm and was fundamentally sound. He would have been a fit at third base or the outfield and been more than serviceable. The decision was made to hand him a first baseman's glove. And that's where he spent the final five seasons of his career.

Mauer and Morneau—the M&M boys—have so much in common. They are both left-handed hitters. Both won MVP awards. Both married Minnesota girls. Unfortunately, both suffered concussions that altered their careers. While Morneau no longer was a run producer, Mauer's offense tailed off too. Mauer batted .278 in five seasons as the full-time first baseman. He hit .305 in 2017, the only season he batted over .300 after moving to first base for good. "It wasn't a tough decision, but it was," Mauer said of moving to first base. "Just because I love to catch and put in so much work to become the catcher that I was."

Mauer's $184 million contract was set to expire after the 2018 season. It seemed likely, at the beginning of the season, that Mauer would return for 2019. But, on May 11, he hit his head while diving for a ball and suffered a cervical strain plus another concussion. That cost him 25 games. Then other developments made retirement more possible. His production was slipping. The Twins started a roster remodeling. He was arriving at the park as early as 1:00 PM before a 7:00 PM game to get physically ready to play, which taxed him. And he was expecting his third child in November. Mauer wasn't going to decide until after the season ended, but it sure seemed like a farewell tour in September. Mauer batted .309 that month, ending the season with a nine-game hitting streak. The September 30 season finale was an emotional one. With former teammates flying in from around the country, with friends and family on hand, Mauer legged out a double in the final at-bat of his career. In the ninth inning, 30,144 fans rose to the feet as a watery-eyed Mauer slipped into catcher's gear for one pitch from Matt Belisle. The Twins got the visiting White Sox to agree that their hitter, Yoan Moncada, would not swing at the pitch—a stipulation Maddie Mauer made. Mauer caught the pitch then left the field.

Mauer waited until mid-November—days before his son, Charles ("Chip"), was born—to make it official. The son of St. Paul became the 22nd MVP to play his entire career with the same team. And Mauer, possibly the best all-around prep athlete in Minnesota history, did it in his home state. He felt he could still produce at a major league level, but the concussion he suffered in May factored in his final, gut-wrenching decision. He finished with a career .306 batting average, .388 on-base percentage, 143 home runs, 923 RBI, and 2,123 hits and led the team in doubles since its arrival from Washington in 1961, with 428.

Mauer was inducted into the Twins Hall of Fame late in the 2023 season. Talk soon turned to the other Hall. What happens if he gets "the call" from Cooperstown early in 2024 to enter the National Baseball Hall of Fame? "Then," wife Maddie said, chuckling, "we're going to have to write another speech." It wasn't a sure thing, as many voters held his five average seasons at first base against him. But not enough of them did. Mauer received 293 votes, four more than needed, and was elected to the Hall of Fame on the first ballot. The St. Paul slam was complete. Winfield. Molitor. Morris. Mauer. All Hall of Famers.

Mauer was born with the baseball gene and the nice guy gene. He never created controversy, was honest with the media, polite to fans and universally liked. He immediately became a full-time dad to his three children but misses stepping into the batter's box four times a night to joust with pitchers. "The beauty of being from Minnesota," he said, "is that I don't have to say goodbye."

Well played, Mauer.

15

Kent Hrbek

Kent Hrbek needed to relax. So he went hunting.

He rose at 5:00 AM one morning in his home in Bloomington, Minnesota, met up with some buddies and headed for Litchfield, about 70 miles west of where he lived. There, the group set up and waited. It was 26 degrees. "Well, the bluebills were flying," Hrbek said. "So we had to give it a try."

Hrbek is a confirmed outdoorsman, as evidenced by his popular television show, *Kent Hrbek Outdoors*, which ran from 2004 to 2010. There was an effort to get Kirby Puckett to commit to the show, which then would have been renamed *The Herbie and Kirby Outdoors Show*, but it never materialized. Just like a pitch over the middle of the plate was in his wheelhouse, holding a rod or shotgun in the great outdoors also was where Hrbek was at his best. It was not out of his comfort zone to awaken at 5:00 AM to be the sportsman. Even on this particular day.

"We did OK," Hrbek said of his hunting trip. "Shot a few ducks."

The date was October 25, 1987. If your ears start to tingle after reading that, then you are a confirmed Minnesota Twins fan. Because anyone who was alive at the time would recognize that as the date of Game 7 of the 1987 World Series between the Twins and Cardinals. That's right. Before playing in the biggest game of his career on the biggest stage the sport provided, Hrbek went duck hunting. There's nothing more Minnesotan than that. And there's nothing more Hrbek-ian than that.

"That's the way I comfort myself," he explained at the time. "People have different ways of comforting themselves."

Later that day, following a nap, Hrbek changed out of his hunting gear and into a Twins uniform. Then he helped the Twins beat St. Louis 4–2, with Hrbek catching the final out when the Cardinals' Willie McGee grounded to Gary Gaetti at third, and Gaetti fired across the infield to Hrbek at first base. After moving to the Twin Cities from Washington, D.C., in 1961, the Twins were finally world champions.

And that made Hrbek a hometown hero and one of the most popular players in Minnesota sports history.

Kent Allen Hrbek was born in Minneapolis but grew up in Bloomington, a southern first-ring suburb. Hrbek could see the lights from Metropolitan Stadium from his home, and dreamed of playing for his hometown team. That dream began at age six, when he started playing T-ball. They didn't have uniforms but his mother hand-stitched a No. 6 on the back of his shirt. It was very appropriate. Since Hrbek lived near the Met, he attended many ballgames as a kid. Either his father would take him, or he would ride his bike there with his friends. They often attended games on Mondays, when tickets were discounted for seniors and those under 16 years old. Hrbek didn't watch every inning of every game. Sometimes his friends would play tag under the stands. Other times, they would sit near the bullpen and talk to the pitchers. When Hrbek did pay attention to the game he focused on his favorite player, Tony Oliva. And Oliva wore No. 6. Hrbek admired how Oliva hit to all fields. Hrbek would grow up to be 6'3½" and 205 pounds as a high schooler, so you would think he wanted to hit long home runs like Harmon Killebrew. Hrbek always thought of himself as a hitter first, power hitter second.

As a high school sophomore, Hrbek began attracting attention from scouts, which led to his first thoughts of being a major leaguer. Prep baseball was growing in the state at the time. The Twins had moved there in 1961, so kids were growing up with Major League Baseball. While Hrbek was turning heads at Bloomington Kennedy High School, Terry Steinbach was starring at New Ulm and Tim Laudner was at Park Center. All would end up playing for the Twins during their careers. Laudner's Park Center team actually defeated Hrbek's Kennedy team in the 1976 state tournament. Hrbek, who ended up teammates and hunting partners with Laudner, couldn't believe the burly major league catcher was Park Center's starting center fielder. "He brings that up," Laudner said. "And I tell him on our hunting trips to South Dakota, 'I'm going to use the old Garry Maddox line. Water covers two-thirds of the Earth; I covered the rest.'"

Paul Molitor had been drafted in the first round in 1977 by Milwaukee following a stellar career at Cretin High School in St. Paul and the University of Minnesota. Molitor then embarked on a Hall of Fame career during which he collected 3,319 hits. But some thought Hrbek had more upside. Angelo Giuliani, a longtime Twins scout, said Hrbek was the best prospect he had seen in 30 years.

The Twins selected Hrbek in the 17th round in 1978. Owner Calvin Griffith even stopped by one of his games at Kennedy to watch him play. The Twins initially offered Hrbek a $5,000 signing bonus, which was rejected. Hrbek had signed a letter of intent to play at the University of Minnesota, but he wasn't a person who had his head in the books all the time, if you catch the drift. The Twins eventually offered Hrbek $30,000, and he accepted. It was too late for Hrbek to join a short-season league, so he reported to Fall Instructional League in Melbourne, Florida—where he landed in hot water with manager Gene Mauch. During a fishing outing with John Castino, Hrbek slipped on a rock and gashed an ankle, requiring 14 stitches. Mauch, who was eager to see him play, chewed Hrbek out for his carelessness. It would not be the only stumble during his first steps to the majors. He dislocated a kneecap while swinging a bat during a spring training scrimmage game, then injured the same knee just 17 games into his stint for Elizabethton, Tennessee, in the Appalachian League for rookies. He returned to the Twin Cities for surgery. Injuries would be a nagging issue for Hrbek through the years, leading some to question what his career would have been like if he'd taken better care of his body. While it's understandable to require an athlete to remain fit, Hrbek wasn't into a lot of conditioning. He would sit out while teammates stretched before games before going to the batting cage, hitting a few line drives and declaring he was ready to go. And he liked beer. Hrbek was the working man's ballplayer—baseball, hunting, fishing and beer drinking. He was gifted in all four. He was in a shape, just not the shape some wanted.

In 1980, Hrbek played at Wisconsin Rapids for manager Rick Stelmaszek. "Stelly" would become a great influence on Hrbek's career and eventually become a bullpen coach under Tom Kelly. Stelmaszek was a stickler for fundamentals, like

Kelly. "He always made me laugh," Hrbek said of Stelly. "I thought he was a hardass, but I thought he was funny too. "Stelly must have said the right words at the right time, because Hrbek began 1981 at Class A Visalia, California, and ended the year in the majors. In 121 games with Visalia, Hrbek batted .379 with 27 home runs and 111 RBI. He was on everything.

While Hrbek was having a season that would lead to a major league promotion, he was devastated to find out that his father, Ed, had been diagnosed with amyotrophic lateral sclerosis—ALS. Better known as the Lou Gehrig disease. A crushed Hrbek wanted to go home and be with his family. The opposite happened. His family traveled to California to visit him and convince him to remain focused on reaching the major leagues. "I got you here," Ed told his son. "I'm going to be at home, taking care of Mother. You keep going with what you are doing here." Hrbek's goal was clear: He had to get the Twins to call him up so he could be home. He just didn't know how soon that would be. Toward the end of Hrbek's explosive season at Visalia, he was called into manager Dick Phillips' office. Hrbek thought he was headed to Class AA. Wrong. He was headed to New York for the Twins–Yankees series. Hrbek had to drive from Visalia to Fresno, then fly to Los Angeles, then fly to New York to join the team. Any promoted player would gladly accept that itinerary.

Waiting for him was another local player who had plenty of experience playing in New York—although he had not heard of Hrbek until that day. It was Yankees outfielder Dave Winfield, who was born in St. Paul and starred at the University of Minnesota. When asked what Hrbek would face beginning his career in such a legendary place, Winfield replied, "The ghosts. You can never replace those guys. If you try, you will hurt yourself. You know all the great things that have been said about the people who have played here? You just hope that when you finish the game they will say the same things about you."

Hrbek found himself in the starting lineup on August 24, facing left-hander Tommy John. Yankees star Reggie Jackson singled during the game. When he got to first base, he asked Hrbek for the correct pronunciation of his name. Hrbek was 1-for-4 with a RBI single when he batted in the 12th inning against George Frazier. Hrbek got a hold of a fastball and drove the pitch over the right field wall for the game-winning home run. Cheers reverberated throughout Bloomington, including the Hrbek household. Hrbek noted the irony of his debut. He spent his first major league game standing in the same spot Lou Gehrig did just several months after his father was diagnosed with ALS. A year later, Ed Hrbek passed away. That was on Hrbek's mind later in his career when he decided to step away from the game following the 1994 season, when he could have continued his career.

After appearing in 24 games in 1981, Hrbek was looking forward to his first full season in the majors. So were the Twins, who had activated a youth movement by giving chances to several players from their farm system. Catcher Tim Laudner, shortstop Lenny Faedo, third baseman Gary Gaetti, left-hander Frank Viola and outfielder Randy Bush were part of the wave. Then the team traded for Tom Brunansky that May. They felt they had something, but it took a while—and a lot of losing—before the Twins won the World Series in 1987 and 1991.

It didn't take Hrbek that long to establish himself as one of the best first basemen in the league. His age-22 season was an impressive one, as he batted .301 with 23 home runs, 92 RBI and a .848 on base-plus-slugging percentage. His season included a 23-game hitting streak during which he batted .308 with five homers and 17 RBI. He received his first and only All-Star Game appointment of his career as he roared into the break batting .332 with 17 home runs and 60 RBI in 74 games. He was a big man with excellent range at first base, able to turn and haul ass well into foul territory to chase down pop-ups. He was such an intriguing newcomer that he landed on the cover of *Sports Illustrated*. The regular guy had hit the big time at age 22.

Hrbek, it can't be stressed enough, did things his way. Spring training, to him, was just a different place for him to go fishing for a few weeks until it got warm enough up north to start the regular season.

"Kirby Puckett needed six or seven weeks of spring training to get ready for the season," Laudner said. "Hrbek was ready after two weeks. He would sit over there smoking cigarettes and say, 'Hey, Skip, when do the freakin' games start?' So we had to find ways to keep him occupied for the last four weeks."

The modern baseball player follows a strict diet. Works out throughout the offseason. Has an in-season physical maintenance plan. Arrives at the ballpark at 2:00 PM to prepare for a 7:00 PM game. And now, some teams have nap rooms available to help with rest and recovery. Wash, rinse, repeat every day. Wash, rinse, repeat every year.

All you need to know about Hrbek can be summed up by Laudner as he talked about the time Hrbek was chowing down on junk food before a game at Comiskey Park in Chicago.

"The clubhouse attendant had an office underneath the stands, and you had to duck your head under a beam to enter it," Laudner said. "He always had a stainless-steel bowl of Oreo cookies on his desk. Well, it's 15 minutes before game time, and I'm sitting in my locker because I wasn't in the lineup that night. Herbie is sitting on the floor in front of his locker and he's got this bowl of Oreos sitting between his legs. And he is hammering these things. I look up and [manager] Tom Kelly had walked out of his office, got past the wall, stopped, came back, looked at Herbie and said, 'What the hell are you doing?' Herbie didn't even look up and said, 'I'm hungry. And if you want two hits tonight you better keep right on walking.'"

In 14 seasons, Hrbek batted .282 and hit 293 home runs. He finished second in Rookie of the Year voting in 1982 behind Cal Ripken Jr. and in front of Wade Boggs. There's a stat called on base-plus-slugging percentage (OPS). On base percentage includes walks, so it shows how often a hitter reaches base. Slugging percentage accentuates extra-base hits. Combined, the two show a hitter's impact on games. An OPS of .770 to .800 is solid. Anything over .800 is very good. Hrbek's OPS in his rookie season was .848. That would be his average OPS for his career. His first three full seasons, his OPS was .848, .855 and .906. His breakout season occurred in 1984, when he batted .311 with 27 homers and a career-high 107 RBI. He finished second to Willie Hernández in MVP voting that year.

Hrbek walked more times in his career (838) than he struck out (798). He never struck out more than 87 times in a season. The Twins would later have a player, Miguel Sanó, who struck out 90 times in 53 games in 2020. Hrbek made contact—and did damage when he connected with pitches.

And he did it with a body that would be out of place on the cover of fitness magazines. He would be needled at times about his workout habits and attempt, at times, to get in better shape. In the end, he was what he was: a big, lovable lug and the best first baseman in Twins history. His favorite moments came after games, when he guzzled beers with teammates and talked shop. And he had the waist to prove it.

"You never saw him down the left field line running," Laudner said. "The only stretching he ever did was when he would go smoke at the landing in the Metrodome behind the two big doors, then yell at whoever was singing the anthem. He would walk around the corner when it was time to take the field. He would squat down, put his elbows inside his knees and push out. Someone would flip him a ball and he would lumber out to first. Someone would ask, 'Herbie, why don't you ever stretch?' He'd go, 'You ever see Secretariat stretch?'"

Laudner, Randy Bush and Gene Larkin would jokingly go over to first base before games and take ground balls. Hrbek would arrive and ask, "What the hell are you guys doing over here?" Bush would say, "Getting some work in over here, waiting for you to break down." "Get the hell outta here!" Hrbek would yell.

Even without the perfect body, the Twins realized what they had in Hrbek. Before the 1985 season, the Twins signed Hrbek to a five-year, $5.9 million contract. He made $560,000 in 1995 followed by $1.06 million, $1.31 million, $1.41 million and $1.56 million the next four seasons. That made Hrbek the first Minnesota athlete to earn $1 million in a season.

As Hrbek matured as a player, the Twins climbed the standings. The 1984 team was in the pennant race entering the final week of the season but lost its final six games. The 1985 and 1986 teams saw the manager's role go from Billy Gardner to Ray Miller to Tom Kelly. Kelly was 12–11 after replacing Miller late in the 1986 season. The 1987 Twins entered the season looking to redeem themselves for their recent failures, and Kelly was the right man at the right time. The players from the 1982 team—Hrbek, Brunansky, Laudner, Gary Gaetti, Randy Bush and Frank Viola—were experienced pros by then. "We had five years together," Hrbek said. "We were looking for more pieces to the puzzle." Pieces were coming in closer Jeff Reardon and leadoff hitter Dan Gladden. They also had Kirby Puckett, their spiritual leader. And Tom Kelly had managed some of them in the minors. Everyone was a good fit on an 85-win team that was hard to beat at the Metrodome.

"Everybody understood everybody's job, and no one stepped on anyone else's toes," Hrbek said. "And T.K. pretty much instigated that. One of his big things was, 'Hey, we all put our pants on the same way as everybody else. Nobody is better than anybody else.' And if you've ever been around, you knew we had Kirby Puckett, who was one of the best players if not the best player in the American League, or in baseball. He was having as much fun as anybody else, but he never walked around like he was a big shot. Gary Gaetti was one of the best third basemen in the game at the time. He wasn't any different than anybody else. We all got along together. And we played as a team. When Boston was coming to town, they weren't playing Kirby Puckett. They were playing the Twins."

Hrbek didn't have a great postseason in 1987. He batted .150 in the ALCS against the Tigers, but the Twins took the series in five games. He did homer off Jack Morris in Game 2. And Hrbek batted just .208 in the World Series against St. Louis with one home run—but he made that long ball count. Down 3–2 in the series, Hrbek blasted a grand slam off a first-pitch fastball from Ken Dayley in the sixth inning of Game 6 to seal an 11–5 win that forced a Game 7. The Twins, of course, won that game too.

The Twins had one more World Series to win but, before that, they needed to lock up Hrbek or risk losing him to free agency following the 1989 season. It took perhaps the first ever "hometown discount," when a player stays with his original team for less than what he would receive on the open market. The Tigers and Mariners offered five-year deals worth a total of $15.5 million and $15 million, respectively. Hrbek accepted $14 million over five years to remain in Minnesota and close to his hunting and fishing spots. And he received the deal after missing nearly 40 games in 1989 due to a separated shoulder. Hrbek was bowling in a league at West Side Lanes in West St. Paul when informed that the deal was done. A side note about West Side Lanes: Twins players, coaches and officials bowled there until the 2010s, when it closed to make way for progress. Hrbek was a regular there. This sportswriter showed up one day to get a quote from Ron Gardenhire and ended up being drafted as an alternate. So I showed up weekly with ears open and waited until a coach said something newsworthy. West Side Lanes was where I learned about the trade for Delmon Young in 2007. For me, the place was Scoop Central.

Hrbek played in 143 games in 1990, batting .287 with 22 homers and 79 RBI. One of those home runs came in April at California off former teammate Bert Blyleven. It was the 400th homer hit off Blyleven, and the right-hander sent Hrbek a framed photo of him standing at the plate during the game with the message, "Thanks for No. 400. Maybe you'll be the guy to hit No. 500. Then again, you fat pig, you probably won't be around then." Hrbek should have played in more than 143 games that season but broke a bone in his ankle while chasing a clubhouse attendant during horseplay, a calamitous ending for a last-place club. "I'm not mad at myself for what happened," Hrbek told reporters afterward. "I've been doing stuff like that for years. I've always been a screw off, and I'm not going to change now."

Hrbek had more health problems in 1991—a strained hamstring, a bruised shoulder, a sprained ankle, then another injured shoulder. He also was being pinch hit for by Al Newman when he slumped at the start of the season. But when the Twins reached the postseason, Hrbek was instrumental to their second World Series championship. The 1987 team was special; it delivered the state's first World Series championship and included several players from the Class of 1982 who were thrown into the fire. The 1991 team was better. Puckett and Gaetti were among the best at their positions. The pitching staff, led by free agent Jack Morris, was deep. Rick Aguilera was a quality closer. And there was Hrbek, who, at the time he signed his contract, was one of the top-10 highest-paid players in the game. And Tom Kelly was known as a master tactician. The Twins won 95 games that season and did not enter the postseason as underdogs. Hrbek eventually got on track, bolstered by a 17-game hitting streak in August.

Hrbek struggled in the ALCS again, batting .143. But the Twins still took out the Blue Jays in five games. Then came one of the greatest World Series ever, as the Twins got a signature performance from Puckett in Game 6 to force a winner-takes-all Game 7. And that game was punctuated by a signature performance by Morris, who went 10 innings for a 1–0 victory.

Hrbek went 2-for-4 and homered off Jim Clancy in Game 1 but went 1-for-22 after that to bat .115 in the series. He was known more for what he did in the field. In Game 2, Atlanta's Ron Gant singled to left and took a wide turn as Gladden's throw skipped by Scott Leius at third. Twins pitcher Kevin Tapani scooped the ball up and threw to first as Gant retreated to the bag.

Hrbek argues that Gant's momentum forced him to come off the bag and fall into Hrbek. Gant, the Braves, Fulton County and the entire state of Georgia claimed that Hrbek pulled him off the bag. Umpire Drew Coble sided with Hrbek. Gant was out. Hrbek received death threats when the Twins arrived in Atlanta for Games 3, 4 and 5, to the point where he didn't leave the team hotel.

"I never talked to Gant about it," Hrbek said. "I wanted to talk to him about it because I wanted his take on it. The guy who ticked me off was the announcer Tim McCarver, who right away said, 'He pulled him off the bag!' So right away everyone in Atlanta and the southern United States thought I pulled him off the bag."

Hrbek was the runner at first base in the 10th inning when Gladden scored on Gene Larkin's pinch hit single to bring Minnesota its second World Series victory. Hrbek had two rings, but he continued to miss games. Injuries limited him to 112 games in 1992, 123 games in 1993 and just 81 games in the strike-shortened 1994 season. Hrbek was 34. He was thinking about his body. He was thinking about his father. He was thinking about being a father to his daughter. On August 4, 1994, Hrbek announced his retirement, citing injuries and his desire to embrace fatherhood even more.

And, that way, he could drink all the beer he wanted and no one would care. Every day was a Saturday with Herbie.

"I think I could have DI I'd for four or five more years but I didn't want to DH," he said. "I didn't like the fact of just going up there and hitting. I liked playing in the field. I enjoyed playing first base. I was getting beat up. My knees were bugging me. They were complaining about me being too big and too fat and this and that. It took them 14 years to find someone to replace me. I decided to retire because I thought maybe somebody else could come in and do a better job. But I think I could go out there and still hit.

"I think I can go out and hit today, what the hell. We all do!"

PART 5

THE MEMORABLE MANAGERS

16

Billy Martin

BILLY MARTIN MANAGED JUST ONE SEASON IN MINNESOTA. But it was a doozy.

Owner Calvin Griffith was looking for a spark after the 1968 Twins were an underachieving 79–83, leading him to fire Cal Ermer. In his place, Griffith put the former player, scout, coach and amateur boxer in the role. Martin proceeded to borrow a little from all those experiences in his one season running the Twins.

Martin came to the Twins as a player in 1961 in a trade with the Milwaukee Braves in exchange for Billy Consolo. Martin was at the end of a career known for his solid defense, clutch hitting, playoff success, imbibing and brawling. In one of his final bouts as a player, he fractured the orbital bone of Cubs pitcher Jim Brewer for throwing at him. Martin served a five-game suspension and was fined. Brewer and the Cubs sued Martin for $1 million but the sides settled for $10,000. Martin played one season with the Twins, batting .246, when he decided to end his playing career. He became a Twins special scout. But by 1965, Martin was back in the majors as a member of Sam Mele's staff, coaching third base and handling the infielders. Zoilo Versalles had the best year of his career in 1965, winning the American League Most Valuable Player Award, and credited Martin's influence for bringing out the best in him. Martin was popular among fans and media, which was odd for a coach to be. There are a few theories as to why. One, he came from a Yankees organization that was the envy of baseball. Two, he spoke his mind. Three, he wore his emotions on his sleeve—and on his knuckles.

The Twins got a taste of how explosive Martin could be during a road trip to Washington in 1966. A disagreement between Martin and traveling secretary Howard Fox began during the flight from Minneapolis. Because of an airline strike, the Yankees were flying back east with the Twins. A couple Yankees players became loud and obnoxious, and Fox asked Martin to ask his former teammates to be quiet. Martin objected. The Twins then arrived at the Statler-Hilton Hotel around 4:30 AM. Martin wanted his room key and became impatient. Either Fox slid it to him and it sailed off the table, or Fox threw it at him. Martin then punched Fox, and the two exchanged a few blows as Harmon Killebrew, Bob Allison, Jim Perry and others stepped in to separate them. Martin was fined. Fox, a longtime ally of owner Calvin Griffith, was not.

Martin was in the middle of a fractured coaching staff that season when differences between manager Sam Mele and a couple of them came to light. Martin was a Mele supporter. Pitching coach Johnny Sain had a different philosophy when it came to handling players. Jim Kaat, who went 25–13 that season, spoke highly of Sain and wanted him retained. Sain was let go following the season, prompting Kaat to pen his objections to the move, which ran in the local papers and ignited a controversy. There is evidence that Martin, who had become Mele's confidant, never forgot Kaat's actions.

Mele lasted 50 games in 1967 before being dismissed with a .500 record. Cal Ermer took over, and the Twins came within one game of winning the pennant. A painful loss to Boston, in the final game of the season, cost them the playoffs. Expectations were high in 1968, but Ermer underachieved. Meanwhile, Griffith asked Martin to leave the club and manage their Class AAA affiliate in Denver. Martin, who had been rumored to be a candidate for the Oakland job the previous offseason, initially declined.

Upon further reflection, he felt that managerial experience would help him land a major league job. It also gave Griffith an opportunity to evaluate Martin. Martin joined a Denver team that was 7–22 and went 65–50 the rest of the season. Martin stressed fundamentals and, of course, aggressive baserunning. He also was ejected from eight games and served a suspension for bumping an umpire. With expansion teams in Seattle and Kansas City beginning in 1969 and rumored to be interested in Martin, he had improved his chances at landing one of those gigs. But Ermer was fired after the 1968 Twins went 79–83, so the Twins needed a manager. Martin was hired shortly after the World Series. "Billy is an inspirational leader and I'm sure he will get us back to playing the kind of hustling ball that all of us want," Griffith said. Martin felt the experience served him well. "I believe that if you treat players like men you don't have to use the weapon of a fine," he said. "But if they act like boys they will be spanked."

Martin's changes included more attention to details and creating an atmosphere in which players could focus on preparation while being able to blow off steam. Despite protests from his son, Billy Joe, children were banned from the clubhouse.

Everyone wanted to know when the drama would begin. Bill Hengen of the *Minneapolis Tribune* wrote, "The 40-year-old is the fourth Minnesota manager in eight years and probably will be the most controversial."

Martin, however, was popular in the Twin Cities—and well known in drinking establishments. He befriended a restaurant owner named Howard Wong, who had a place in Aberdeen, South Dakota, called the Capitol Cafe and Lounge. The two became inseparable, going on hunting and fishing trips together. In 1966, Wong opened a restaurant in his name in Bloomington, Minnesota, where a few beverages were consumed through the years. Donna Baker, Howard's daughter, became friends with Martin's second wife, the former Gretchen Creswell. "She was just a great person while putting up with Billy's erratic behavior," Baker said.

It was at Howard Wong's where Martin met Kaat for lunch before the season to lay out his dilemma: he was going to have two pitching coaches on the staff. "Billy liked Art Fowler because they were drinking buddies," Kaat said. "He said, 'I gotta have Early Wynn because of Calvin. Fowler is my pitching coach. You listen to Artie. You don't have to listen to Early Wynn at all.'"

Martin was in control in the dugout. Speed was a big weapon for him. He believed that speed forced defenses into mistakes, and he loved putting pressure on his opponents. César Tovar, Rod Carew and Tony Oliva had the green light to run. Tovar stole a career-high 45 bases. Carew swiped 19, which was two more than his two previous seasons combined. Oliva stole 10 bases but was thrown out 13 times—a result of being more aggressive on the basepaths under Martin. Carew embraced Martin's push to be aggressive, swiping home seven times during the season. Martin taught him how to get a walking lead, giving him some momentum if he decided to take off.

The epitome of "Billy Ball" occurred on May 18 against Detroit. Tovar beat out an infield hit and was balked to second. Carew followed with a walk. The two pulled off a double steal, then Tovar stole home. Carew stayed at second on the play, but then he stole third base too. Sure enough, Carew took off on a pitch and stole home. To recap the inning: One infield hit. Five stolen bases. Three steals by Carew. Two steals of home. One round of thunderous applause from fans at the Met.

On June 4, the Twins pulled off a triple steal, with Carew scoring while Harmon Killebrew and John Roseboro advanced a base. Martin didn't stop there. He called for suicide squeezes when the situation called for it. With runners on first and third, he had the runner on first stray off the bag enough to draw a throw. As soon as the throw left for first, the runner on third would take off for home. In that May 18 game, Harmon Killebrew, not known to be fleet of foot, stole twice in one inning. Everybody ran, as the Twins swiped 115 bases that season, fourth most in baseball. Killebrew stole eight bases in 1969—more than his previous 10 years combined. It didn't take away from his normal game, either, as he was the American League Most Valuable Player that season while tying a career high with 49 home runs. He also led the league with 140 RBI and 145 walks. Carew won his first batting title with a .332 average. Oliva led in hits and doubles.

The diamond became a campus of chaos under Martin. And once opponents realized that Martin could throw literally anything at them, it sped up the game on them. And that's when mistakes are made. The Twins lost their first four games in 1969 but finished April 13–7 as Billy Ball began to flourish. Oakland, led by 23-year-old Reggie Jackson, hung around until midseason. The Twins won the second game of a doubleheader at Kansas City on June 29, during which Oliva went 5-for-5 with a 517-foot home run off Dave Wickersham. That victory kicked off a 20–4 run by the Twins that gave them a four-game lead over the Athletics. Oakland crept within a game a couple of times the rest of the season, but the Twins put them away in September with a 17–12 spurt.

Fans, players and media got the full Billy Martin experience in 1969. He complained about umpires, stadiums, the schedule and even his farm system. Martin was ready to take on the entire Griffith family when they sent pitching prospects Charley Walters and Bill Zepp to Class AA Charlotte instead of Class AAA Denver. That probably didn't sit well with the owner. Walters ended up having a short baseball career but a lengthy one as a sportswriter for the *St. Paul Pioneer Press*.

Kaat pitched on a Saturday in Cleveland around the time his father suffered a stroke. Kaat asked Martin for permission, and received it, to visit his father in Michigan. When Griffith asked where Kaat was, Martin told him that he had missed the flight. Once back in Minnesota, Griffith called Kaat into his office to confront him about leaving the team. Kaat explained that he had received permission to leave. "I'm finding out that Billy has lied to me about a few things this season," Griffith replied. It's not a good sign when the owner loses trust in his manager.

The big eruption came on August 7 while the Twins were in Detroit. Players and coaches were at the historic Lindell Athletic Club, located down the street from Tiger Stadium. Right-hander Dave Boswell—on the way to his first and only 20-win season—was confronted by Fowler for not getting his wind sprints in earlier in the day. An argument ensued, with Bob Allison pulling Boswell out of the bar to calm him down. Somehow, Boswell decked Allison. Martin rushed out of the bar to engage Boswell, who eventually ended up unconscious.

How Boswell ended up there was a matter of contention. Martin said Boswell went after him and landed the first punch. Boswell said he was held by four people while Martin worked him over. Boswell woke up in a hospital, needing stitches over his left eye and his upper lip. Martin disputed that people held Boswell up, asserting that Boswell sucker-punched him to start the skirmish.

"I was staying on the same floor as Boz," Kaat said. "When I got up in the morning, he had come out of his room at the same time. I said, 'What happened to you?' His eyes were black and blue, and he was headed back to Minnesota. There are two sides to every story and only one is right. When Billy took him back there, I can't believe he did what he did by himself. I think he had a couple of his posse from the Lindell AC take him back there, because he took a pretty good beating."

Boswell was 6 feet, 3 inches tall and 185 pounds. Martin was 5 feet, 11 inches tall and 165 pounds—and 40 years old. Does amateur boxing make that much of a difference? Griffith flew to Washington, D.C., to meet with the combatants, then fined Boswell. What was confirmed was that Boswell punched Allison. The origin of Boswell's injuries, whether it was one-on-one or one-on-four, were not determined at the time. Griffith, in his biography, said he never learned the truth about what happened that night until five years later. "They were the tightest-lipped people I ever saw," he said. "I found out somebody held up Boswell and Martin beat on him."

Boswell missed two weeks but came back strong, finishing the season 8–4 with a 2.79 ERA. It was the pinnacle of his career. He pitched tremendously in Game 2 of the ALCS, matching the Orioles' Dave McNally for 10 innings. But he felt excruciating pain in his shoulder while striking out Frank Robinson to end the 10th. He went back out for the 11th and walked two while getting two outs. He yielded to the bullpen, and Ron Perranoski gave up a walk-off RBI single to Curt Motton to end the game. Boswell was never the same pitcher.

The Twins led Oakland by just 5½ games at the start of September but promptly won six of their first seven games—which included taking three of four at Oakland—to put plenty of cushion between themselves and the A's. The Twins won the final game of the series in a 16–4 rout that included a grand slam by Killebrew. The scuffle between Martin and Boswell had blown over by then. When Martin received a shotgun late in the season, he gave it to Boswell because he knew it was the gauge he was looking for. The Twins clinched on September 22, and Martin was pictured drinking champagne out of an oversized glass. "What I did as a player never impresses me," he said. "But as a leader of a team that has won, that impresses me much more." Martin was ejected from three games during the season, lipped off to everyone and punched out his pitcher. But he was the talk of the town. The *Minneapolis Star* even published a story that included Martin's recipes for spaghetti sauce and meatballs.

The division championship was a showdown between Billy Ball and the Earl of Weaver for the AL title. Baltimore skipper Earl Weaver loved the three-run homer and had a strong starting rotation anchored by 20-game winners Mike Cuellar and Dave McNally. The series turned out as lopsided as Boswell versus Martin. Baltimore won the first two games of the series in extra innings. Jim Kaat, who had beaten the Orioles twice during the regular season, was ready to pitch in Game 3. Martin instead started Bob Miller, whose 5–5 regular season record was dwarfed by Kaat's 14 wins. Part of Martin's reasoning was that Miller pitched well during the heat of the playoff race. Miller failed to make it out of the second inning in Game 3, and the Orioles ran out to 11–2 winners to knock the Twins out of the postseason. And Kaat never pitched in the series.

"Sure, a lot of people wanted Kaat to pitch today, and they are just second-guessing," Martin said. "If Miller throws a one-hitter, I'm a genius. If Kaat starts and gets bombed, then these second-guessers would ask why I didn't go with Miller."

Well, the owner, Calvin Griffith, wanted Martin to start Kaat in Game 3. Going against the owner's wishes—regardless of whether he's meddling in areas he shouldn't—is not a good idea. Not when the manager has been controversial, fought his pitcher, given a blow-by-blow account of it and questioned the acumen of the minor league director.

Fans and media were stunned when Griffith announced that Martin would not return as manager. He had led them to 97 wins. The team reflected Martin—scrappy, hard-nosed and unyielding. Several players had career years. They did not know what was behind the scenes. Bill Rigney replaced Martin and led the Twins to 98 wins in 1970, but Baltimore swept them in the playoffs for the second consecutive season.

Martin would go on to be one of the more memorable managers in baseball history. Everywhere he went, teams improved. Everywhere he went, he would eventually tick someone off and get fired. But he made the playoffs five times, winning two pennants. His one World Series title came with the Yankees in 1977. New York was where Martin and owner George Steinbrenner became one of the most combustible couples in baseball.

Those behind the scenes saw Martin's other side. "If social media was around then..." Kaat said. "If you could put him in the dugout and let him run the game and then lock him in his room it would have been perfect. He was a great game manager."

The Twins won World Series titles in 1987 and 1991 and lost a World Series in 1965. It can be argued that Martin's bunch in 1969 was the fourth-best Twins team ever.

17

Tom Kelly

CARL POHLAD PURCHASED THE TWINS FROM CALVIN GRIFFITH in 1984, and the club remains under family control. There have been plenty of highs and lows during that time.

Pohlad is remembered for his attempts to motivate the state legislature to build a new revenue-generating stadium. He was willing to contribute money to the deal, but it was discovered that it was only a loan that would be paid back to him. He threatened to sell the team to someone who would move it to North Carolina, but a stadium bill there fell apart. Then he threatened to contract the team, but a judge ruled that the team had to honor its lease at the Metrodome.

On the field, Pohlad ordered a payroll purge that led to 18 rookies being used in 1999 as well as 2000. Consequently, some fans don't view the Pohlad family in a positive light. Many hoped he would sell the team to someone who would keep it in Minnesota.

But there are a couple things Pohlad was spot-on about. One was hiring Andy MacPhail as general manager then later promoting him to executive vice president of baseball operations. The other move was settling on Tom Kelly as manager.

Kelly was not the first choice. Pohlad had offered a two-year contract to Jim Frey to run the team, but Frey turned it down because he wanted a longer deal. Frey eventually signed with the Cubs' broadcast team as an analyst. They also spoke with Joe Torre and Chuck Cottier. Kelly was only 36 at the time, which gave Pohlad pause. Pohlad was not a baseball man but understood that the best organizations have the right decision makers at various levels. He hired MacPhail and, eventually, signed off on Kelly. Those two moves set the Twins up for two World Series runs.

Who had a better 1987 season, Jim Frey from a broadcast booth or Tom Kelly holding the Commissioner's Trophy?

Kelly might have been 36, but he acted—and looked—older than that. He had a good feel for players and believed that the game is about them, and he could put them in the best position to win games. Kelly would have had problems with modern research departments handing him data to help him manage games. "All that analytic stuff they use today," Kent Hrbek said, "it's already up in T.K.'s head."

And just because Kelly was 36 didn't mean he was inexperienced as a manager.

He was an eighth-round pick by the Seattle Pilots in 1968. He ended up in the Twins organization in 1971 and toiled there before he was called up for 49 glorious games in 1975. On May 26, he hit the only home run of his career, coming off Detroit's Vern Ruhle and landing in the overhang in right field at Tiger Stadium. That was his statistical highlight. He batted .181 in his only big-league stint.

Kelly spent a season with Rochester (New York) of the Orioles organization before returning to the Twins, and Tacoma, in 1977. But his role had expanded. At age 26, Kelly was named player-manager of Tacoma. Tacoma was 40–49 when he took over, then 28–26 under his watch. He returned to managing two years later, after exhausting every chance to return to the majors. He managed two years at Class A Visalia then two years at Class AA Orlando. He was named manager of the year in each of his last three seasons. So when Kelly joined Billy Gardner's staff in 1983, he had some games under his belt. He understood the nuances of the game and the importance of fundamentals. He was there for two-plus seasons of Gardner then, after Gardner was fired during the 1985 season, 100 games under Ray Miller. Kelly was Miller's right-hand man, the only coach allowed to dress in Miller's quarters in the Metrodome. As a third base coach, he took calculated risks based on how the game flowed. When Miller was fired on September 12, 1986, club president Howard Fox named Kelly interim manager for the final 23 games of the regular season.

Kelly made it clear to the players that he wanted the job. When he expressed his intentions, he was talking to a club-house with several familiar faces. Tim Laudner, Gary Gaetti, Frank Viola and Greg Gagne were among the players Kelly had managed in the minors. They understood his tendencies and knew he was firm, yet fair. And they knew he went with his gut when he felt it was appropriate. Kelly knew they could play. It was a good fit for a first-time major league manager.

"T.K. was always a real student of the game," Hrbek said. "He was already thinking about the seventh inning when it was the second or third inning, who is coming up or whatever. I know many times in the dugout he would ask Dick Such, the pitching coach, 'What should we do here?' Such would say,

'We probably should bunt him over.' T.K. says, 'Fuck it, we're going to let him swing.' He was asking for opinions but still went with his gut."

Kelly went 12–11 in those 23 games, which was met with favorable reviews. Bert Blyleven did not play for Kelly in the minors but noticed that his arrival had a calming effect on the players who had experience with him as well as the rest of the team. Blyleven saw good things around the corner, to the point that, after the final game of 1986, he grabbed a microphone and told fans that a special season was possible in 1987 if everyone worked to be the best they could be.

MacPhail noticed the same things, as well. And that influenced his decision to recommend Kelly for the job to an owner who had some reservations about going with such a young manager.

"You know, I really wasn't terribly concerned about it," MacPhail said. "I've said on many occasions, really the last 23 games of '86, the team played with so much more energy and enthusiasm that to me, with the pick of T.K., there wasn't much risk in it from my point of view because it was already apparent that the players trusted him, they responded to him. So it took me a while to get that across the finish line with ownership."

Kelly was 36, MacPhail was 33. Ralph Houk, a baseball lifer, was hired as vice president of baseball just to have someone with experience around while the two youngsters took the franchise to new heights.

First, there was spring training in 1987. Kelly used his first camp to stress fundamentals and individual improvement, like Tom Brunansky being more selective at the plate, Frank Viola learning how to problem solve on the mound or Greg Gagne becoming more of a base-stealing threat. MacPhail continued to add players, trading for closer Jeff Reardon just before camp opened then adding Dan Gladden in a March trade. The Twins also had to keep Kirby Puckett out of jail, as an Orlando police officer threatened to arrest him because his batting practice home runs were smashing cars that had no business being parked on the other side of the fence. MacPhail had done his part to give a Kelly an improved roster that didn't include any criminals.

Kelly's first full season was a grind, as the Twins went 85–77 and were outscored 806–786. Puckett, Hrbek, Gaetti and Brunansky all belted at least 28 home runs. Dan Gladden stole 25 bases while providing speed at the top. The starting rotation lacked depth but had two of the best pitchers in the league that season in Frank Viola, who was 17–10 with a 2.90 ERA, and Bert Blyleven, who was 15–12 with a 4.01 ERA. Juan Berenguer brought the heat as a setup man, and Reardon saved 31 games.

Kelly made it all work. His approach was simple: play the game the right way and he would make a few moves in the final innings to win. The Twins were nails at the Metrodome that season, going 56–25 for a gaudy winning percentage of .691. They were terrible on the road, going 29–52 for a .358 winning percentage. The Twins tried several things to improve their luck on the road, including hanging pictures of the Dome in visitors' clubhouses to inspire them. No such luck.

One of the crises Kelly had to navigate was road success, or lack of it. Especially in August as the Twins held on to a lead in the AL West. They were five games ahead of Oakland heading into a six-game road trip to Detroit and Boston. They were outscored 26–3 while getting swept in Detroit. Then they were swept in three games at Boston, blowing a 4–0 lead on getaway day. Their lead was down to two games as they walked out of the visitors' clubhouse at Fenway Park and headed for the charter bus to take them to the airport.

"Guys are going, 'What the hell? We are scoring seven runs and we can't win a game,'" Roy Smalley said. "Guys were grousing a little bit about pitching not holding up. I was walking and listening to the little comments and I'm looking around and I don't see T.K. anywhere. I was a little worried about the manager hearing talk like that. I didn't see T.K. anywhere. We all get on the bus, and T.K. is the last one. He gets on and he tells the driver to wait a second.

"He stands in the middle aisle at the front of the bus and says, 'OK, listen. We're all rowing this boat together. It's going to be with us all pulling the oars together. So I don't want to hear anything about pitching because there are going to be times where hitters let them down and vice versa. We've got what we've got and we're going to try to win this thing rowing the boat at the same time in the same direction.' Then he turns around and sits down. I hadn't heard too many manager meetings, whether they were called or whether they were spontaneous, like that one where the message was as needed as that one was, and the impact was as great."

It wasn't about changing their fortunes on the road. It was about keeping the clubhouse from imploding to a point where it didn't matter if they were on the road or at home when they lost. The Twins won 17 of their next 27 games after that, then clinched the division the next week. It was their first division title in 17 years and Kelly, now 37, had brought them there. The Twins knocked off the favored Tigers in five games to reach their second World Series.

As speculation mounted over Kelly's ability to manage under National League rules, another side of the rookie skipper was coming into view. Kelly wasn't used to being second-guessed. At that time in his career, he bristled at times when questioned about his strategy. But that is going to happen when a manager occasionally makes decisions based on the book, his personnel or his guts. Hours before Game 6 at the Metrodome, Kelly confronted *Star Tribune* sportswriter Dennis Brackin about a story he wrote in which Game 6 starter Les Straker said his back and right shoulder were sore. He also wrote a story about Kelly opting for a three-man rotation for the series, which didn't allow Blyleven to be available for Game 6. Kelly exploded with profanities as Brackin explained his reasoning. Kelly then stormed off.

Kelly had a humorous side, was eloquent at his best moments and showed, occasionally, that he could be sympathetic. He didn't show these sides often. He was driven to get players to perform up to their capabilities.

My first season as a Twins beat writer was 1998, right after the Twins traded Chuck Knoblauch to the Yankees. I was not as good as I thought I was, which was evident when Kelly would get mad when I wanted to know why a certain left-handed hitter wasn't starting against a left-handed pitcher. I should have known the matchups and the history between the hitter and pitcher. It forced me to begin predicting the next day's lineup as soon as I was off deadline the night before, or at least the next morning. It took a while to screw my head on straight, but I was better prepared when I walked into his office. He was less prickly about explaining his decisions as the years went by, if questions about strategy were phrased the right way. He also mitigated scrutiny with an opening monologue about how the game had gone.

Kelly was known to snap at anyone. But there were moments when he was insightful and enlightening. He also had a thing for the television series *Murder, She Wrote*, starring Angela Lansbury. I would walk into his office, particularly on the road and particularly in Cleveland, to find Kelly either reclining or laid out on a sofa while watching the show intently. I would chat him up for a couple of minutes, then move on and wait for the official media pregame session. Those were the moments he seemed to be the most human.

But there were times when his laughter could he heard through the clubhouse. Like everyone else, he liked having his fun. And he liked jokes. There was one spring training in Fort Myers, Florida, when I was in the minor league facility interviewing Jim Rantz, the farm director, about a few prospects. I was about to leave for the major league clubhouse when Rantz asked if I could take a box of supplies earmarked for assistant general manager Wayne Krivsky with me because it had been delivered to the wrong location. So this slightly husky sportswriter walked out of the minor league offices and headed for Hammond Stadium with a large box balanced on a shoulder. I walked past one of the practice fields while Kelly was working with some players. From about 100 yards away, I hear Kelly bellow, 'Hey La Velle, is that your lunch?!' as players broke up with laughter. I laughed too, as I imagined what I must have looked like walking with a big box on my shoulder. Later that day, I walked into his office and said, 'Man, you don't miss anything.' Kelly chomped on his cigar and replied, 'Thats why I get paid the big bucks." Too bad Kelly didn't show that side more often. My baseball editor—Dennis Brackin—often wished I had someone easier to deal with during my early years on the beat. I respectfully disagree. Tom Kelly helped me become a better beat writer.

By the time I got on the beat, Kelly had won two World Series. When the Twins vanquished the Cardinals in 1987, there was a dogpile at home plate as the final out was made. Kelly, however, hung back by the dugout, content to watch his players celebrate rather than join in. "Stay here," Kelly told first base coach Wayne Terwilliger. "This is better right here. This is the best place in the house." Kelly had just become the youngest non-playing manager to win a World Series since John McGraw in 1905, but it was about the players.

The next time he won a title, Kelly ventured out on the field a little further. You would too, after being part of one of the greatest World Series ever.

In 1990, the Twins finished in last place in the American League West division with a 74–88 record. Gary Gaetti and Juan Berenguer departed as free agents. The Twins needed upgrades, and executive vice president of baseball operations Andy MacPhail found new ingredients to throw into the pot in third baseman Mike Pagliarulo, designated hitter Chili Davis and right-hander Jack Morris. They also gave rookie second baseman Chuck Knoblauch a chance to prove he was ready for the majors.

MacPhail believed the 1990 season wasn't bad as the record showed. But no one believed that the offseason moves were enough to make the 1991 Twins a contender. The returning players felt 1991 was going to a redemption campaign.

The campaign needed time to get on track, as the Twins started off 20–24. Then Scott Erickson went on a run during which he won 12 consecutive decisions and became the darling of baseball. He wasn't the only one who got on a roll. The Twins went on a 24–3 tear that had them in control of the division in June. Kelly had a juggernaut on his hands. The Twins pulled away from the pack in August and clinched the division title with seven games remaining. The Twins defeated the Blue Jays in five games to win the AL Championship and the right to face the Atlanta Braves, led by Bobby Cox. Both teams had finished in last place in their respective divisions the previous season.

Much of the talk before the series was about Kelly having to manage by National League rules when the games were played in Atlanta. Could he use the double switch effectively? How would he handle pitching moves late in games because of their presence in the lineup? A better question would have been if Kelly was ready to age 20 years in the span of two weeks. The Twins and Braves proceeded to have a series for the ages. Five games were decided by one run. Four were won in the final at-bat. All those close games meant both managers were pushing buttons like a court stenographer to try to squeeze more runs out of the lineups. And it can get nerve-racking for a manager when those plans fail.

By Game 7, the series was already considered one of the best ever. The "Puckett Game" allowed the Twins to tie the series at 3–3, with star outfielder Kirby Puckett stealing an extra-base hit from Ron Gant then hitting a walk-off homer in the 11th. Game 7 was the stage for another tremendous individual effort—brought on by Kelly's internal battle between his head and his guts. Right-hander Jack Morris had pitched out of a two on, no out jam in the eighth inning, followed by a 1-2-3 ninth. Morris headed for the dugout knowing he wanted to remain in the game.

Kelly approached Morris and told him he couldn't ask for anything more from him. Rick Aguilera was warming up for the 10th inning. But Morris wanted the 10th. "Jack said he was fine," Kelly said. "[Pitching coach] Dick Such said he was fine. What the heck? It's just a game."

Morris pitched a 1-2-3 10th inning. Gene Larkin's pinch hit single in the bottom of the inning scored Dan Gladden with the winning run. And the party was on. Modern managers aren't letting their pitchers throw beyond seven innings, let alone 10. If the 1991 World Series had been played in 2021, there's little chance Morris is allowed to pitch into the 10th. Kelly's decision was one of the greatest gut decisions ever.

Success in baseball often is through a collaboration between talent and leadership. Can a manager lose a clubhouse and create a toxic culture of losing? Absolutely. But good players often make coaches and managers look good. The best movie directors love working with professionals, or the show is not going to be fit for even community television. Tom Kelly was the same with baseball. He didn't mind teaching the game but was a master at running it. But in the years following the 1991 series, the Twins' roster nosedived. Kent Hrbek retired after 1994. Kirby Puckett was forced to retire because of glaucoma after 1995. Scott Erickson was traded in July of 1995 for Scott Klingenbeck and Kimera Bartee. After 1992, the Twins had eight consecutive losing seasons. The talent cratered.

By the late 1990s owner Carl Pohlad, who was frustrated over not getting a new stadium, reduced the payroll. Kelly had 18 rookies to deal with in 1999 and another 18 in 2000. Kelly, in 2000, won his 1,000th game. At the behest of a team official, he took a moment to tip his cap to the crowd before a video tribute was played on the scoreboard. Kelly had to be cajoled. It's about the players, not the manager.

Around this time, there were rumblings that Kelly was too hard on young players and that the game was passing him by. There was a lot of losing, there were many teaching moments and Kelly would jump down a few throats and bench players if they weren't playing the game the right way. Kelly pulled right-hander Joe Mays from a start in Seattle after two innings when it looked like Mays had lost his composure over strikes that were called balls. There was a game at Kansas City during which Kelly blamed Torii Hunter for missing a sign. When Hunter objected, Kelly held a re-enactment after the game. Kelly stopped the Kauffman Stadium ground crew from raking the field and put Hunter on first base, third base coach Scott Ullger in his box and Denny Hocking as the batter. Ullger, like he had during the game, flashed a sign. Hunter responded. Hunter and Kelly then got into a heated discussion about what sign was given.

Despite playing with the major league club for most of 1999, Doug Mientkiewicz and Todd Walker were cut during the following training camp. Mientkiewicz said playing for Kelly was like "walking on eggshells," while Walker demanded a trade. Kelly's approach rubbed some players the wrong way. Others credit Kelly for helping them play the game the right way.

Hunter said that, later in his career, he better understood Kelly's methods. He was more cerebral as a hitter and used all fields more—things Kelly worked on him about. "I went back to T.K. later in my career and said, 'Man, I want to apologize because I could have been a little more respectful. And I can understand what you were trying to do.'" Hunter said. "He couldn't put it into words, but his message was that he was trying to help you. When you get wiser you actually see what he was trying to teach me. What T.K. did for my career, it actually gave it longevity."

The same day Kelly won his 1,000[th] game—May 7—the *Star Tribune* learned that the Twins were looking at expanding the role of executive Chris Clouser. A couple weeks later, Clouser was named the Twins' first-ever CEO. Clouser pushed to re-sign right-hander Brad Radke to a four-year, $36 million extension before he reached free agency. He pushed to have an outdoor series played in a temporary stadium in Bloomington in September, which was turned down by the league because of time constraints. And his main goal was to drum up support for building a new stadium.

Clouser also wanted to replace Kelly as manager, which, of course, didn't go over well with the skipper. Before Kelly's fate could be determined, Clouser abruptly resigned in December, stating that Pohlad should be the one making key decisions. Kelly was motivated to prove Clouser—and those who felt he was a relic—wrong. He was optimistic. By September of 2000, the Twins were playing better. There were fewer mistakes; players had gained confidence and become a tight-knit group. Kelly had good reasons for optimism. The 2001 Twins began the season 50–31 before slumping to an 85–77 finish. The program was on the upswing, as the Twins won six division titles in the 2000s. And Kelly's work was done. He retired following the 2001 season, citing wear and tear through the years. But he stuck it to the doubters on his way out. "I heard more than once that some people thought the game had passed me by," Kelly said the day he announced his retirement. "That really upset me. I knew I wanted to do it one more year to see if we did the right things with the people we invested our time with. I think we did."

Kelly won 85 games in his first full season as a manager. And he closed his career by winning 85 games in 2001. There were a few tumultuous moments along the way, but few head coaches or managers of professional sports teams in Minnesota were as successful as Tom Kelly was. There is one—Cheryl Reeve, who won four titles with the Minnesota Lynx of the WNBA. The NFL Vikings lost four Super Bowls. The NBA Timberwolves and the NHL Wild have not even reached a championship series. There's not a lot of company with him at the top.

And keep in mind that the only reason Kelly was hired before the 1987 season was because of the 23-game tryout he had in 1986. Howard Fox could have waited until after the season to fire Ray Miller. Instead, he gave Kelly a chance to prove himself worthy. And he did.

"We had the opportunity to watch him manage 23 games," MacPhail said, "or history would have been different."

18

Ron Gardenhire

THE TWINS WERE EMERGING FROM THE CONTRACTION ZONE in 2002. Contraction was Major League Baseball's threat to convince Minnesota lawmakers that the Twins were going to be disbanded if they didn't approve funding for a new stadium. The Twins weren't going to be contracted, but no one was sure of that at the time. So the Twins, their employees and their fans had one nervous offseason before the 2002 campaign.

Not long after the conclusion of the 2001 season, MLB owners voted 28–2 to contract two teams, one being the Twins. Instead of following the Twins' efforts to improve an already talented offense in an attempt to return to the postseason for the first time since 1991, fans were tormented by the possibility that their beloved Twins would cease to exist. Could owner Carl Pohlad really accept a check to disband the team? Was it a hollow threat?

No one knew then that Hennepin County judge Harry Crump was going to save baseball in Minnesota by ordering the Twins to honor their lease at the Metrodome. Right after GM Terry Ryan declined an interview request from Toronto for a similar role, he pushed Pohlad to proceed as if there were going to be a 2002 season. Ownership realized that employee retention would be a growing problem the longer they waited to see if Crump's ruling would be overturned.

It was getting too close to spring training for the Twins to learn of their fate, so they proceeded as if they were going to play. Tom Kelly had stepped down following the 2001 season. So it was time to name Kelly's successor and start planning spring training workouts. The choice was Ron Gardenhire, the confirmed "futility infielder" as a player, who had been on Kelly's coaching staff for 11 seasons and become a valued lieutenant. He would be the Twins' 12th manager in their history.

Gardenhire came to the Twins as a player, in a trade with the Mets before the 1987 season. He failed to make the team out of spring training and missed out on the 1987 World Series run. Al Newman, who would one day coach under Gardenhire, beat him out for the utility role. Gardenhire spent that season playing for Class AAA Portland then began his managing career at Class A Kenosha in 1988. After three seasons managing in the minors, Gardenhire joined Kelly's staff in 1991 and was the third base coach for the Twins' second World Series run. He has joked that his big mistake was not running alongside Dan Gladden as he scored the winning run in Game 7 on Gene Larkin's single over a drawn-in outfield. Gardenhire would have been in all the photos and video clips. Instead, Gardenhire went to the stands to shake commissioner Fay Vincent's hand. He would not make such a blunder as manager.

After interviewing with San Francisco, Kansas City, Colorado and the Cubs—losing out to Dusty Baker, to Bob Boone and twice to Don Baylor—2002 was Gardenhire's chance to run a major league club. And it was a good one. The 2001 Twins were 50–31 at the season's halfway point. It was a dangerous mix of young players with upside and a few veterans. The Twins fell apart during the second half, with a shoulder injury suffered by shortstop Cristian Guzmán—which cost him 33 games—being the biggest blow. Guzman still led the league with 14 triples that season after hitting 20 the year before. Wait 'til next year, because the Twins were about to turn the corner.

The media had joined fans in suffering from contraction fatigue by that point. The future of the team was still up in the air, but pitchers and catchers were due to report to Fort Myers, Florida, in a month's time. Gardenhire's hiring was a reason to talk baseball again. And Gardenhire was asked during a post–press conference huddle what his lineup was going to be.

"Jacque Jones is my leadoff hitter," Gardenhire said, to the surprise of the questioner.

Jones had experience batting leadoff, but more experience batting lower than that. Gardenhire believed in Jones, feeling that the outfielder had gotten into a rut the year before and never recovered. He was going to be Gardenhire's everyday left fielder. The season opener was in Kansas City, and Jones led off the game with an opposite-field blast over the left-center field wall, an outcome predicted by teammate Denny Hocking. Jones hit 11 leadoff home runs that season while batting .300 with 27 home runs and 85 RBI—the best season of his career. And his 11 leadoff homers tied for the fourth most ever. Teammates called Jones "1–0" because of his proclivity for hitting leadoff home runs. Jones ordered a vanity license plate with the nickname, spelling it 1NUTHIN'.

That's one effect Gardenhire had on players. He knew the ones he could ride and the ones who needed support. He was sharp, enthusiastic, humorous and, as Michael Cuddyer said, "a great guy." Most importantly, Gardenhire, who spent five years with the Mets and jokes that he was Rusty Staub's personal pinch runner, always kept in mind how long the season is and how hard it is to play the game. That influenced how he dealt with players through the years. He wanted his players to play with free minds, promising them that it was the best way for their talent to show.

Gardenhire was a down-to-earth fellow you wouldn't mind having for a next-door neighbor. He was born in Butzbach, West Germany, where his father, Clyde, was a first sergeant in the Army. The family moved to Oklahoma when he retired from the service. Ron Gardenhire grew up in Okmulgee, Oklahoma, located about 40 miles south of Tulsa down Route 75, a working-class town that enjoyed supporting sports. Gardenhire was an All-State baseball player there before moving on to Paris (Texas) Junior College, then the University of Texas, where he set a school record with 10 RBI in one game. The Mets drafted him in the sixth round in 1979 and he debuted in the majors two years later. "I learned pretty quick that I would be a utility infielder," he said. He did form a connection with Staub, a Mets legend who excelled as a pinch hitter later in his career. And if Staub reached base, Gardenhire often pinch ran for him. Staub was a restaurant owner, and Gardenhire spent hours dining with him and talking baseball.

Gardenhire played one season for Class AAA Portland, on a team that went 45–96 but one, Gardenhire said, that he learned a lot from. Charlie Manuel, who would manage Cleveland and Philadelphia in the majors, was Portland's skipper then. Future Twins Billy Beane, Sal Butera, Chris Pittaro, Gene Larkin and Allan Anderson were among Gardenhire's teammates. Butera was there for only 10 games, but it was a memorable 10 games.

A couple of Gardenhire's best stories are from that 1987 team. One was when he was using the bathroom but could hear Manuel—who was nearby and talking to fans in the stands before a game—berating all his players. The other was after another blowout loss. Manuel was berating the team when he spotted Butera and asked, "How many games you been here, Sal?"

Butera: "I've only been here 10 games."

Manuel: "How many games you won since you've been here?"

Butera: "We've won one."

"Chris Pittaro yells, 'Get rid of Sal!'" Gardenhire said. "Charlie spins around and was like, 'Fuck you guys.'"

Years later, someone told Manuel Gardenhire's version of the story.

"I think it was Gardy who said that," Manuel said.

Gardenhire was a change of pace from the rigid and occasionally acerbic Kelly. But Kelly did win two World Series titles that way. Fundamentals, attention to detail and playing the game with honor were important to Kelly, and that rubbed off on Gardenhire. They just went about things differently. The contrasting personalities were evident among players. "He was definitely a player's manager," said outfielder Torii Hunter, a five-time All-Star and nine-time Gold Glove winner. "All of us who came to Gardy in 2002 were T.K.'s products. We were happy to have Gardy because he was the one we all had relationships with. We'd talk to Gardy or his coaches, Jerry White and Scott Ullger. We didn't have that type of relationship with Tom Kelly."

Hunter also won two Silver Slugger awards, at ages 33 and 37, as he got smarter as a hitter and realized he was applying a lot of things Kelly tried to teach him. He apologized to Kelly later in his career for not realizing it sooner. But, with Gardenhire, he could walk into his office and talk with him about anything—as long as he didn't pick up anything on his desk. Gardenhire didn't have a great relationship with everyone. But most of the players on his watch enjoyed their time with the Twins.

"He played several pranks on me," Hunter said. "The one I liked, I was nervous about it. He asked for an autograph. I grabbed the ball and I grabbed the pen and when I pressed down on it, it shocked me. My heart dropped. I was like, 'What's happening?' He was on the ground laughing and crying. I actually saw him give someone a hotfoot. This is our manager, giving hotfoots. I'm like, oh, I like him even more now."

Gardenhire could have used instant replay during his career. But it didn't exist, and he ended up getting tossed from 71 games—a Twins record—then 13 times in two-plus seasons running the Tigers. He set the Tigers' single-season ejection record with eight in 2019. Gardenhire would rather take the fall than see his player get booted from a game and hurt the team. Players appreciated that.

He wasn't afraid to show his human side when players had off-the-field issues. He comforted Corey Koskie and let him be with his family when his wife suffered a miscarriage. And he immediately let Michael Cuddyer join his family when his father-in-law passed away.

"It was no questions asked," Cuddyer said. "He said, 'You need to be on the first flight out of here to get home to Virginia. Then you come back when your wife's ready for you to come back.' That always spoke volumes and always really meant a lot to me. Because it's our job and it's a pressure-packed job and you can't afford to spend time away from the team because of everything that's involved. But at the same time, we're humans and we have families and there's other people that are impacted by our profession and by our career. And Gardy never really lost sight of that."

But when everyone was comfortable, Gardenhire made things uncomfortable. His desk was a minefield of props. It had a pen, a calculator and a can of soda, all designed to shock anyone who tried to use them. There was a box with a sliding top that had a fake mouse attached to a wire; when someone opened the box, the mouse would hop out and nip their wrist. He was the manager who pranked his players. He used the exploding golf ball trick on David Ortiz at a charity tournament, although Ortiz screwed up the bit by missing the ball. He asked Mike Pelfrey, who attended Wichita State, to give a pep talk to the Shockers before they played in the NCAA tournament one year. Pelfrey yelled into the speakerphone while left-hander Glen Perkins and clubhouse attendants were on the other end, pretending they were members of the team.

He was occasionally a victim of his own pranks. One morning during spring training, I walked into Gardenhire's office to say hello. I had no idea he had a busy morning that included cutting players from camp, something managers hate doing. "Hey, I've got a lot of shit going on today," he said. "I've got to send down some players. I've got injuries. I don't have a lineup yet because I've got guys in the trainer's room." While he was rattling off his to-do list, Gardenhire shuffled items that were on his desk, like schedules and lineup cards. Then he grabbed the can of soda. "Ah! I shocked myself!" he yelped. I wished him a good day and left his office.

Eventually, we'll get back to baseball. In 2014, Gardenhire was named the recipient of the Mike Augustin Media Good Guy Award at the annual Diamond Awards banquet, an award voted on by writers who covered the team. Truthfully, he could have won every year he managed the Twins. He was a reporter's dream. As a player, he helped legendary New York writer Marty Noble win contests for the best quotes. Gardenhire knocked it out of the park during his first press conference as manager. When asked about running his first spring training camp, the balding manager replied, "Maybe I'll come up with something different. Maybe I'll wear hair." Then he was asked if he could go without being ejected from games like Kelly, who was tossed five times over 2,385 games. "Absolutely not," Gardenhire said, "I'm not as diplomatic as T.K."

One year during spring training, Gardenhire was asked about the fitness of portly left-hander José Mijares. "Is Mijares in shape?" a reporter asked. "He's in *a shape*," Gardenhire replied.

Even when he was inducted into the Twins Hall of Fame in 2022, he had a quip for the few dozen former players who traveled to Minnesota for the ceremony. "Some of these guys got me fired," he said.

Some of those guys also were responsible for Gardenhire winning six AL Central titles, the first coming in his inaugural season of 2002. The team was hungry after its second-half fade the year before. Jacque Jones thrived under Gardenhire that season, leading the team with 5.5 WAR. Corey Koskie, who had spent previous offseasons taking grounders from Gardenhire at the University of Minnesota to improve his defense, batted .267 with 15 homers, 69 RBI and 72 walks and tied for the team lead with 37 doubles. Hunter was selected for his first All-Star Game and hit .289 with 29 home runs, 94 RBI and 23 stolen bases. Rick Reed, traded to the Twins by the Mets during the previous season, went 15–7 with a 3.78 ERA. Closer Eddie Guardado saved 45 games and headed a bullpen that included two other talented lefties in J.C. Romero and a young Johan Santana.

They all knew Gardenhire the coach. They were about to get Gardenhire the manager. Same guy. Different role. More pranks.

"I expect players to work hard and play hard," he told the *Minneapolis Star Tribune* before his first game as manager. "But in general, my philosophy is, 'There's nothing wrong with having a little fun at the ballpark.'"

If a baseball season was a horse race, the Twins had a good trip in 2002. They were 16–11 in April and played above-.500 ball in each month. A six-game winning streak had them in first place on May 4, and they never fell out of first the rest of the season. That didn't stop fans from fretting about a repeat of the crash of 2001. This time, the Twins led the White Sox by 7½ games at the break and didn't relinquish it. They had lost Brad Radke, Joe Mays and Eric Milton to various injuries during the season, but decent starting depth and a terrific bullpen made up for their losses. Gardenhire, while dealing with injuries during the first half of the season, also saw inconsistent play. He decided to rest his regulars more during the second half in hopes of making them fresher and more productive later in the season. "All I know is I keep hearing from Chicago that they're in a better position than we are," Gardenhire said, while rolling his eyes, at the All-Star break.

The Twins put their foot on the throats of the rest of the AL Central division the rest of the way. The lead reached double digits on July 17. Radke, who missed two months, and Mays, who missed three months, returned to the rotation during the second half. The defense was excellent. The bullpen, a rock. When the Twins clinched the division on September 15, their first return to the postseason since 1991, Gardenhire called his wife, Carol, and told her to grab a beer and pour it over her head.

It was the first of six division titles under Gardenhire. It was also the team that advanced the furthest in the postseason during his tenure. They rallied from a 2–1 deficit to Oakland to win the division series. They won Game 1 against the Angels in the American League Championship Series as Mays pitched the game of his life, holding Anaheim to an unearned run over eight innings. The Twins thought they were on their way to the World Series. The Angels were just catching their breath after knocking the Yankees out in the Division Series. The Angels won the next four games and moved on to the World Series. The Twins' bullpen ran out of gas in the seventh inning of Game 5 as the Angels sent 15 batters to the plate.

The Twins resolved to go a step further in 2003, but they were eliminated by the Yankees in the ALDS. They won their third consecutive AL Central title in 2004—but met the same fate in the postseason. They won Game 1 against the Yankees before losing three straight. Game 2 was an epic 7–6 loss in 12 innings, despite Hunter's homer in the 12th that gave them a 6–5 lead. All-Star closer Joe Nathan entered his third inning of relief in the 12th but couldn't tame the Yankees.

That was one of a few decisions Gardenhire was second-guessed on. Like how he took it easy on Johan Santana and Brad Radke down the stretch when home field advantage was at stake. Jesse Crain was warmed up in the 12th in Game 2, but Gardy stuck with Nathan. Instead of going to his bench, he let Jason Kubel face Mariano Rivera—and Kubel looked bad while striking out in a key moment. "They can fire at me all they want. That's fine," Gardenhire said after the series was over. "Just don't fire at my players."

The heartbreak would continue. After a slow start in 2006, the Twins finished 70–33 to win the division on the final game of the regular season. Justin Morneau won the AL Most Valuable Player award. By the time they caught their breath following a big run to the postseason, they were done. Oakland swept them in the Division Series. They won the final four games in

2009 to force a game 163 against Detroit, which they won in 12 innings. Morneau, however, was lost for the season after September 12 with a stress fracture in his lower back. Then they were swept by the Yankees in the ALDS while scoring a total of six runs in three games. Another year, more heartbreak in 2010. Morneau suffered a concussion at midseason that ended his year. The Twins still won the division but were swept again by the Yankees, scoring seven runs in three games. Damn Yankees. Gardenhire was 6–21 in the postseason by then, 2–12 against the Yankees.

Overall, Gardenhire was 1068–1039 as the Twins' manager. He was the first Twins manager to lead a team to 90 wins in three consecutive seasons. He was Manager of the Year in 2010 and runner-up five times. He brought much joy to Twins territory. Fans kept glued to the television after games to see if Gardenhire would, once again, look into the camera and tell his wife to get the hot tub ready. But the Twins could not go on a lengthy postseason run during his career. And they lost their last 12 postseason games under Gardenhire. The playoff malaise carried over into other administrations, as the Twins entered the 2023 season with an 18-game postseason losing streak that was the longest in North American professional sports. Of his playoff teams, the 96-win team of 2006 might have been his best. So it is a little baffling how they were swept by Oakland in the first round that season.

The playoffs can be a crapshoot at times. And the Twins kept running into the Yankees, who were never an underdog in those series. Mauer and Morneau—the M&M boys—played in the postseason together once because one of them was injured and unavailable the other three years they qualified. But the Twins and Gardenhire were blamed, fairly or not, for not having more postseason success.

But the 2000s saw the Twins establish themselves as the best team in the AL Central division. They had MVPs in Morneau (2006) and Joe Mauer (2009). Johan Santana won two Cy Young Awards. Joe Nathan was a dominant closer.

Things cratered after 2010. The Twins lost 90 games for four consecutive seasons. After going 70–92 in 2014, general manager Terry Ryan decided to fire Gardenhire and replace him with Paul Molitor. Gardy didn't just pack up and leave the building after he got the pink slip. He showed up at a press conference to express how he understood the change. "I've been here a long time," Gardenhire said the day he was fired. "Sometimes people need to hear a different voice, and I have no problem with that." Gardenhire, the Army brat, wouldn't leave his post until the end.

Gardenhire joined Arizona as a bench coach in 2017, a move he warned would be a short stay because he was looking to become a manager again. But he had to leave in early April when he needed prostate cancer surgery. He returned in five weeks and finished out the season. He got the managerial job he sought a year later with Detroit but stepped down late in the 2020 season because of health concerns. He was 132–241 with the Tigers, bringing his career record to 1200–1280. It does not tarnish the work he did with the Twins, as his teams frequently reached the playoffs. His teams just couldn't beat the Yankees.

Gardenhire appears at special events at Target Field, where he's cheered by fans. He maintains a home in the Twin Cities. His retirement, however, created two unanswered questions.

One, why couldn't Gardenhire reach the World Series even once?

Two, what is he doing with all those props?

PART 6

THE MEMORABLE SEASONS

19

2001
(Contraction)

THE TWINS IN THE EARLY 1990S WERE ONE OF THE BEST-RUN franchises in baseball. Their farm system had produced the core of World Series champions in 1987 and 1991. Their trades and free-agent signings brought in players to round out the roster—like Jack Morris, who pitched 10 innings in Game 7 of a World Series. And the employees were, for the most part, loyal. And that made success sustainable.

And they were able to retain their good players, something Twins fans in the 2000s and 2010s lamented. Following the 1989 season, the Twins signed Kirby Puckett to a three-year, $9 million contract. For about a week, Puckett was the highest-paid player in baseball. Before that, Kent Hrbek had become the first Minnesota athlete to make $1 million in a season.

When they needed to add players, they acquired Dan Gladden. Bert Blyleven, an original Twin who spent time with three other teams following his first stint there, was brought back. The bearded Jeff Reardon was traded for—forcing the team to abolish its ban on facial hair.

Owner Carl Pohlad didn't know a lot about the game, but he picked the right people to run baseball operations, and the franchise succeeded.

By the mid 1990s, baseball's financial landscape had changed and so had the Twins' fortunes. In 1991, Roger Clemens made $2.5 million annually. In 1997, Albert Belle earned $10 million, $2.75 million more than Ken Griffey Jr.

The Twins weren't drawing well by the mid-'90s. Puckett's career was derailed by glaucoma. Hrbek retired unexpectedly. After winning 90 games in 1992, the Twins finished under .500 for eight consecutive seasons while larger markets enjoyed a sizeable advantage in revenue. Baseball was headed to a showdown between large-market and small-market teams over competitive balance and the generation of revenue. Labor wars dominated the mid-'90s as the 1994 season was shortened to 113 games because of a players' strike and the start of the 1995 season was delayed.

As the Twins reached the new millennium, the franchise that had won two titles threatened to launch itself into extinction and leave Upper Midwest baseball fans without a major league team to cheer for. Missteps were made that changed opinions about Pohlad. And it was a turbulent ride, to the point where they were presented as candidates for contraction.

Make sure your seatbelts are securely fastened. There were a series of attempts to leverage state legislators, who represented constituents who were skeptical of subsidizing millionaires, into caving in and passing a sweet deal to provide a state-of-the art stadium that would satisfy Pohlad's profit margin. Time and time again, stadium bills were turned down. Contraction was Pohlad's last big swing at them, and it was a doozy. Pohlad, who bought the Twins in 1984 for a reported $38 million, threatened to cease operations and walk away with a bunch of loot.

Carl Ray Pohlad was born in 1915 in Valley Junction, Iowa, before it was renamed West Des Moines. He was one of eight children raised by father, Michael, a railroad brakeman, and mother, Mary, who cleaned houses and did laundry. He went to California and sold used cars before landing a scholarship to play football at Gonzaga. After two years, he returned to Iowa and worked for a finance company before being drafted into the U.S. Army from 1943 to '46, marching through Germany, France and Austria. He was wounded in action, receiving a Purple Heart and a Bronze Star Medal. He was also a cook but found time to run a small loan business out of a mess tent. Following the war, he returned home and met his future wife, Eloise, on a blind date.

Pohlad took everything seriously. He was focused, driven and unyielding. He showed those traits as he collected loans and foreclosed on farms during the Great Depression. With the help of a partner, he acquired Marquette Bank in the 1950s. That was the first of several business ventures that helped build his net worth to $3.6 billion by the time he passed away in 2009—quite a journey from his hardscrabble days in Iowa. He was a dealmaker and regularly raked in a high rate of return for his investments. He worked until he was physically unable to and remained mentally agile well into his eighties. I visited his 38th-floor office in early 2001 for an interview, just a couple months after buying my first home. He walked into the room I was waiting for him in and said, "I heard you just bought a new house. Why didn't you finance it through us?" I didn't take it as an attempt to get in the good graces of a media member. He wanted my business for his bottom line.

Pohlad was viewed as a hero when he bought the Twins from Calvin Griffith in 1984. He felt it was his civic duty to preserve Major League Baseball in Minnesota. Keep in mind that, in 1983, Griffith flew to New York to meet with Donald Trump, when the future president of the United States offered $50 million for the team. Griffith, perhaps worried about the team possibly leaving town, instead accepted Pohlad's lesser offer. Trump owning the Twins? That would have been wild.

But feelings toward Pohlad changed in the mid-'90s. Fair or unfair, Pohlad's legacy as the owner of the Twins would be defined during that time as he sought funding for a new stadium that would increase revenues and—this is how he and his family shaped it—would allow them to retain their best players and be more competitive. How he went about it would draw the ire of Twins fans throughout the region, as the future of the franchise in Minnesota was in doubt.

The first time owner Pohlad uttered the words "new stadium" was in 1994 during a meeting with the Metropolitan Sports Facilities Commission—12 years after the Dome opened. By this time, the Twin Cities suffered from stadium fatigue. Norm Green had moved the Minnesota North Stars of the National Hockey League to Dallas, where he received a lucrative stadium deal while simultaneously dealing with sexual harassment claims. That rendered the Met Center, where the North Stars played, vacant. Wolves owners Harvey Ratner and Marvin Wolfenson—affectionately known as Marv and Harv—had built Target Center but were losing money and sought a bailout. They endeared themselves to no one when they tried to sell the team to a group—led by boxing promoter Bob Arum—that wanted to move the team to New Orleans. The NBA Board of Governors stopped that sale, saying it "wasn't complete enough."

Now Pohlad let it be known that he wanted a new ballpark, and the timing could not have been any worse. By now, you should have arrived at the conclusion that Minnesota has had a contentious history with stadium pushes. And the debates about helping a billionaire build a stadium raged on.

Pohlad explained how much a new stadium would help while claiming that baseball was working to get into a stronger financial position. That was weeks before the players' strike and subsequent labor wars that contradicted Pohlad's optimism.

The 1995 team finished last in the American League Central division while drawing 1,057,667 fans—its lowest attendance since 1983. The script on the Twins had been flipped when they agreed to move to the Dome. Metropolitan Stadium, where the Twins were born in 1961, was built for a baseball team, while the configuration wasn't ideal for the Minnesota Vikings of the NFL. The Dome was a multipurpose stadium that had better sightlines for football than baseball. While the Twins raked in more concession and parking revenue at the Met, the Vikings received parking, suite and signage income at the Dome.

Baseball was in revenue overdrive by then. Oriole Park at Camden Yards in Baltimore was the first of a run of retro-style stadiums built near the urban core that spurred economic development. Luxury suites were the rage. Naming-rights deals were blossoming across the league—Jacobs Field in Cleveland; Coors Field in Denver; Tropicana Field in St. Petersburg, Florida; Bank One Ballpark in Phoenix; and Safeco Field in Seattle were coming. All reflected the latest trends in stadium construction, except Tropicana Field, which resembled a crashed spaceship. They increased revenues and inflated franchise values. Pohlad saw this and wanted to join the cool kids at school.

But remember, the Dome had opened in 1982 and was not that old. It was going to be a tough sell to the public that a new stadium was needed, especially if public money was required. And it was going to be a lot of money. The Minnesota Vikings of the NFL, co-tenants at the Dome with the Twins, were not going to sit idle and let the baseball team get funding for a new stadium. If that happened, they desired their own new facility. That "what about us?" approach made frosty relations between the franchises even frostier. To make all of this happen, it would take around a half-billion dollars. The public would be taxed. Stadium wars had returned.

A referendum effort early in 1996 failed to gain any traction. The smartest thing Pohlad and stadium bill supporters did is not push the issue later in 1996, which was an election year. Candidates didn't want to tackle the stadium issue and risk their political careers. But talks continued behind closed doors that came to light later in the year. There was a sense of urgency to resolve the stadium issue: The Twins had an escape clause in their lease with the Dome that allowed them to leave following the 1998 season.

The movement received a jet-propelled boost in early 1997, when Pohlad agreed to provide 44 percent, or $158 million, toward a $354 million retractable-roof ballpark. The plan also included 49 percent of profits from any future sale of the team going to the state. It included an $82.5 million cash injection.

Then the jet lost fuel and crash-landed. It was discovered that the Twins' contribution was more like a loan that would have to be repaid to them, hopefully with interest, whenever they sold the team. Negotiators should have known better, *Star Tribune* columnist Patrick Reusse wrote:

"A longtime observer of Pohlad said this: 'When I saw the $82.5 million figure, I had no idea why I was naive enough to think that Carl was just going to give that away. Money is very important to Carl. When he dies in 20 years, there will be a 21-hearse funeral—one for Carl and 20 for his money.'"

On top of it all, the deal was announced during a nonsensical press conference before it had been finalized. Some of the key figures in negotiations had not read all the details. Then the group touted the plan as innovative and creative while misleading viewers on one big item—that Pohlad was going to get all his money back, and then some. There was another detail left out too—that the state had to produce more than $200 million to get the stadium built, and it had to pass muster with the state legislature.

The deceptive financial details and deliberate omissions, combined with a poll in which 69 percent of residents opposed the deal, led to it unraveling in the coming days. Pohlad's credibility was in question. Sports talk radio had exploded in the 1990s, and Pohlad's stadium push filled many segments. And a public sensing it was being hoodwinked had an outlet to vent their frustration. Pohlad was not a very popular figure in the town by then.

But the fact remained that the escape clause still existed. And Pohlad was not finished trying to persuade the state to pass a stadium bill. Emboldened by a suggestion from one of Governor Arne Carlson's aides, Pohlad was going to play poker. His 6-7 off-suit hand was going to be portrayed as a pair of aces. In his book *Stadium Games: Fifty Years of Big League Greed and Bush League Boondoggles*, tireless former *Star Tribune* reporter Jay Weiner wrote that Bernie Omann, Carlson's chief of staff, suggested the Twins concoct a threat to move the team.

After the most recent stadium bill failed in the legislature, the Pohlads let it be known that they would begin looking to relocate. This came after Carl Pohlad had vowed to keep the team in Minnesota. Pohlad would talk on both sides of the issue occasionally. *Minneapolis Star Tribune* columnist Sid Hartman, who considered Pohlad one of his "close and personal friends," frequently wrote that Pohlad was serious about moving the team.

Solutions were being offered from both sides of the Twin Cities. Minneapolis mayor Sharon Sayles Belton took Pohlad on a tour of a riverfront site in which a new stadium could help spur development. St. Paul mayor Norm Coleman tried to produce a plan to bring the Twins to St. Paul. But in September reports surfaced that Pohlad had an offer from North Carolina to purchase the team. Within a couple weeks, Pohlad begins discussions with nursing home magnate Don Beaver, who wanted to bring the team to a part of the state known as the Triad—an area anchored by the cities of Greensboro, Winston-Salem and High Point. Many were skeptical that the area was large enough to support a major league team because it was about half the size of the Twin Cities.

The sides struck a tentative deal for a reported $140 million. The state had until November 30 to get a stadium deal done or Beaver would buy the team, let it play the 1998 season in Minnesota and then take it to North Carolina.

Many believed that Pohlad was a puppet master, pulling Beaver's strings until Minnesota legislators gave in and approved a taxpayer-funded stadium. The family didn't dispute that. Carl Pohlad's son, Bob Pohlad, told the *St. Paul Pioneer Press*, "People have said that this is orchestrated to put pressure on the legislature. Well, it *is* orchestrated to put pressure on the legislature. Of course it is."

Pohlad also had an $80 million offer from Clark Griffith, son of the former owner Calvin Griffith. Pohlad didn't seem to take Clark's offer seriously.

Minnesota governor Arne Carlson called a special session to tackle the stadium issue. Other big news was happening in the Twin Cities around then, as Wolves star Kevin Garnett signed a six-year, $125 million contract extension—a professional sports record. Meanwhile, the Twins couldn't get the state legislature to budge on a stadium funding deal.

Pohlad claimed he was losing money. Major League Baseball commissioner Bud Selig, who enjoyed weekly phone calls with Pohlad, claimed baseball's finances were in danger. Were they really? In 1993, the Colorado Rockies and Florida Marlins joined the league as expansion franchises, each paying $95 million to join the Rich Kids' Club. In 1998, the Arizona Diamondbacks and Tampa Bay Devil Rays were joining the club for $130 million each. If baseball was in so much trouble, why were cities eagerly wanting to join? In Minnesota, fans were torn. They loved their Twins and loved Major League Baseball. But they found it hard to justify building a stadium for a billionaire. And despite hiring a gaggle of advisors and strategists to help shape their stadium strategy, Pohlad could not reverse public sentiment.

The special session began on October 23. A day later, Pohlad offered $111 million, which he would get back over a 20-year period through stadium revenue, including naming rights, stadium advertising, season tickets and suites. The state of Minnesota would contribute $250 million. The City of Minneapolis and Hennepin County would be on the hook for $50 million for land acquisition and infrastructure costs. Legislators did not want to try to sell the public on a tax increase. They wanted to raise their share through user fees, but Pohlad's offer meant he gripped every revenue stream.

The final bill was defeated 84–47. "I think my patience has finally run out," Pohlad said. Hartman, in his *Star Tribune* column, vowed that those legislators who voted against the plan would not win re-election.

It looked like the Twins were on their way to North Carolina. Major League Baseball appointed a five-member committee to help with the sale to Beaver. "The [November 30] deadline is a very real and significant one," said Bud Selig, who would head the committee. "If there's no new ballpark, baseball will not survive in Minneapolis." But a stadium needed to be built in North Carolina before the sale could go through. And guess what? Voters in May of 1998 rejected a bill to build Beaver a ballpark. Pohlad, who never signed the deal with Beaver, was believed to prefer Charlotte, anyway. Before fans had to worry about Charlotte swallowing up their team, the Twins and the Metropolitan Sports Facilities Commission extended the team's lease through the 2000 season, seemingly enough time to revisit the stadium issue. Following the deal, Hartman kept up the pressure on legislators by writing, "You can kiss the Twins goodbye if they don't have a stadium in the works by the middle of the 2000 season."

And those who felt that the Triad wasn't big enough for a major league team were right. More than 25 years later, the area still didn't have a team.

Clark Griffith continued efforts to buy the team from Pohlad, offering $111 million in September 1998. Pohlad turned it down after examining it for two months, saying it didn't include enough cash. A new governor was elected in November, but Jesse "the Body" Ventura did not believe in taxpayer-funded stadiums. He thought the Metrodome was a fine facility.

One of the people Ventura beat in the gubernatorial election was Norm Coleman. The election forced him to return to his job as the mayor of St. Paul. And he had his eyes on bringing the Twins to the capital city. Coleman began meeting with the Twins, and Pohlad had leverage once again. Both cities began working on plans. But Coleman delivered a master stroke—Pohlad would sell the team to local owners as part of a stadium deal. Pohlad would recover the money he'd lost through the years. St. Paul would get 2.5 million fans roaming through its streets.

Would new owners and new city lead to a new stadium? It seemed possible enough that St. Paul bar owner Al Baisi Jr. purchased season tickets so he could have priority in getting seats at the new park. His dream was to have his employees wear shirts from his bar, Alary's, while sitting behind home plate during televised games. Free advertising! His bar was located a couple of blocks from one of the proposed sites and less than a mile from another. St. Paul business owners were dreaming about what 81 home games would do for their bottom line.

A group led by Minnesota Timberwolves owner Glen Taylor and Minnesota Wild co-owner Bob Naegele struck a $120 million deal to buy the team from Pohlad contingent upon—insert sad trombone noise here—voters approving a tax increase for a $325 million open-air stadium.

Coleman's ballpark pitch was treated like a hanging curveball, as the stadium tax was rejected 58 percent to 42 percent. A possible change in ownership did not change views on taxpayer funding.

As the 2000 season approached, the Pohlad family expressed optimism that baseball was going to solve its revenue sharing problems, leading to a better bottom line. And they hoped that public opinion would change toward stadium funding. This was said while the team was losing $10 million a year.

The 1998 Twins, with veterans like Paul Molitor, Bob Tewksbury, Terry Steinbach, Ron Coomer, Otis Nixon and others, lost 92 games with a $26 million payroll. The Twins decided they could lose that many games with cheaper players. In 1999 and 2000, the Twins played 18 rookies each season while having a $16.3 million payroll (29th of 30 teams) in 1999 and $15.6 million in 2000 (30th). The Twins went 63–97–1 in 1999 and 69–93 the following year. There didn't seem to be a plan to pull them out of the depths of the league. And they still lost money.

It was going on six years since Pohlad had asked for a new stadium. Since then, he had been dealt setbacks through the legislature and victimized himself by disguising loans as contributions. Every lever he reached for broke, as a threat to move the team to North Carolina fell apart—although he never signed the agreement to sell the team to Beaver—and an attempt to build a stadium in St. Paul was beaten back by voters. Now he had a team that was among the worst in baseball and a franchise that was among the worst in revenue. It was rock-bottom baseball, all around.

The first reports of Major League Baseball considering contraction came in 2000, when as many as four teams would be bought out and dropped by the league as it worked to get its financial house in order. Colorado Rockies owner Jerry McMorris initially brought it up in 1999, but the subject was being talked about more a year later as baseball dealt with revenue disparity and concern about Montreal's inability to get a stadium deal.

Large-market teams were outspending small-market teams like the Twins. Texas, following the 2000 season, signed shortstop Alex Rodriguez to a $252 million deal. The Twins franchise was valued at $99 million that year by *Forbes*. In fact, the Twins' valuation didn't surpass that Rodriguez deal until 2007, when it reached $288 million. During the first four days of the annual winter meetings, where many trades and free-agent signings are announced, $738 million had been guaranteed to 24 players. For the offseason, $1.043 billion had been spent on 49 players. The Twins had not signed a single player.

"There's been a lot of conversation about [contraction]," Pohlad said during an interview with the *Star Tribune* in December of that year. "We do not like that. Our whole motive and objective is to keep baseball here." By March 2001, Major League Baseball commissioner Bud Selig confirmed that owners were seriously considering the plan. It seemed impossible. Even without MLB's four weakest links, teams like the Yankees and Dodgers enjoyed swift revenue streams that allowed them to outspend mid-market and small-market teams for the best players. Major League Baseball wasn't sharing all its television revenue like NFL teams did. The MLB Players Association was a tough group to negotiate with, and it was against a salary cap. But surely, there were other ways baseball could get its financial house in order—not contraction. It seemed like another lever was being pulled to force governments in Minnesota and Montreal to approve stadium bills. The one fishy thing about it all was that the team that could benefit from the elimination of the Twins was the Milwaukee Brewers, who were once owned by Selig. And there was the possibility that Selig and league owners would pull the lever to force the players association to give in to a few demands during the upcoming collective bargaining meetings. *We are about to cut 50 jobs. What will you give us to not do so?*

While *contraction* was the dirty little word that crept into newspapers across the country—along with mentions of the Twins as a candidate—there was a revival on the diamond. After spending two years bottoming out, the young Twins players who took their lumps in 1999 and 2000 began to deliver their own blows. The rotation was led by Joe Mays, Brad Radke and Eric Milton. "Everyday" Eddie Guardado led the bullpen. Corey Koskie and Torii Hunter fueled the offense. The Twins played excellent defense, stole bases, hit for enough power and had enough pitching. And they had fun while doing so. The outfield of Hunter, Jacque Jones and Matt Lawton called themselves "the Soul Patrol." Koskie, catcher A.J. Pierzynski and bullpen coach Rick Stelmaszek answered by calling themselves "the Pole Patrol." The infield of Koskie, a third baseman from Canada;

Cristian Guzmán, a shortstop from the Dominican Republic; Luis Rivas, a second baseman from Venezuela; and Doug Mientkiewicz, a first baseman from Florida, called themselves "the League of Nations." They laughed, played practical jokes on each other and won. The 2001 Twins were 50–31 by the season's halfway point. They were young—with upside—and dangerous. It was safe for Twins fans to come out again.

Unfortunately, a shoulder injury to Guzmán during the All-Star break—some believed he injured himself during an All-Star Game workout—and other setbacks led to a second-half collapse during which they went 35–46. They finished second in the American League Central, six games behind Cleveland. Still, the Twins went 85–77 overall for their first winning season since 1992. As the season ended, the excitement over what the 2002 Twins could do took hold. What the Twins almost did after that season was fold.

As the World Series played on, reports surfaced that owners were going to vote on contracting the Twins and Expos, sending shockwaves across baseball but especially the Twin Cities. The Twins tried to conduct business as usual—manager Tom Kelly stepped down following the season and a search was underway—but the fan base was rocked. I received a flood of emails from fans, all asking some version of "How could baseball take away my beloved Twins?" Pohlad stood to receive a check for $250 million to go away. That would double what he had invested in the team through the years. At the same time, his family would have been ostracized for being the ones who erased a franchise that had won two World Series titles over the previous 15 years and was the first American League franchise to draw 3 million fans. The owners of the remaining 28 teams would pay about $18 million each to contract two teams, but projections suggested they would make up the money in a handful of years.

A stadium bill that hit a wall in the spring of 2001 was expected to be brought up again early in 2002. Was this the latest scare tactic to get a ballpark approved? Could they risk not taking it seriously?

On November 7, Major League Baseball owners voted 28 to 2—the "no" votes coming from the Twins and Expos—to contract two teams before the 2002 season. What followed was the expected blowback. Local politicians were split. Some took the threat seriously, while others doubled down on not helping billionaires build ballparks. A local group of businessmen and attorneys attempted to band together to purchase the team from Pohlad. The MLB Players Association told its membership that there wasn't enough time to contract two teams before the 2002 season. Minnesota attorney general Mike Hatch planned to sue the league for violating antitrust laws. Minnesota senator Paul Wellstone introduced a bill to revoke baseball's antitrust exemption.

Meanwhile, Twins fans were in turmoil over what seemed to be the biggest threat to lose their team during Pohlad's time as an owner. It appeared that Pohlad was fed up with years of losing stadium battles and had thrown his hands up. A fan sent me a miniature lobby card from the movie *The Sting*. The faces of Paul Newman and Robert Redford were replaced with images of Pohlad and Selig.

And it wasn't just the fans. There were hundreds of Twins employees in various departments who would lose their jobs. In a letter sent to some staff members, Jim Pohlad, one of Carl's three sons, acknowledged for the first time the plan to eliminate the franchise.

"Our willingness to go along with contraction, if the Commissioner so decides, has come from a feeling of hopelessness," Pohlad wrote. "Within the context of baseball's commitment, when we are posed the question, 'Why should the

Minnesota Twins not be contracted?' we are unable to find a plausible answer."

Dave St. Peter, the Twins' senior vice president in charge of business affairs, had to be prepared for anything. While he crossed his fingers that the Twins remained entrenched in the Twin Cities for the long haul, he also had a "doomsday" plan in mind if contraction was carried out and artifacts needed to be preserved. "I actually called the state historical society and said, 'Look, I'm not ready to go there yet. But I wanted you to know that if this were to really happen, I'm going to want to have a conversation with you about how we are going to preserve this history.' Again, I never was definitively told that this was going to happen or believed it was going to happen. But I knew it was a possibility."

The Pohlads met with employees on November 9 and offered staffers an incentive program to keep them from seeking jobs with other major league organizations. But staff members already had their incentive to stay following the actions of general manager Terry Ryan.

Ryan, born in Janesville, Wisconsin, pitched for the University of Wisconsin-Madison and was a 35th-round pick of the Twins in 1972. He was 14–3 over four minor league seasons before an arm injury ended his career. He re-enrolled at the University of Wisconsin-Madison and earned a degree in 1979. He returned to baseball as a scouting supervisor for the Mets but joined the Twins as their scouting director in 1986. He understood what baseball meant to the region.

Ryan replaced Andy MacPhail as general manager in 1994 when MacPhail left to join the Chicago Cubs. Ryan's staff was minuscule compared to the layers of departments that make up today's organizations. Ryan relied on a small group of versatile assistants. He was fair, respectful and quick-witted, with the integrity of a scoutmaster. The type of fellow you'd want for a next-door neighbor.

While Twins owners were meeting with employees, it was revealed that the Toronto Blue Jays had asked the Twins for permission to speak to Ryan about taking over their baseball operations department. Ryan learned of their interest as the Twins contingent left Chicago following the general managers' meetings to drive back to the Twin Cities. Ryan was behind the wheel, while assistant general manager Bill Smith sat next to him and special assistant Wayne Krivsky sat in the back seat. Ryan knew all along that he would stay with the Twins. But the three began discussing Toronto's organization and started opening files. As they drove back, they broke down Toronto's top prospects, payroll, stadium lease, upcoming free agents, coaching staff, etc. By the time the trio returned to the Twin Cities, they had the Blue Jays' entire organization broken down and analyzed.

"It's all true," Ryan said, "but when you've got six hours, what else have you got to do?"

Ryan was prepped for an interview, but never took one. If there was a franchise in Minnesota, he wanted to stay. Many people in the organization believe that if Ryan had left, there would have been an exodus of staffers.

Even if Ryan wanted to go, he would have had problems doing so. His wife, Karilyn, frequently cut negative stories out of the local papers so their children, Tim and Kathleen, would not read bad press about their father. Well, Karilyn didn't make it to the paper before Tim did on the morning the story about Toronto's interest in Ryan ran. She was elsewhere in their Eagan, Minnesota, home when she heard Tim, who was around 10 at the time, yell, "We're going to TORONTO?!" Karilyn felt the same way.

"My wife said, 'If you are going, you are going by yourself,'" Ryan said. "So that was one reason. I wasn't gonna go because I

THE FRANCHISE: MINNESOTA TWINS

had a lot of loyalty, and we had a club that was starting to turn the corner." Ryan stayed. So his staff stayed, despite the possible end of the franchise. Some were more prepared than others. St. Peter's doomsday plan included a marketing campaign. "It would be heavy on nostalgia and history and everything this franchise has meant to this community," St. Peter said in March of 2002.

Opinions of the Pohlads were so low that they couldn't have beaten Robert Hanssen in a popularity contest. But Selig continued to defend the family, arguing that they were "grossly, unfairly castigated" while claiming that Major League Baseball in Minnesota could not survive without a ballpark, leaving an opening for the Twins to be saved.

By Thanksgiving, the tentacles surrounding the fate of the Twins were large and numerous enough to wrap around Moby Dick. There were spirited legal battles between owners and players as the stage was being set for the next round of negotiations for a new collective bargaining agreement. The owners faced a challenge from the Twins' landlord, the Metropolitan Sports Facilities Commission. A group of fans presented Selig with 110,000 signatures on petitions asking him not to contract the club. Legislators called Selig to Washington, D.C., for hearings as they examined baseball's antitrust exemption. Free agency was affected, as teams waited to see if teams would be contracted, which would send their players into a dispersal draft. Agents wanted to see how that affected players with no-trade clauses in their contracts. Twins players had few answers when asked for updates. A group of Twins players were in the middle of an offseason golf outing when a cameraman rushed up to them in the middle of someone's backswing to ask a question about being contracted.

"I feel like we're sitting in the dugout watching the tarp being pulled over the field," said Twins infielder Denny Hocking at the time. "I really think we are going to play in 2002, but we have to wait until the tarp gets pulled off first."

If things weren't confusing enough, someone approached the Twins and Major League Baseball about buying the team. Donald Watkins, an Alabama attorney who ran a bank and had a share of an energy company, announced in November of 2001 that he wanted to purchase the team from Pohlad. This came out of nowhere. Reports estimated his net worth as $1.5 billion, but there was no strong evidence of that. He was not listed on *Forbes'* annual list of wealthiest individuals. But Watkins traveled to the Twin Cities to meet with fans, then later claimed he could buy the Twins for cash and then build a privately funded stadium. Watkins would have been the first African American owner in baseball history. It was too good to be true.

But how could the ownership bid co-exist with a contraction push? There was some sort of contraction story in the papers every day—especially if you included columnist Sid Hartman's musings, as he claimed there was a 99 percent chance the Twins were going away. It was hard for Minnesotans to enjoy the holiday season. And the near future didn't look much better, as Selig claimed the league could announce contraction as late as February of 2002.

The Twins, unable to make many moves during the off-season while awaiting their fate, could not wait or risk losing on-field staff. In January, the Twins officially announced Ron Gardenhire as their new manager, announced the coaching staff and signed Joe Mays to a contract extension. January 4, 2002, was the rare calm moment—during turbulent times—that baseball was discussed. Gardenhire named Jacque Jones his leadoff hitter and Eddie Guardado as his closer.

What no one knew on that day was that one man had put the Twins in position to not only play the 2002 season but remain in Minnesota for the long haul. That man excelled in skiing, long-range marksmanship, home building and—most importantly—law. On November 16, 2001, Hennepin County district judge Harry Crump ruled in favor of the Metropolitan Sports Facilities Commission as it sought to force the Twins to meet the terms of their lease agreement and play the 2002 season at the Metrodome. That meant they could not be contracted. "Clearly more than money is at stake," Crump wrote at the time. "The welfare, recreation, prestige, property, trade and commerce of the people of the community are at stake. The Twins brought the community together with Homer Hankies and bobblehead dolls."

On January 22, an appellate court upheld Crump's ruling and refused to hear an appeal, severely damaging Major League Baseball's chances to contract teams before the 2002 season. Then the Minnesota Supreme Court—which included former Vikings defensive end and Hall of Famer Alan Page—upheld Crump's ruling by refusing to hear the case.

Minnesota Twins: safe! Contraction: out!

"That's the end of the line as far as we are concerned," Twins president Jerry Bell told jubilant staff members at the Dome.

That saved the Twins from contraction in 2002. Then in May, in order to keep financial secrets from being revealed in court, Major League Baseball agreed not to pursue contraction before 2003 if the MSFC agreed to drop a lawsuit. The Twins were guaranteed at least two seasons at the Dome. It would take until 2006, but funding for a $545 million ballpark named Target Field was approved to ensure the franchise's future in the Twin Cities.

The 2002 Twins could now focus on the season and finishing what they threatened to do in 2001: win their first division championship since 1991. They would have to knock off the defending division champion Cleveland Indians, who had become their archrival. The Twins went into that season full of confidence and no longer burdened by contraction thoughts. Hocking, the reliable utility player, boasted to reporters before the season opener in Kansas City that new leadoff hitter Jacque Jones would lead off the first inning of the first game with a home run, which we all snickered at. On the second pitch from Jeff Suppan, Jones blasted a home run over the left field wall. Hocking went to the top step of the dugout, looked up toward the press box and held out his arms in triumph. It was the first of 94 wins during that AL Central title–winning season.

Contraction was in the rearview mirror. But was it ever a real, viable threat? Or was it the most diabolical scheme Pohlad was willing to be part of to shake the state capital into decisive action on a stadium bill while also being a chip for the league to play in its CBA discussions with the union?

"Well, [Pohlad] was frustrated," Selig told the *St. Paul Pioneer Press* in 2014. "The guy tried everything. I know. I was up there. I thought we had a deal two or three times and every time it fell apart, mainly for political reasons.

"Contraction had nothing to do with Minnesota. Baseball was really struggling at the time, losing a fortune as a sport. There were owners who believed that contraction might help. I wasn't of that particular view, but the owners were searching around."

For Pohlad, it was nearly 12 years of sparring with the state over a stadium bill that included the threat of contraction. Yes, he bought the team and kept it in Minnesota. Yes, he hired the right people who helped win two World Series titles. And, since 1991, the Minnesota Lynx of the WNBA are the only major pro sports team to win championships in the state. Not the NFL Vikings. Not the NHL Wild. Not the NBA Timberwolves.

But he burned some goodwill along the way. The tactics used in his attempts to get a stadium deal are a drag on his legacy.

Carl Pohlad passed away in 2009, but his family still owns the franchise. His three sons collaborated on ownership duties before Jim Pohlad eventually settled into the role. Before the 2023 season, Jim relinquished some of his duties to his nephew, Joe. The Pohlad family was set up for 60 years of ownership.

Future success will be factored in the final assessment of the family patriarch. For Carl Pohlad, deception masked his offers. He threatened to move the team to North Carolina. He gutted the roster and lowered payroll, spawning a generation of fans who still call the family "cheap Pohlads." And he appeared willing to take a check and walk away from it all while the franchise would have been jettisoned into oblivion.

Pohlad preserved baseball twice: once when he bought the club in 1984 and again when Target Field's funding was secured in 2006. But he caused a hell of a lot of problems between those two checkpoints.

"I think, at the end of the day, Carl probably paid a lot of money to some people for some bad advice and for some bad counsel," said Dave St. Peter, who has since become the team president. "Mistakes were made. And the Twins, we stumbled mightily. But I feel badly about that because Carl and his family felt the brunt of that. They were in the spotlight, and that's not a fun place to be."

One person's legacy is as clear as a cloudless night in the Northwoods. Harry Crump saved major league baseball in Minnesota.

20

2020

THE 2020 TWINS WON THE AL CENTRAL TITLE FOR THE second consecutive season. Right-hander Kenta Maeda finished second in the Cy Young Award voting in his first season with the Twins. Nelson Cruz led the team in home runs. Luis Arraez batted .321. Taylor Rogers led the team in saves.

That Twins team won 60 percent of their games before running into the Houston Astros in the first round of the postseason. They entered the postseason battered. Josh Donaldson was out with an injury and Mitch Garver was banged up. Byron Buxton played in Game 1, a 4–1 loss, but served only as a pinch runner in Game 2 because of what was suspected to be a concussion. Things were so dire that the Twins started rookie outfielder Alex Kirilloff in right field in Game 2 against Houston. Kirilloff was making his major league debut!

The Twins were swept 2–0 in the AL wild card series by Houston, scoring two runs in the entire series. It ran their postseason losing streak to 18 consecutive games, at the time the longest losing streak in North American sports playoff history. There were two running themes during the streak that began in 2004. One, the Twins lost 13 of those 18 games to the Yankees. Two, they forgot that games are won by putting the bat on the ball.

Once again, there was no opportunity for a postseason run. Once again, they were swept. The streak dated back to the Ron Gardenhire years, continued through Paul Molitor's stint as manager and now was Rocco Baldelli's problem to figure out. A generation of Twins fans had not experienced the thrill of their team winning a playoff game.

It was time to look ahead to next year.

In more ways than one.

Most people wouldn't think of 2020 primarily as the year the Twins extended their postseason futility. It was the year cold water was splashed on the face of America as it was shut down by the COVID-19 pandemic and racial tensions were stoked into a red-hot blaze by the Minneapolis Police Department's murder of George Floyd and the subsequent demand for racial justice.

Before I delve into the year we would like to forget, it's important to understand that before the 2020 Twins, there was the Bomba Squad.

The 2019 season was Baldelli's managerial debut and the third in which the front office was run by chief baseball officer Derek Falvey and general manager Thad Levine, occasionally nicknamed "Falvine." Owner Jim Pohlad, following in the footsteps of his late father, Carl, agreed to build out the baseball department under Falvine. Analytics became the guiding light in many of their decisions. The way players were coached, trained and fed was altered. State-of-the-art technology helped pitchers with spin rate, release points and efficiency. Hitters looked to increase their exit velocity and sharpen their launch angle.

Rest and recovery became ever important, as Baldelli frowned upon players who showed up at 7 AM for spring training workouts. Get your rest, then get to the park and work smartly. Right-hander José Berríos, an avid early riser and workout fiend, joined Anytime Fitness to get workouts in before reporting to spring workouts at the team's facility in Fort Myers, Florida. A nap room was created at Target Field.

The Twins' notable signing during the previous offseason was Nelson Cruz, who signed because the Twins had "really good young guys with a lot of talent." When Cruz, during one meeting, asked if the Twins had a nap room, the response was, "We do now."

Everything clicked. The 2019 Twins won 101 games. And they did it largely through achieving the greatest feat in baseball—hitting home runs.

Shortly after a May 24 game during which the Twins belted three home runs in an 11–4 drubbing of the White Sox, Eddie Rosario was quoted as saying, "When you're hitting a lot of bombas, everybody's hitting bombas, everybody's happy." And the Bomba Squad was born.

T-shirts were printed, bobblehead dolls were handed out. It was A Thing all summer as the Twins set a major league record with 307 home runs, topping the Yankees, who hit 306 homers that season. Eight Twins hit at least 20 home runs. Five Twins—Cruz, Rosario, Miguel Sanó, Max Kepler and Mitch Garver—hit at least 31 homers. Cruz, at age 38, hit 41.

All five Twins starting pitchers won at least 10 games with José Berríos and Jake Odorizzi earning All-Star honors.

And the Bomba Squad was swept in the first round of the postseason by the Yankees. Remember, they were in the middle of a streak.

The Twins hit four home runs and scored seven runs while losing the three games. I went down on the field before Game 2 at Yankee Stadium with ESPN's Marly Rivera, who spoke to a few of the Latin players in Spanish and translated for me. When we got to Sanó to ask about the offense, he simply said, "We have lost our minds."

Soon, the Twins were out of the playoffs and left to figure out how to return and have a longer run in 2020.

They signed Josh Donaldson, a three-time All-Star and the 2015 AL MVP, during the offseason. The thinking was that the brash and ultra-confident Donaldson would provide toughness and the edge that they believed they needed. The Twins' recruiting push included a video during which Sanó pledged to move from third base to first to accommodate Donaldson. Former top-10 tennis pro Mardy Fish, a lifelong Twins fan and a friend of Donaldson's, was playing with him in the celebrity bracket of an LPGA event in January when he heard the news. "Ever since it came out that he was thinking about the Twins offer, I was on him," Fish told the *Minneapolis Star Tribune*. "Text messages, FaceTime, Twitter. So many that it got to the point where he was not returning my messages. Maybe I was going in a little hard, but I told him about the people, all the great golf courses there, the ballpark, the team. I know the lineup top to bottom, and I told him how great a fit he would be."

Veteran left-hander Rich Hill was signed to add depth to the starting rotation. The Twins signed Tyler Clippard and brought back Sergio Romo to boost the bullpen. Like Hill, Clippard and Romo had been on teams that reached the World Series. The

Twins also worked a trade right before spring training began for right-hander Kenta Maeda from the Dodgers.

These cagey veterans were expected to join forces with the Bomba Squad to give the Twins the boost that would help them through the regular season and beyond. The disappointment of 2019 was supposed to lead to the success of 2020.

Baldelli openly spoke of winning a title during spring training.

"Guys are going to come in knowing what to expect and what we want out of spring training and out of the year," Baldelli said on the first day pitchers and catchers worked out at the Twins' base in Fort Myers, Florida. "We have a good group. We have a group that we believe is going to win a lot of games and go out there and do a good job."

The start of the 2020 season could not come soon enough for the Twins and their fans. The novel coronavirus, however, derailed baseball, the country and the world.

COVID-19 was the first of two developments that made the 2020 season difficult for sports fans and the country to handle. The virus was believed to have originated in China but quickly spread worldwide. Most countries had no experience in dealing with a pandemic, and figuring out a way to treat and live with it polarized the country along political lines.

The sports world eventually ground to a halt. But during the first week of March, teams disinfected their spring training facilities and figured out ways to engage fans safely. Twins players signed baseballs to toss to fans instead of signing autographs near them. "Coronavirus balls," closer Taylor Rogers said. "Good idea."

But things turned for the worse. NBA player Rudy Gobert became the first player in the league to test positive for the virus on March 11, the same day that the World Health Organization officially declared COVID-19 a pandemic. More than 4,000 people globally had been killed by the virus at that point and there were nearly 120,000 cases. It was two days earlier that Gobert had playfully touched microphones and recorders while discussing safety with reporters. Now he had tested positive. His team, the Utah Jazz, then had its game against Oklahoma City postponed. Hours later, the NBA shut down the league.

The Twins lost 3–2 to the Braves in an exhibition game on March 11. Their March 12 game against Baltimore was cancelled. Then Major League Baseball shut down spring training and delayed the first two weeks of the regular season, although many expected the delay to be longer. Meanwhile, citizens began stocking up on supplies, with bottled water and toilet paper disappearing off shelves. Many of us, from slightly husky sportswriters like me to the President of the United States, believed the virus would leave us in a few weeks. We were terribly wrong.

No one knew when baseball would be played. The Twins' highly anticipated season was paused. Some guessed it would be a month or so. The bigger problem was that no one knew when life in general would return to normal.

By Sunday, March 15, the Twins had sent most of their players and coaches home. Access to the team had been significantly reduced by then. Police blocked the entrance to the Twins' spring training headquarters, and I argued with the Twins' senior director of baseball communications, Dustin Morse, to interview whoever was still on campus. I offered to do so from a distance. This was a worldwide story now. That request was denied.

What was a bustling Lee County Sports Complex (then still named the CenturyLink Sports Complex) a few days earlier suddenly looked like spring training had never started. Tourism throughout Florida, a vital revenue generator for the state, quickly suffered. On March 17—St. Patrick's Day—bars in downtown Fort Myers were full of revelers clad in various shades of green and behaving like nothing was wrong. Then governor Ron DeSantis announced around noon that bars and nightclubs would have to close for 30 days, and restaurants would be limited to half of capacity. By 5:00 PM, spring break was officially over. And the rest of the country was shutting down as well.

A few days later, I flew back to Minnesota. I cleaned my townhome like never before. I bought a new computer and joined Amazon. Within two weeks, I upgraded to Amazon Prime. It was time to settle in and wait to cover games again. The thought that the virus could blow through in a month was folly. The coronavirus was on its own clock, forcing us to work remotely, download Zoom, study contact tracing, stock up on masks and spread out when we were allowed in restaurants.

The *Minneapolis Star Tribune* had no games to cover. So we audibled. We revisited past moments in Minnesota sports history. I wrote about how Kent Hrbek became Minnesota's first pro athlete to earn a $1 million salary in a season. I contacted a Twins scout in South Korea to explain what contact tracing meant. The sports department held a virtual draft of the best sports movies ever. I was excited that *Ali* was still available in the third round. We held a virtual chat with Frank Viola while airing one of the Twins' World Series games from 1987.

Twins players worked out at home and communicated with coaches and trainers through Zoom and FaceTime. One month became two months. Then three months. Baseball didn't resume until late July; in June, MLB had announced a 60-game schedule after talks with the players' association for a longer season hit snags. Mainly, there were disagreements about compensation and revenue sharing. Any season with more than 60 games would have to be played with prorated pay less than 100 percent. Owners stood to lose billions in revenue and argued that the players had to assume some of the risk. Of course, the union rejected that.

Games were played in empty stadiums, generating no revenue. The Toronto Blue Jays played their games at the home of their Class AAA affiliate in Buffalo due to travel restrictions in Canada.

The abbreviated schedule for the Twins had them opening on July 24 against the White Sox in Chicago. Baseball was back, and sorely needed, in more ways than one. It was a sign that the country was figuring out how to move forward in a pandemic.

But, by then, America was faced with another challenge. And Minnesota was ground zero.

On May 25, a Minneapolis resident named George Floyd, a 46-year-old Black man, purchased cigarettes with a suspected counterfeit $20 bill. Employees called the police. Within 20 minutes of the first squad car arriving, Floyd was dead. And the actions of four members of the Minneapolis Police Department led to his death. The image of one officer, Derek Chauvin, placing his knee on Floyd's neck as he was handcuffed and lying on the ground, was unforgettable and ignited a public already concerned about racial justice and police brutality.

While onlookers pleaded with the officers to aid Floyd, who was struggling to breathe, Chauvin kept his knee on Floyd's neck for nine minutes. Nine minutes that changed America.

Chauvin and the other three officers—Tou Thao, Thomas Lane and J. Alexander Kueng—were fired the next day, and all were charged for their actions. Chauvin was eventually sentenced to 22½ years for violating Floyd's rights.

The world was horrified by the video of Floyd's death, leading to protests across the country and all over the world. Nowhere was more passionate than the Twin Cities of Minneapolis and St. Paul. Thousands of protesters gathered to object to police brutality and systemic racism. The people demanded change.

Businesses were destroyed in both cities. But the worst was in Minneapolis, where protests turned into riots while Minneapolis mayor Jacob Frey and Minnesota governor Tim Walz pointed fingers as to who delayed the deployment of the National Guard. Meanwhile, rioters set fire to the Third Precinct police headquarters and watched it burn.

In many protests, there are three groups of folks. One group consists of peaceful protesters. Another group consists of rioters looking to commit crimes of opportunity. The third group are anarchists who travel to hot spots across the country with the sole purpose of contributing mayhem. The second and third groups damaged 1,500 Minnesota businesses during the riots, and parts of Minneapolis will never be the same.

"It's unbearable to think about what's happening in our city and throughout the country," Twins star outfielder Byron Buxton wrote on Instagram at the time. "but things have to CHANGE. African Americans have been slaughtered left and right for nothing more than the color of our skin. That is the reality, and it has been ignored for far too long. DEMAND PROGRESS—DEMAND JUSTICE for George Floyd."

We were waiting for baseball to return. We were amid a pandemic. And now we were in the throes of a national debate on race relations in America. It was a summer of discontent.

There were tough conversations throughout the summer. Many came my way. I'm a Black man, so the assumption was that I was a Black Lives Matter supporter—I support change, but not violence. I'm a media member. And I'm left of center on the political scale. So I had difficult conversations throughout the summer—regardless of whether I wanted to or not. The sociopolitical climate was so volatile and so polarized that I came home mentally drained from debating people with differing opinions from six feet away. I feared that we were moving away from being the United States of America to being a bunch of states on the same island.

Twins players and athletes across the country had similar discussions—clubhouses of players who were on opposite ends of the political spectrum and approaches to dealing with the pandemic.

"It puts your mind in just a completely altered place, like you don't even know what to do and how to think and how to act sometimes because there's so much going on at the same time and you're trying to stay grounded and you're trying to think about things rationally," Twins manager Rocco Baldelli said. "You're trying to use your mind and do what you think is right. Say what you think is right. But it's hard to feel like yourself when you're experiencing all these things in real time. For me at least, I know."

Athletes in other professional sports began taking a knee during pregame ceremonies, which rankled many who believe that doing so disrespects the flag and those who defend it. This even though there's a lengthy history in this country of athletes making political statements.

"Just like any other workplace," Twins right-hander Trevor May told reporters in July of that year. "The common adage with politics, religion and money. You usually don't go into those. Only go in those with your closest friends and your family, right? So this kind of gets into a more serious nature of things, but it's phenomenal that I think guys are really, really open to have the conversations, and you're hearing things from guys that you've never heard before and that is kind of the key.

That is the point of this whole thing, is to have the conversations and to listen to stories and to get some context."

By then, the delayed start to the 2020 baseball season was approaching. The Twins opened the season in Chicago against the White Sox on July 24. Twins and White Sox players gathered on the field during pregame ceremonies and held a black ribbon in support of racial justice and equality. Many took a knee. Buxton, who was recovering from a foot sprain, drove from the Twin Cities to Chicago just to be part of the ceremony. He then drove back. It wasn't an easy decision for Buxton to take a knee during the national anthem. His brother, Felton Buxton III, is in the Navy. The brothers spoke in advance to make sure Felton wouldn't be offended by Byron's actions.

Life was easier when we just had to worry about the Twins bullpen. The nation was healing in the aftermath of the George Floyd riots. Players were being tested regularly for the coronavirus. Many of us couldn't wait for vaccines to be produced. And the debates over how to achieve racial justice were ongoing.

Meanwhile, it was time to cover baseball again.

Games without fans made stadiums turn into supersized libraries. Everything on the field could be heard. Luis Arraez, while playing second base, would call strikes before the umpire would offer his ruling. Detroit Miguel Cabrera talked between every pitch, a constant commentary in Spanish. If a close pitch went against a team, complaints that usually weren't in earshot of the umpire were easily heard. Umps would look frequently into dugouts for the culprits. Sergio Romo nearly ignited a brawl with the Royals when a call went his way, he heard the Royals complain about it, then he yelled at them to pipe down.

Covering baseball has allowed writers to see the country. We saw it in a different way during the pandemic. It takes about $12 in tolls to get through Illinois, another $12 for the Indiana part,

$20 to travel across the Ohio Turnpike and another $8 once you cross into Pennsylvania. The *Minneapolis Star Tribune* covered every road game during the 2020 season. The most challenging trip was a Pittsburgh–Kansas City–Milwaukee swing in August. I made the 14-hour drive to Pittsburgh (that's a six-cigar drive, by the way), then met the team in Milwaukee while a colleague covered the Kansas City games. I showed up at PNC Park in Pittsburgh before the first game just as the Twins' bus pulled up. I chatted up Rich Hill as we were separated by a fence. It was the closest I had been to a major league player since March 10.

The 2020 Twins went 36–24 to win the AL Central Division. Then they were dispatched by the Astros in two games at Target Field. By then, a limited number of spectators (but no fans), which ended up being mostly Twins employees, were allowed in the stadium. The Twins offense was anemic once again, and the season was over. The best part of the 2020 season was that it ended.

By then, there was an empty space outside Target Field where Calvin Griffith's statue used to be. In the aftermath of George Floyd's death and the resulting riots, there was an effort to re-examine anything and anyone with ties to racism. Despite bringing Major League Baseball to the Twin Cities, Griffith had made racist statements during his tenure as owner during a speech at the Waseca Lions Club on September 28, 1978. What Griffith got away with in 1978 could not withstand the wave of social justice that swept the world in 2020.

Griffth's insensitive remarks about race led to the *Minneapolis Star* demanding that he sell the team. Griffith owned the Twins until he sold the team to Carl Pohlad in 1984. His statue went up when Target Field opened in 2010. The post–George Floyd focus on race prompted the Twins, whose owner, the Pohlad family, had donated $25 million to fight racial injustice, to examine what they stood for as a franchise. That's when the decision to remove Griffith's statue was made.

"We're very pleased he was there for 10 years, and we're sad to see him go," Calvin's son, Clark, said.

By the end of the season, the country was worn down from living with the virus and trying to repair race relations. The 2020 season will be remembered for being a season like no other. A season no one wants to see repeated. Because that would reveal that we have learned nothing.

"It was relentless. It was kind of a gauntlet every day, showing up where 95 percent of what we did here felt like it was not related to baseball, which made it real hard," Baldelli said. "We tried our best in every way to let our players focus on baseball. But you're also dealing with individuals that are going to live their lives and do the things and say the things that they that they want. And you know, you can't reprogram an entire team, nor do you want to. But we're trying to find a way to just thread the needle of functioning successfully as a team throughout the course of this season in territory that nobody understands, and no one knows what's going on. So every day it was trying to gather everyone here, so everyone is on the same page."

21

1991

THE 1987 TWINS WERE LED BY TWO STANDOUT STARTING pitchers, a relief ace and a maturing lineup. They were unstoppable at home, unwatchable on the road and winners of a weak division. But when the postseason came, the Twins got on a roll, used their Domefield advantage, blasted a couple of grand slams and rode the arms of Bert Blyleven and Frank Viola to make history in the Twin Cities.

The 1991 Twins had their own traits. "A different group of guys," first baseman Kent Hrbek said. "A different vibe. We were a lot better team, I thought, in 1991. I've always said that." The core that had won it all four seasons earlier was whittled down to a Big Two of Hrbek and Kirby Puckett. Blyleven and Viola had moved on, with Jack Morris, Scott Erickson and Kevin Tapani left to form the backbone of the starting rotation. The ends of games no longer saw Juan Berenguer preceding closer Jeff Reardon. Carl Willis and Steve Bedrosian were the warmup acts for closer Rick Aguilera.

There was also resolve to bounce back after finishing dead last in the American League West division in 1990. Resolve had served the Twins well in the past. The 1964 Twins were 79–83 and 20 games behind the Yankees. A year later, they won 102 games and reached the World Series. In 1986 the Twins were 71–91 and 21 games behind the Angels. A year later, they won 85 games and proceeded to win the World Series. In 1991, the Twins went from 74 wins the year before to 95 wins and a second World Series championship—the first team to go from finishing last in their division to a title the following year.

Indeed, there was a bad taste in a few Twins' mouths at the conclusion of the 1990 season. The offense scored just 666 runs, as Hrbek, Puckett and Gary Gaetti all had down seasons. Gaetti was frustrated after batting a career-low .229. Hrbek was the only player with more than 20 home runs with 22. And he missed the final 10 games of the season with a broken ankle suffered while chasing around a clubhouse attendant. Puckett was in the middle of a run of 10 consecutive All-Star Game appointments. He had led the league in hits four times, hit .356 in 1988 and won a batting title a year later. On July 15, 1990, Puckett hit two homers in a game against Baltimore. He would not hit another homer for the remainder of the season. On June 2, the Twins were 29–20 and 4.5 games out of first place in the division. They proceeded to lose 11 of their next 12 games and 20 of 26. By the end of June the Twins were 13 games out of first place and never heard from again.

As the losses mounted, fans began to boo the performances. Even Hrbek, the hometown hero from Bloomington, was not spared. He was in the first year of a five-year, $14 million contract and fans expected more. *Star Tribune* columnist Patrick Reusse's "Turkey of the Year Award" went to Hrbek for his less-than-inspiring performance for a last-place club. Hrbek wasn't pleased. In his book *Tales from the Twins Dugout*, Hrbek wrote, "I certainly didn't think I deserved to be the Turkey of the Year. I didn't shoot anyone or rob a bank, did I?"

Clearly, work needed to be done following an abysmal 1990 season. "I didn't think we were as bad as the record," then general manager Andy MacPhail said. "Maybe I was just oblivious, but you know there were certain things that we needed to improve." The challenge got even tougher when Gaetti left for California as a free agent. His 10-season run with the Twins had ended, with a drop-off in production in his final two seasons. Gaetti had become deeply religious by then, and the fiery player who would curse out pitchers who wouldn't throw him fastballs had stopped showing that edge. Regardless of whether his stronger faith was the reason for his tailing off, the Twins needed a third baseman for the first time since 1980. And there was no internal candidate.

MacPhail pivoted a couple of times as he searched for the right players during the offseason. And the roster building lasted right up to a couple weeks before pitchers and catchers reported. More than 30 years later, Twins fans scoff and scratch their heads when the Twins go into January with holes still in their roster. But it doesn't matter when the moves happen if they work.

There was a heated debate among Twins scouts and staffers about how to fill third base. Jim Presley, who hit .242 with 19 homers and 72 RBI for Atlanta in 1990, had the support of many club officials except one—manager Tom Kelly. Kelly wanted Mike Pagliarulo, who batted .254 with seven homers and 38 RBI the previous season with San Diego.

MacPhail was attempting to mediate the spirited discussion when the lightbulb went off.

"It was one of those moments in your career where you have an epiphany," MacPhail said. "It was pretty clear to me that Tom Kelly wants Mike Pagliarulo. And it's pretty clear to me that the scouting organization prefers Jim Presley."

The scouting department nearly won out, but MacPhail had to be honest with himself.

"Why would I stick my manager with a third baseman that he doesn't want?" he said.

So the Twins inked Pagliarulo to a $605,000 deal. He proceeded to hit .279 in 1991, the highest average of his career to that point. As for Presley, he signed a month later as Pagliarulo's replacement in San Diego—but played in just 20 games in what would be the final season of his major league career. Pagliarulo wasn't a core player, just a reliable player. The Twins would have had to scramble in-season for a replacement if they had gone with Presley.

The Twins still sought another bat in the lineup and that search nearly led them away from Chili Davis. MacPhail said the club had early interest in former World Series hero Kirk Gibson, a free agent who had played in just 160 games over the previous two seasons. But Gibson signed a two-year, $3.3 million contract with Kansas City in early December. Another option was Franklin Stubbs, who had belted 23 homers and added 71 RBI in 1990. Stubbs could also play first and some outfield if needed. But a few days after Gibson signed with the Royals, Milwaukee inked Stubbs to a two-year deal.

MacPhail went into the new year without a designated hitter, but Davis was still available. Davis had hit .265 with 12 homers and 58 RBI the previous year with the Angels. Kirby Puckett did have a role in getting Davis to come to Minnesota before the 1991 season. But Dan Gladden also was vouching for his buddy, Charles Theodore Davis. The two lived in the Phoenix area during the offseason and were teammates in San Francisco.

"I told them Chili was the perfect fit," Gladden said. "He's a designated hitter. He's a switch hitter."

On January 29, the Twins signed Davis to a two-year deal. And Davis provided what, at that point, was a career year: .277 average, 29 homers, 93 RBI, .892 on base-plus-slugging percentage, while leading the club in several categories. Davis also homered in Games 2 and 3 of the World Series against Atlanta. And he was great for team chemistry. Gibson hit .236 with 16 homers and 55 RBI for Kansas City. Stubbs batted .213 with 11 home runs and 38 RBI. MacPhail looked like a genius.

MacPhail also sought starting pitching. Early in the offseason, he offered Mike Boddicker, a 17-game winner with Boston the previous season, a three-year deal worth just over $8 million. Boddicker, an Iowa native, signed with the Royals for a little more than $9 million over three seasons.

As the start of spring training neared, there was one notable free-agent pitcher still on the market—Jack Morris. Having been born in St. Paul and grown up in the Highland Park area, he had a chance for a homecoming. Morris, 35 at the time, was a horse. He had averaged 31 starts and 231 innings over his previous 13 seasons. He had finished in the top five in Cy Young voting three times. He had won at least 14 games in 10 consecutive seasons—and the 14 wins came in the strike-shortened season of 1981. He was 15–18 with a 4.51 ERA in 1990. It wasn't his best work, but he posted a 2.83 ERA over his last eight outings. At the worst, Morris would lengthen the rotation. But the Twins felt he would set a great example for the rest of the staff.

The Twins tried to sign Morris before the 1987 season—think about what that would have done for them—before deciding to return to Detroit. The Twins had a better chance this time, but MacPhail was a little leery of agent Dick Moss, who indicated that Morris was leaning toward signing with the Twins before 1987 but re-signed with the Tigers. This time,

Toronto was interested. And Detroit offered him a three-year deal worth $9.3 million to return to the Tigers.

The Twins could not match Detroit's offer, but MacPhail had an idea. He offered Morris a three-year contract worth $7 million, with incentives that could push it to as much as $11. And MacPhail included an opt-out clause after each of the first two years of the deal. It was a novel idea at the time. Morris, if he remained durable, could earn $11 million. If he had a big year, he could leave after a season and seek a larger payday.

On February 5, 1991—the same day that the Baseball Hall of Fame banned Pete Rose from being on any future ballots—Morris agreed to the deal. The opt-out clause, which eventually became a standard contract enticement for top players, made the difference.

"My rationale was a., If I don't do this, he's not likely coming," MacPhail said. "And b., Would I sign him to a one-year deal for $3 million? Of course I would."

It capped a successful offseason for MacPhail. Gaetti and Berenguer were gone. But he added Pagliarulo, Bedrosian, Davis and Morris. Each would play a role in the Twins winning a second World Series title. What is mind-blowing about these additions is that they could have ended up with other players. It's dangerous to play the "What if?" game, because it could lead you down a road to nowhere. But MacPhail could have followed his scouts' advice and signed Presley instead of Pagliarulo. Boddicker could have taken the Twins' offer. And Davis was signed after they got nowhere with Gibson and Stubbs. If any of these moves had been reversed, history could have been rewritten. Instead, the Twins made history once again.

The 1991 Twins were a product of trades (like Kevin Tapani, Rick Aguilera, Dan Gladden, Al Newman and Greg Gagne), free-agent signings (like Davis, Morris and Pagliarulo), prospects

(Hrbek, Puckett, Chuck Knoblauch and Scott Erickson), a minor league free agent (Brian Harper) and even a Rule 5 draft pick (Shane Mack). A last-place team had been augmented by several moves by MacPhail—including gambles on Pagliarulo and Davis that paid off. "You look back at that roster and you didn't rely on one element at all," MacPhail said. "You used all of them."

The Twins went 21–10–1 during spring training, their first in their new facility at Fort Myers, Florida. Spring training numbers mean nothing. But the players judged themselves by how they prepared and saw evidence that they were a better team. But how much better? There were several new faces, but the lineup had six players 31 years old and over. Morris, at 36, was expected to be the ace, leader, mentor and guidance counselor for the pitching staff. A lot to ask of a 36-year-old. Preseason predictions had the AL pennant going to anyone other than the Twins. But the Twins went into the season confident they were better.

The pundits were right, at first. A 3–9 stretch had them at 20–24 and in sixth place in the AL West on May 27. Hrbek was batting .224. Puckett was batting .339 and others were producing. The pitching staff had a 3.82 ERA in May, but one man in particular was thriving.

Scott Erickson began the season 0–2. Then he threw back-to-back compete game shutouts in his fourth and fifth starts of the season. The day after the Twins fell to 20–24, Erickson tossed eight shutout innings at Texas to move to 7–2. Uh-oh. His next five starts: win, win, win, win, win. The 23-year-old Erickson, a fourth-round pick in 1989—the same draft the Twins selected Chuck Knoblauch and Denny Neagle—had won 12 straight decisions.

"To me, he was as dominant of a pitcher over a stretch as I had ever seen," MacPhail said. "He's an unsung hero because his elbow was barking pretty good by the end of 1991, and he really gutted it out. He never got the credit he deserved for doing what he did toward the end of that season. He was throwing bricks up there," MacPhail said. "They couldn't hit him. He was breaking bats."

Erickson was a phenomenon. He loved the color black, threw fastballs that would drop like an anvil when they reached the plate and couldn't lose. He was the talk of baseball—so much so that a crowd of 50,525 fans came out on a Saturday night in June to see Erickson go for No. 13 against the White Sox. But he gave up seven runs on 11 hits—including one that nearly took his head off—over 6⅓ innings. The streak was over, but Erickson had tied Bobby Witt for the longest winning streak since Roger Clemens won 14 straight in 1986.

But the job had been done. The 1991 season will be known for Erickson being dominant at the beginning, Kevin Tapani being consistent all season and Morris, with a 2.27 ERA over his last 11 starts, dominating at the end. And Erickson's run coincided with a ridiculous surge by the entire team. The Twins won three straight, beginning with Erickson's game against Texas. They lost a game, then won 15 straight. Rick Aguilera blew a save in Baltimore, then the Twins won four more. That's how close they were to a 20-game winning streak. The 15-game run was the second longest in the majors since 1961, the year the franchise moved in from Washington. When they defeated Cleveland on June 16, for their 15th straight win, they moved into first place in the AL West. They had the lowest team ERA, highest team batting average and second-best fielding percentage. The machine was working perfectly. The Twins were 22–6 in June that season, a month they historically had struggled in. And they were in first place for good.

The Twins fell into a first-place tie with California and Texas once each in July. And their lead shrank to one game in August over the surging White Sox. But they won 10 of their last 15 games that month to enter September with a seven-game lead. They clinched the division title on September 29, but not on the field. The Twins lost 2–1 to Toronto as sore-elbowed Scott Erickson pitched eight innings in a bid to win his 20th game of the season. The Twins climbed onto two buses and headed for the airport in Hamilton, Ontario, to fly to Chicago. While on the bus, the White Sox lost to Seattle. Magic number: 0. But only one bus knew. This thing called the cell phone was just landing in people's hands. Tom Kelly and traveling secretary Remzi Kiratli were listening to final outs of the White Sox–Mariners game. After the final out, Kelly stood up and announced the news. The bus driver then contacted his dispatcher, who alerted the driver of the second bus. Players waved and gave thumbs-up as the buses traveled down Queen Elizabeth Way. There were hugs at the airport followed by a charter flight to Chicago, where a ballroom was set up for them to celebrate in. And celebrate they did, as repairs were needed after the party.

The Twins had dropped eight of 12 games to Toronto during the regular season, and here were the Blue Jays in the other dugout for the American League Championship Series. Toronto was powered by Devon White, Joe Carter and future Hall of Famer Roberto Alomar. Todd Stottlemyre, Jimmy Key and David Wells each won at least 15 games during the regular season. Tom Henke and Duane Ward combined for 55 saves. Erickson led the Twins with 20 wins and Morris added 18. It was the Metrodome in Minneapolis versus SkyDome in Toronto. It would not be like 1987, as the Twins actually lost a playoff game at the Dome. Toronto won Game 2 to even the series. But the Twins swept the three games in Toronto to take the series, scoring 17 runs over the final two games. Puckett, who batted .429 with two home runs in the series, was named ALCS Most Valuable Player. And he was just warming up as the Twins headed back to the World Series.

Both the Twins and Braves had finished last in their respective divisions the previous season.

The stage was set.

The first World Series was held in 1903. And it's been more than 30 years since the Twins and Braves met for the Commissioner's Trophy in 1991. That's a lot of World Series. And the 1991 tussle between the Twins and Braves continues to be considered one of the best series ever. It was a movie that gained momentum as each scene unfolded. Heroes, villains, gasps, tears, love, hate, intensity, collisions, controversies, homers, hankies, gut-wrenching decisions, iconic moments—it had it all. Five games decided by one run. Four games decided in the final at-bat. Three extra-inning games. And, perhaps, two of the greatest individual performances in World Series history: Kirby Puckett putting the team on his back in Game 6 and Jack Morris pitching 10 innings in Game 7.

Greg Gagne broke open Game 1 with a three-run homer off Charlie Leibrandt in the fifth inning, helping the Twins win 5–2. That game also was known for Dan Gladden upending Braves catcher Greg Olson in the fifth as he tried to score from third. The picture of an upside-down Olson as Gladden looked to see if he'd held on to the ball ended up on magazine covers. The Twins took Game 2 as well, as rookie Scott Leius' home run off Tom Glavine in the eighth won the game.

The Twins were halfway to a second title. They flew to Atlanta that night amid controversy. In the third inning during Game 2, Ron Gant singled with Lonnie Smith on first. Smith advanced to third as pitcher Kevin Tapani cut off a throw from

Gladden. Tapani looked to first and fired over. Kent Hrbek took the throw as Gant, who had rounded first, attempted to return to the bag. Smith's momentum appeared to carry him into Hrbek. But Hrbek appeared to have a hold of Gant's leg as he came off the bag. It looked like Hrbek pulled Gant off the bag. "I saw that he was going to come off the bag, so I put the tag on him," Hrbek said. "That's exactly what I did." First base umpire Drew Coble agreed and called Gant out. The Braves protested to no avail. Hrbek became the villain. He stayed in the team hotel during the entire trip to Atlanta after he began to receive death threats. Teammates couldn't resist. They stayed away from him when they took the field for warmups, telling him they didn't want to be near him if shooting started. "They still don't like me down there," said Hrbek more than 30 years later. Hrbek was booed during pregame introductions and every time he went to the plate.

Atlanta won Game 3 5–4 in 12 innings, walked off the Twins again in a 3–2 win in Game 4, then jumped all over Tapani in Game 5, winning 14–5. The Twins returned to the Dome down 3–2 in the series. As they prepared for Game 6, Hurricane Kirby blew into the clubhouse and said, "Jump on my back. I'm driving the bus." It was something Puckett said often, but it had a calming effect on his teammates. But he was inaccurate. Puckett didn't just drive the bus in the Twins' 4–3, 11-inning, Game 6 victory; he built the frame, assembled the engine and installed the flooring—and he had actually installed flooring in Thunderbirds for a while in Chicago. Puckett: 3-for-4, three RBI, two runs scored. In the third inning, he jumped and levitated to the plexiglass in left center to steal a hit from Ron Gant. And he ended the game in the 11th with a home run off Charlie Leibrandt. Jack Buck signed off with one of the great broadcasting calls ever, "And we'll see you tomorrow night!"

There had already been four series games decided by one run. How about a fifth? And how about waiting until 11:00 PM to determine the winner? Jack Morris walked out of the Dome following Game 6 after playing Marvin Gaye's "Let's Get It On" in the clubhouse. He returned to the Dome the next afternoon looking to get on the mound and bring the state a second World Series title.

Nine innings and 118 pitches later, the game was still scoreless. The Twins had threatened to score in the eighth and ninth innings but were thwarted. Lonnie Smith led off the Braves' eighth with a single. Then he took off for second as Terry Pendleton followed with a drive to left that split the defense. However, as Smith neared second, Chuck Knoblauch pretended to field the ball and flipped air toward Greg Gagne to start a double play. Smith pulled up for a moment, then advanced to third. He would have scored if he hadn't slowed down. Braves players were celebrating the run being scored, until it wasn't. Why did Smith stop? No one knows. Morris got out of the inning three batters later when Sid Bream hit a grounder to first, where Kent Hrbek started a first-to-home-to-first double play that's hard to pull off during spring training drills.

Now the 10th inning was coming up. Tom Kelly was ready to take Morris out of the game. He didn't want Morris to lose after such an effort. Pitching coach Dick Such told Kelly, "I think he's OK." Morris told Tom Kelly he had gas left in the tank and there was no game tomorrow. "This is my game. I'm fine. I feel good." A movie script couldn't have contained as much drama as Kelly sent Morris back out. "It would have taken a shotgun to get him out," Kelly said after the game. Morris needed eight pitches. Pop-up, strikeout, groundout.

Dan Gladden led off the bottom of the inning with a Dome double on a broken-bat sinking fly ball that bounced between the left and center fielders. Knoblauch bunted Gladden to third.

Atlanta manager Bobby Cox intentionally walked Kirby Puckett and Kent Hrbek to load the bases. A ground ball could have led to a force out at home plate or, if hit to the right spot, a double play.

Kelly countered with sore-kneed pinch hitter Gene Larkin. If he had hit the ball on the ground, the inning would likely have ended with a double play. Atlanta's outfield was brought in because a deep fly ball would have ended the game anyway. On the first pitch from Alejandro Peña, Larkin lofted a fly ball over Brian Hunter's head in left field. It bounced. Gladden bounced home. The Twins bounced around home plate. One of the most thrilling Game Sevens of one of the most thrilling World Series ended with the Twins holding the trophy. Morris, of course, was named World Series MVP. But of all the players on both teams who had opportunities to drive in runs that would have made a difference in the series, the big swing came from a guy playing on one leg.

"It was probably the greatest World Series ever," then commissioner Fay Vincent said.

Two World Series titles. Two different teams. Each one stood out. The Twins' first title in 1987 was more emotional because they weren't expected to win but surged once the postseason arrived. The 1991 Twins had more talent, but their title was more emotionally draining because of all the tightly contested games. Seven players—Kent Hrbek, Kirby Puckett, Al Newman, Greg Gagne, Randy Bush, Dan Gladden and Gene Larkin—played on both title-winning teams.

"Momentum switched back and forth from dugout to dugout," Gladden said, "and either team could have won any of the games at any time."

Same dogpile near home plate, though. And each title team had home field advantage, where the Dome Gods awaited them.

The Twins could not repeat the magic in 1992, as a 90–72 season was not enough to topple Oakland. Many folks who believe in curses point to a late-July game at the Dome when Eric Fox hit a three-run homer off Rick Aguilera in the ninth to pull off a 5–4 comeback win. The Twins didn't recover from that moment for nearly a decade. Could it have been a curse? Maybe. The Twins had some other setbacks that were more troubling.

Less than 24 hours after winning the 1991 World Series, Jack Morris opted out of his contract, became a free agent and eventually signed with Toronto. GM Andy MacPhail traded for John Smiley, who went 16–9. But it wasn't enough, as Scott Erickson dropped to 13–12 after his 20-win season. The next blow came when Kent Hrbek retired following the 1994 season. His daughter was born in 1992, when thoughts of retiring first entered his mind. He had won two World Series. But he was starting a family and getting banged up. So he let his contract run down.

Then, in 1996, Puckett was forced to retire because of glaucoma. The Twins had been looking forward to Puckett playing in the same lineup with their latest free-agent signing, Paul Molitor. Molitor, who had led the league in hits twice, was the latest St. Paul native to play for his hometown team. Molitor hit .341 his first year with the Twins while leading the league, for the third time, with 225 hits. There's more. Chuck Knoblauch had a career year, batting .341 with 45 stolen bases and 62 extra-base hits. Plop a healthy Puckett in that lineup and the Twins could have hit their way into the postseason.

The Twins couldn't recover from these setbacks. By the end of the decade, owner Carl Pohlad—while trying to get a new stadium—ordered payroll to be slashed. They headed into the new millennium on the heels of a 63–97–1 record.

But they had 1987. And 1991.

22

1987

THE FIRST ONE IS ALWAYS THE MOST MEMORABLE.

Once a bunch of inexperienced pushovers who took their lumps at the major league level, the 1987 Twins shocked the baseball world. They only won 85 games during the regular season to win a weak division. They played below-.500 ball after the All-Star break while doing so. They survived with basically a two-man rotation. This team succeeded because the whole was greater than the sum of its parts. They were disciplined and cohesive, clutch when it was called for. Their fires were stoked from past failures. They had a manager in Tom Kelly who thrived in putting players in the right position at the right time to be productive. And they were determined to reward a fan base yearning for success.

"I've had chats with Terry Steinbach of late [about] when he was playing for the Oakland A's back in the day," Hrbek said in a 2023 interview. "And Terry said that [manager] Tony

La Russa was always impressed by the way we played together as a team. And they knew they were going to have a fight on their hands when they played the Twins because of the way T.K. managed the game."

The 1987 season was the first real special memory the Twins created in the Dome. It was their first World Series championship since moving to Minnesota in 1961. It was the first pro sports championship won in the state since the NBA's Minneapolis Lakers in 1954. Names like Puckett, Hrbek, Gaetti, Laudner, Blyleven and Viola are legendary. Some of them might still be drinking for free in town. They made grown men cry and children squeal and sportscasters gush.

This great team started at the bottom. The first steps were taken in 1982, when Billy Gardner's squad went 60–102. Outfielder Tom Brunansky, third baseman Gary Gaetti, first baseman Kent Hrbek, catcher Tim Laudner, left-hander Frank Viola, infielder Ron Washington and outfielder Randy Bush were all rookies on that team who developed together. No one knew then how long that road would be.

But in 1982, let's just say that there was a lot of development going on. The Twins were 23½ games out of first by mid-June and had streaks in which they lost 14 straight and 23 of 25.

Hrbek and Brunansky thrived in their first full seasons in the majors that year. Hrbek, the burly slugger from suburban Bloomington, Minnesota, batted .301 with 23 homers and 92 RBI. He finished second in American League Rookie of the Year voting, between future Hall of Famers in Cal Ripken Jr. and Wade Boggs. Brunansky, the California kid, hit .272 with 20 homers and 46 RBI. Gary Ward was the veteran presence, belting 28 homers to go with 91 RBI. And even though Gary Gaetti batted just .230 in 1982, he added 25 home runs and 84 RBI. There were things to work with there.

But the Twins burned through 17 pitchers that season. Only one starter, Bobby Castillo, had an ERA under 4.00. Terry Felton, who worked predominantly out of the bullpen, was 0–13. Viola took his lumps as a 22-year-old, going 4–10 with a 5.21 ERA. The offense had potential. The pitching was brutal. As a result, the 1982 Twins were outscored by 162 runs during the season.

Turnover was constant, as it usually is with 100-loss teams. And a series of trades suggested to the players that owner Calvin Griffith was making deals for financial reasons and not baseball reasons. In April 1982, the Twins sent Roy Smalley (whom they would eventually get back in a trade) and Gary Serum to the Yankees for Paul Boris, Ron Davis and Greg Gagne. Davis had been a setup man for Goose Gossage in New York but was immediately installed as the Twins' closer. He often tormented fans with outings that became fraught with peril. Yet this ended up being a bad trade for the Yankees because they lost their complement to Gossage, and they also sent the Twins a shortstop in Gagne who debuted the next season and became a mainstay in the lineup.

On consecutive days in May, the Twins sent Rob Wilfong and Doug Corbett to the Angels for Brunansky, Mike Walters and $400,000. Then they dealt popular catcher Butch Wynegar and pitcher Roger Erickson to the Yankees for Pete Filson, Larry Milbourne and John Pacella. The clubhouse was in an uproar, mostly over the trade for an unproven Brunansky (who would soon prove his worth). "What is he, 74 years old?" Davis asked of Griffith. "They ought to put him in an old folks' home. Trade the owner; that's what they ought to do." Davis would be lectured the next day by Gardner, especially after he provided quotes to the *St. Paul Pioneer Press* that were even more critical of the club. The roster shake-up brought an array of responses.

"The only reason I ain't gone," Hrbek said, "is because I live here."

"But Calvin likes you," someone said.

"He liked Butch, and he liked Roger," Hrbek responded. "The season is still young."

The Twins had moved into the shiny new Metrodome a month earlier, drawing 52,279 to their first home game. The next night attracted 5,213. And the remainder of the season didn't encourage many more to enjoy the new-car smell of the Dome. The season ended in front of 5,085 during a loss to the White Sox. The Twins finished 60–102, the first time the club had lost 100 games. But seeds were being planted. Some stats suggested that Brunansky was the best player on the team that season. Catcher Tim Laudner, who would win two World Series titles with the team, was called up when Wynegar was traded and received his big-league baptism. Gagne would be called up the next season. The building blocks were falling into place.

The kind of comments Hrbek made usually come from a veteran, so they revealed confidence that belied his experience. Gaetti, a first-round pick in 1979, had the same demeanor. They were young and took their lumps on the field but backed down to no one. That was exemplified on July 20 when the Twins and Brewers brawled. Hrbek had knocked Brewers second baseman Jim Gantner out of the game with a takeout slide at second. In retaliation, Robin Yount went out of his way later in the game to throw a block into Lenny Faedo as he tried to turn a double play. The benches emptied, and Hrbek ended up taking a punch from Ted Simmons and leaving the field with his left shoe in his hand and no glove. Hrbek believed that the Brewers had it in for him because he did so well against them. Hrbek and Brewers pitcher Bob McClure, a future Twins coach, were ejected from the game. Another Brewers player involved in the brawl that day was a guy from St. Paul: Paul Molitor. Molitor went on to a Hall of Fame career, which included three seasons with the Twins. He also managed the Twins from 2015 to '18.

But the brawl showed that while the Twins were young, they were unafraid to stand up for themselves. It would not be the last time they got into it with the team from Sudsville. Another reason not to mess with these young Twins: they had a right-hander named Albert Williams from Nicaragua. Williams was with the Pirates organization in the late 1970s but was released when his government wouldn't approve a visa for him to come to the United States. So he joined the freedom fighters and was part of the Nicaraguan Revolution prior to joining the Twins.

Gardner saw young, hungry players on his team and expected improvement in 1983. They did improve—just not as much as Gardner had hoped, as they went 70–92. The development was ongoing. The 1984 season was when the Twins' potential began to turn into victories. They remained relevant throughout the season and led the American League West division by five games as late as August 25 before sputtering to a 13–21 finish. They relinquished the division lead on September 24, then lost six straight games to end the season.

That was a lesson about finishing out a season. Hrbek, who batted .311 with 27 home runs and 107 RBI, and Brunansky, who batted .254 with 32 home runs and 85 RBI, had the best years of their still-young careers. Mickey Hatcher hit .302. Viola went 18–12. Mike Smithson was 15–13 and showed the staff the benefits of pitching inside. Davis had 29 saves to go with a 4.55 ERA. And some rookie named Kirby Puckett batted .296 with no home runs in 128 games.

Minnesota fans responded to a team in contention. After drawing 858,939 in 1983, the 1984 edition saw 1,598,692 visit the

Metrodome. Despite stumbling over the final week of the season, about 1,000 fans were on hand at the Minneapolis-St. Paul airport to greet them as they arrived from their season-ending series in Cleveland. "They choked, and in a big way," Twins fan Teresa Doherty of Plymouth, Minnesota, told the Associated Press, "but it was still a great season."

The highly anticipated 1985 season ended up being a dud. The Twins lost nine of their first 11 games. Hrbek got off to a poor start, batting .230 on June 15, and battled shoulder problems. Brunansky got off to a terrific start, batting .345 over his first 40 games, but crashed to earth during the second half. They suffered from a top-heavy rotation, with Mike Smithson and Frank Viola leading the way. Ron Davis saved 25 games, but cried in the clubhouse after giving up a game-winning home run to Don Mattingly at Yankee Stadium on May 13. By then, the Twins were 2–8 in one-run games and Davis had given up three walk-off homers. An 8–22 stretch in May and June sealed their fate. They had some good players, but others were still gaining experience. The pitching staff lacked depth. They lost a lot of close games. The 1985 Twins finished 77–85. Gardner was fired after 62 games and replaced with Ray Miller, who never played in the majors but had been a coach on a World Series–winning team with Baltimore. Twins president Howard Fox made the hire by calling the Orioles and asking who their candidates were before hiring Earl Weaver. So it wasn't much of a search. The hope was that Miller, Weaver's protégé, would bring that winning mentality to the Upper Midwest.

The results did not reflect that. Miller didn't last the season, as he was fired after going 59–80. He had a .456 winning percentage in parts of two seasons with the Twins, third worst in club history at the time. Miller was considered a pitching guru, but the Twins' 4.77 ERA in 1986 was 14th in the American League. The offense showed promise, as Puckett broke out with 31 home runs to go with a .328 batting average. Gaetti hit 34 home runs and had 108 RBI. Hrbek walloped 29 home runs with 91 RBI. Tom Kelly was named interim manager for the season's final 23 games.

After the final game of the season, Bert Blyleven, who had won a World Series with the "We Are Family" Pittsburgh Pirates in 1979, grabbed the microphone and told a crowd of 7,208, "If we can, going into next season, get together as a unit and 25 guys having the best years they are capable of having, we can bring a World Series to Minnesota." Blyleven felt that Kelly, who had managed many of the players in the minors, created a comfortable atmosphere. "I just sensed a really good clubhouse," Blyleven said. "Everybody got along. Puck, of course, was there. I felt something was good."

Changes were coming. Andy MacPhail had joined the organization in 1984 and was named general manager in 1985. He would have input on the next manager. The Twins were 12–11 in 23 games under Kelly, winning six of their last eight. MacPhail recommended Kelly for the job, but owner Carl Pohlad first offered the spot to Jim Frey. Frey turned it down because it came with just a two-year contract. On November 24, 1986, Kelly was named manager as part of the reorganization of the baseball department. Ralph Houk was hired as vice president of baseball. Bob Gebhard, a Minnesota native, was named director of major league personnel. MacPhail's title changed to executive vice president. Howard Fox no longer had day-to-day baseball operations duties.

Kelly was 36 when he was hired, making him the youngest manager in baseball. But his managerial experience went back to when he was 26 and player-manager for Class AAA Tacoma for a season. MacPhail was 33. As young as they were, these two men reshaped the franchise.

The 1987 season was the final exam for the Class of '82. Six Twins—Gaetti, Laudner, Brunansky, Hrbek, Viola and outfielder Randy Bush—were part of that baptismal season. The lessons had been learned. How to get out of slumps; hitters not blaming pitchers, and vice versa; how to grind out wins; how not to blow a pennant. It was time to apply what they had learned. Kirby Puckett was already a star. Bookmakers, noting the Twins had gone 71–91 the previous season, gave them 150-to-1 odds of winning the World Series.

Twins players reported to spring training prepared to return to their winning ways. Viola wondered when the organization's patience would run out with the group that had taken its lumps over the previous five seasons. "I think this is time to put up or shut up," he told the *Star Tribune* during spring training.

Hrbek agreed. "We knew we had something. We knew we had a pretty good nucleus of players. We had a lot of confidence in our team. We weren't cocky. We were confident that we knew we could play. It was just being able to get a couple extra players here and there."

Viola was from Long Island and had the accent to prove it. He starred at St. John's University, and was selected by the Twins in the second round of the 1981 draft and fast-tracked to the majors. He won 11 games over his first two seasons before breaking out with an 18–12 season in 1984. A writer claimed that when Viola pitched there was "sweet music in the Metrodome." He ended up with the nickname "Sweet Music." He was a force in 1987, going 17–10 with a 2.90 ERA.

Hrbek, the local product from Bloomington, was heading into his seventh major league season in 1987. He hit .267 with 29 home runs and 91 RBI in 1986. But there were concerns about his weight and he had battled some shoulder problems in the past. He reported to camp in 1987 weighing 240 pounds.

"He's doing a lot better," said Jeanie Hrbek, his wife at the time. "I can see the difference in his love handles, or whatever those things are called." Hrbek responded with a career year in 1987, batting .285 with 34 homers and 90 RBI.

Gaetti, from Centralia, Illinois, was a first-round pick in 1979 and played in nine games in 1991 before finishing fifth in Rookie of the Year balloting in 1992. Nickname: G-Man. To Hrbek, he was like a brother. The two were roommates from their rookie year through the late 1980s. Many viewed Gaetti as the heart and soul of the team. Gaetti talked trash and backed it up. If he struck out on a slider, he would tease the pitcher for not having the guts to throw him a fastball. He batted just .257 in 1987 but hit 31 homers with a team-high 109 RBI.

Brunansky, born in California, was traded to the Twins from the Angels in 1982 and quickly became a core player. He hit at least 20 home runs in each of his first eight seasons while playing all three outfield positions. The 1987 season would be his final full season with the Twins. But he made it a memorable one by hitting 32 homers to go with 85 RBI, one of his best years in the majors.

Laudner, who was born in Iowa but went to high school in Brooklyn Park, Minnesota, was the catcher. He had the demeanor of a police sergeant and spoke with similar authority. He was reliable behind the plate and could occasionally park one in the seats. Laudner hit just .191 in 1987 but walloped a career-high 16 home runs.

Bush, born in Delaware, was drafted out of the University of New Orleans. Laudner, his confidant, was his roommate on road trips—even when they could afford their own rooms. He played at the corner outfield spots, first base and designated hitter. He also was a pinch hitter deluxe, batting .242 in his career in those situations. He hit .253 with 11 homers in 1987.

This was the core with much on the line in 1987. MacPhail did his part. The team moved on from the human roller coaster that was Ron Davis by trading for proven closer Jeff Reardon. His 31 saves did the job. Roy Smalley, in 1987, was in the third year of his second go-round with the Twins. He hit .275 with eight home runs over 110 games. Juan Berenguer was added for bullpen depth. The quest for speed in the outfield led to a trade for Dan Gladden, who ended up in the leadoff spot. He stole 25 bases while batting .249. MacPhail was on top of his game with the Gladden move. He had a center fielder in Kirby Puckett who hit like a corner outfielder. The Twins needed a fast left fielder to stop ground singles in the Dome from rolling to the wall. Enter Gladden, who also brought a hard-nosed, gritty style that gave the Twins another dimension.

Puckett already was a star, coming off a .328 season with 31 home runs and 96 RBI in 1986. At 26, the Chicago-born Puckett was the spiritual leader of the Twins, fearless, charismatic and clutch. And almost thrown in jail before Opening Day in 1987. During spring training, an Orlando officer walked onto the Twins' practice field and threatened to arrest Puckett because his batting practice home runs were damaging cars parked behind the wall. MacPhail had to defuse the situation.

This was the cast of characters Kelly had to work with. Oh—Blyleven needs to be mentioned whenever the word "character" is used. A product of Zeist, Netherlands, Blyleven's presence helped Viola thrive on the mound. His jokes and humor kept teammates loose—and on their toes. Blyleven was the master of the hotfoot, the art of sneaking up on someone and lighting their shoes on fire.

Truthfully, the players felt Kelly used the right approach with a team that believed success was coming.

"Even though he had his quirks, like T.K. has, he just let the guys play," Blyleven said. "He had a lot of confidence in us, and it came down on the players that, hey, the manager had faith in them so why shouldn't I?"

They played that way from the start. Hrbek hit a bases-loaded single in the 10th inning to beat Oakland 5–4 on Opening Day. Puckett hit a two-run homer in the third inning and robbed Mickey Tettleton of a homer in the top of the 10th. George Frazier replaced Blyleven in the ninth and pitched two scoreless innings to pick up win No. 1 of 85. The Twins won seven of their first nine games, marking the best start in club history.

That game would be part of a trend that season, as the Twins played in 46 games decided by one run. They won 24 of them, including 16 in their last at-bat, which would be a useful trait in October. The Twins could never run away with the division, though. And no one in their division could take advantage while the Twins fought to gain traction.

MacPhail tried to help by acquiring 42-year-old Joe Niekro on June 6 for catcher Mark Salas. Niekro won his first two starts for the Twins before suffering a slight shoulder separation on June 17 during another benches-clearing event with the Brewers. He was 2–9 with a 6.75 ERA after that. He also was busted during an August 3 game for scuffing baseballs. Replays showed Niekro trying to distract umpires while he tried to slip an emery board out of his pocket. He also was found with sandpaper. He was tossed by umpire, and Minnesota native, Tim Tschida. Niekro served a 10-game suspension for the infraction, but he made the most of it. He appeared on *Late Night with David Letterman* wearing a utility belt adorned with a power sander, a nail file, sandpaper, toenail and fingernail clippers, Vaseline, emery boards and other items.

But June ended up being a notable month for the Twins, as they moved into first place on June 9 and never relinquished it. As summer arrived, so did the crowds. Games at the Dome became destination viewing.

Blyleven and Viola formed one of the best one-two punches among starting pitchers, but the Twins struggled to find a third wheel. "Blyleven and Viola started 45 percent of our games," MacPhail said, "which wouldn't happen today." The bullpen was solid, with Reardon, Juan Berenguer, George Frazier and Keith Atherton. Les Straker finished 8–10 with a 4.37 ERA and was the de facto No. 3 starter. Mike Smithson had a 5.94 ERA. Niekro injured his shoulder then tailed off. They tried Mark Portugal and 42-year-old Steve Carlton, with no luck. It was easy to see why the Twins couldn't pull away with the division.

At the All-Star break, the Twins were 49–40. And Puckett was their only All-Star. Hrbek, who was snubbed, said he would never play in another All-Star Game. "I'm peeved, not just for myself, but because it shows nothing for the whole team," he told reporters then. "I accepted not making it when we weren't doing well. This I don't accept. If those guys ask me to go again, they can kiss my ass."

The Twins were 36–37 following the All-Star break. Not exactly putting away the division. They struggled mightily on the road. They went 1–7 during a midseason trip and lost all six games during a Detroit–Boston swing in August. The team hung about 20 pictures of the Dome around Detroit's visitors' clubhouse to try to break the road hex. "We tried everything," Hrbek said. It only worsened. They lost three games there to the Tigers then went to Boston and were swept. But Dome, Sweet Dome. The Twins won 56 games at the Metrodome in 1987. They were used to dealing with the turf, the baggie, the blind spots, the roof and the noise. Opponents weren't. And the Twins gladly played that fact to their advantage.

On the road, the Twins took wins however they could get them. Puckett went 4-for-5 with two homers during a 12–3 victory in Milwaukee. The next day, he went 6-for-6 with two homers and two doubles in a 10–6 win. He tied the major league record for the most hits in consecutive nine-inning games. Even though the games were played at County Stadium, the Brewers hung a sign acknowledging Puckett's accomplishment in the press box of Miller Park (renamed American Family Field in 2021) for several years.

MacPhail tried to trade for another starter before the August 31 deadline to have postseason rosters set. Unable to do so, the Twins looked at adding a veteran hitter. They considered Jim Dwyer, but he would not agree to waive his no-trade clause. The Twins then turned to Don Baylor, a wise old soul who still had some power and had led the league in getting hit by pitches eight times. MacPhail approached Smalley, who had played with Baylor with the Yankees, for his thoughts. "I'm just going to tell you, if you don't [sign Baylor], then you're not nearly as smart as I and everybody else think you are about this stuff," Smalley told him. MacPhail laughed and said, "Well, I think we're going to do it." The Twins sent minor league pitcher Enrique Rios, who would be out of baseball following the 1988 season, to Boston for Baylor.

Baylor hit .286 with a .397 on base percentage in 20 games with the Twins, but his lifetime of baseball lessons was just as impactful on a team looking to close out the division. By now the Dome was bursting at the seams with fans. Between 5,000 and 10,000 fans were turned away from a September 5 game against Milwaukee that drew 51,122. The final home game saw a record 53,106 fans attend an 8–1 win over Kansas City. Puckett, Gaetti and Hrbek all homered as the Twins' magic number to clinch the AL West dropped to one. A few hundred Twins fans traveled to Texas for the September 28 game at Arlington. One held a sign that read THE CLINCH IS A CINCH as Reardon closed out a 5–3 win for the Twins' first division title in 17 years. Their lead had shrunk to a half game at the start of the month before they pulled away to qualify for the postseason. The Twins exhaled, losing the final five games of the season. But 6,000 fans greeted them at the airport upon their return. What else was there for the fans to do around those times? Watch replacement football?

The Twins' rotation lacked depth during the regular season, yet was a strength in the postseason. Because of off days so teams could travel during the playoffs, both Blyleven and Viola could be available for multiple starts in a seven-game series. The Twins also had home field advantage in the ALCS, despite having a worse record than Detroit. Back then, the East and West Divisions rotated home field advantage, and it was the West Division's turn. That meant four games, if needed, at the Metrodome. Or Thunderdome. Or Terrordome. However the fans wanted to describe the racket they made under the Teflon ceiling.

Detroit had won 98 games during the regular season. They had last won the World Series in 1984 with Alan Trammell, Lou Whitaker, Kirk Gibson, Chet Lemon and Jack Morris still on the team. The Tigers were solid all around and picked as the favorites in the series.

Many of the Twins made their postseason debuts on October 7, 1987. And so did Homer Hankies. The hankies were inspired by the Pittsburgh Steelers' Terrible Towel, which debuted in 1975 and was an instant hit. And tens of thousands of Homer Hankies were waving as the Twins took the field for Game 1 of the ALCS.

The tone was set in Game 1. Gaetti homered twice. But the Twins trailed 5–4 in the eighth when Gladden led off with a single that kick-started a four-run rally and an 8–5 Twins win. After falling behind 2–0 in the second inning of Game 2, the Twins scored three in the bottom of the inning and got a two-run single from Gladden in the fourth and a Hrbek home run in the fifth. They vanquished Jack Morris to go to 2–0 in the series. It was off to Detroit for Game 3.

After the Tigers won the 1984 World Series, there was mayhem in the streets as celebrating fans damaged their city. One person was killed, a police car was burned and the city's finest moment was stained. MacPhail remembered this as the Twins headed for the Motor City, so he was worried about the safety of the traveling party if they were too spirited while supporting the Twins.

"I'm like, 'Fellas, we've got to low-key this," MacPhail said. "I'm telling my wife to don't start jumping up and down and screaming when we score. Just win the games and go home. Lo and behold, Bert Blyleven's wife brings a whistle. Every time the Twins did something good, she started blowing the whistle. The next thing I know, shit, Carl and Eloise [Pohlad] got whistles and they are blowing them. I'm like, I don't want security to have to cordon off our fans."

He didn't have to worry about that in Game 3. Pat Sheridan, the No. 9 hitter, socked a two-run homer off Reardon as Detroit rallied for a 7–6 win. But the Twins won Game 4 by a 5–3 score to take a 3–1 lead in the series. That game was known for the defensive play of the series. Down 4–3 in the sixth inning, the Tigers had Dave Bergman on second and Darrell Evans on third with Lou Whitaker at the plate. Gaetti, the Twins' third baseman, knew that Evans would take a big lead. Whitaker was a left-handed hitter, so the Twins' catcher, Tim Laudner, had a clear throwing lane. Gaetti signaled for a pickoff play. Twins pitcher Juan Berenguer fired a pitch that was in the dirt. But

Laudner caught the ball and fired to third. Gaetti slapped the tag on Evans' back for the out. The Twins were rolling.

In Game 5, the Twins scored four runs in the second, two coming on a Brunansky double. With a 6–4 lead in the ninth, the Twins added three more runs, one on a Brunansky homer. The Twins won 9–5 to become American League champions. Brunansky hit .412 with two home runs in the series. Gladden batted .350. Blyleven won both his starts. And legendary Tigers skipper Sparky Anderson went over after the game to personally congratulate Tom Kelly. Gaetti, who batted .300 with two homers, was named MVP.

As the team flew back to Detroit, the players were told that a crowd was forming at the airport to greet them, so they should smile and wave. Then they were told that the crowd was getting big and was being sent to the Metrodome. Then, while on the bus from the airport to the Metrodome, they were told there could be as many as 15,000 fans there. Players noticed people on the street as the bus approached the stadium. Then they went inside. "When that door opens and we see it, it was amazing," MacPhail said. The Dome was full at 11 o'clock at night. By the time they arrived back to the Twin Cities, newborn babies were being wrapped in Homer Hankies. It was fandemonium. And the World Series was five days away.

More than 3 million fans filled Busch Stadium in 1987 to watch Jack Clark drive in his fleet-footed teammates. Clark smashed 35 homers, drove in 106 runs and walked 136 times during the regular season. The Cardinals had five players with at least 16 stolen bases, including Ozzie Smith with 43 and Vince Coleman with 109. Five players hit .285 or better. St. Louis' rotation lacked a clear ace, as three pitchers had 11 wins each. But they were led by Whitey "the White Rat" Herzog, who, like the Twins' Tom Kelly, played chess during games while other managers played checkers. Herzog, however, had done it over 16 seasons to Kelly's one.

The Twins would not have to worry for a couple of reasons. One, they played in the Hubert H. Humphrey Metrodome. The Teflon roof, the drab background, the trash bag covering the vampire seats in right, the air vents keeping the roof inflated. The 1987 World Series welcomed indoor baseball for the first time, and national media folks were trumpeting the complaints that the Dome was more of a warehouse than a ballpark. It was not the way baseball was meant to be played.

The other reason was injuries. Clark, the fulcrum of the Cardinals offense, was pulled from the World Series roster with an ankle problem. Then starting third baseman Terry Pendleton was limited to designated hitter duties because of a pulled rib cage muscle. Clark and Pendleton had combined for 47 home runs and 202 RBI during the regular season.

Injuries, plus the Twins having home field advantage in that dastardly Dome, had some observers picking them to win the World Series. They couldn't be taken for granted anymore.

A crowd of 55,171 piled into the Dome for Game 1, but Twins operators were besieged with calls from upset fans who saw empty seats in the second deck behind home plate. That area was reserved for visiting media and was covered in cloth that made it appear to be empty seats. That's what the demand for tickets was like. And the fans who couldn't get to the Dome that night missed a show. The Twins showed it all—pitching, defense, speed, power—as they thrashed Joe Magrane and the Cardinals 10–1. The Twins scored seven runs in the fourth inning, including a grand slam by Dan Gladden, to blow the game open.

It was more of the same in Game 2. The Twins broke the game open with six runs in the fourth inning. Gary Gaetti and

Tim Laudner homered. Bert Blyleven held St. Louis to two runs over seven innings in a game the Twins won 8–4. The top three hitters in the Cardinals' lineup were 2-for-24 over the first two games. "That's a buzzsaw over there," Herzog said. Herzog sang another tune after that, mentioning that the Twins had won just nine road games after the All-Star break and that their two-man rotation worked well, with the scheduled off days in the postseason keeping their lack of starting pitching depth from becoming an issue.

Right-hander Les Straker was supposed to be the easy mark of the Twins' rotation. To the contrary, Straker threw six score-less innings in Game 3, although he had to work out of a couple jams. It was the bullpen that let a 1–0 lead in the seventh slip away, as Juan Berenguer gave up three runs and Cardinals won 3–1. Game 4 saw Tom Lawless, who batted .080 in 19 regular season games, connect for a three-run blast off Frank Viola during St. Louis' six-run fourth. The Twins ended up losing 7–2.

If Game 4 was the time to get concerned, Game 5 was time to panic. The Cardinals beat Bert Blyleven and the Twins 4–2 to take a 3–2 lead back to the Dome. St. Louis did not have a single extra-base hit in the game but stole five bases while playing to its strengths. The Twins had Straker going in the must-win Game 6. And things didn't start well when Straker served up a home run to Tom Herr in the first inning. The Twins scored twice in the bottom of the inning to take a 2–1 lead, but they trailed 5–2 in the fifth. Then the Twins got to John Tudor in the fifth with four runs, including a two-run blast by Don Baylor. Four big runs came in the sixth on Kent Hrbek's grand slam off Ken Dayley. Kirby Puckett went 4-for-4 on the game's biggest stage. An 11–5 victory set up Game 7.

Game 7 was the best game of the World Series, as both teams had plenty of fight left despite dueling over the previous six games. The home team had won every game, and nothing changed in Game 7. Puckett was Puckett, collecting two hits, including an RBI double in the fifth. He also made a big running catch in the ninth on Tom Herr's sinking fly. Umpires were in the middle of four close plays. Lee Weyer had two bang-bang plays at first, including one in which he called Greg Gagne safe as he beat out an infield hit that allowed the winning run to score in the sixth. St. Louis' Vince Coleman threw out Baylor at home in the second and Gary Gaetti at home in the fifth—both plays that might have been reversed in the era of instant replay. In the end, the player of the game was Frank Viola, who pitched eight innings, giving up two runs on six hits. Kelly didn't hesitate to bring in Jeff Reardon for the ninth, and Reardon got a fly out—on Puckett's catch—a pop out and a groundout to close out the series.

The team that many believed was flawed during the regular season was nearly flawless in October. Twins players popped champagne in the clubhouse after the final out, dousing each other—and some media members—before returning to the field some 45 minutes later to salute fans who had remained at the Dome to revel in their first World Series title. The fans had fallen in love with their team, and the Twins showed them the same love. Kelly, as he had when the Twins clinched the division and when they defeated Detroit in the ALCS, hung back in the dugout and clubhouse as his players celebrated. To him, it was always about the players. A few days later, they were headed to Washington, D.C., for lunch with President Ronald Reagan.

"We knew that we had a pretty good group of guys coming up that could play with anybody," Hrbek said. "We had a lot of confidence on our team. We weren't cocky. We were confident. We knew we could play well."

Acknowledgments

THE AUTHOR WOULD LIKE TO THANK THE FOLLOWING: Minnesota History Center, Gale Family Library, South St. Paul Library, Minnesota Twins, the Webb Family, the Skahen Family, Patrick O'Brien, Robert Wagner, Baxter

Sources

Books

Dennis Brackin and Patrick Reusse, *Minnesota Twins: The Complete Illustrated History,* MVP Books, 2010

Dick Bremer and Jim Bruton, *Game Used: My Life in Stitches with the Minnesota Twins,* Triumph Books, 2020

Rod Carew and Ira Berkow, *Carew,* University of Minnesota Press, 2010

Calvin Griffith and Jon Kerr, *Calvin: Baseball's Last Dinosaur,* Wm C. Brown Publishers, 1990

Thom Henninger, *The Pride of Minnesota: The Twins in the Turbulent 1960s,* University of Nebraska Press, 2021.

Kent Hrbek and Dennis Brackin, *Tales From the Minnesota Twins Dugout,* Sports Publishing, 2007

Jim Kaat and Douglas B. Lyons, *Good as Gold: My Eight Decades in Baseball,* Triumph Books, 2021

Minneapolis Star Tribune, *Magic! The 1987 Twins' Enchanted Season,* Star Tribune, 1987

Stew Thornley, *Minnesota Twins Baseball: Hardball History on the Prairie,* The History Press, 2014

Jay Weiner, *Stadium Games: Fifty Years of Big League Greed and Bush League Boondoggles,* University of Minnesota Press, 2000

Dean Urdahl, *Touching Bases with Our Memories: The Players Who Made the Minnesota Twins.* North Star Press of St. Cloud, 2004

Newspapers
Minneapolis Star Tribune
New York Times
St. Paul Pioneer Press

Websites
Baseball-Reference.com
ESPN.com
Fangraphs.com
MLB.com
Newspapers.com